Black Noise

MUSIC / CULTURE

A series from Wesleyan University Press

Edited by George Lipsitz, Susan McClary, and Robert Walser

Published titles

My Music by Susan D. Crafts, Daniel Cavicchi, Charles Keil,
and the Music in Daily Life Project

*Running with the Devil: Power, Gender, and Madness in
Heavy Metal Music* by Robert Walser

Subcultural Sounds: Micromusics of the West by Mark Slobin

*Upside Your Head! Rhythm and Blues on
Central Avenue* by Johnny Otis

*Dissonant Identities: The Rock'n'Roll Scene in
Austin, Texas* by Barry Shank

*Black Noise: Rap Music and Black Culture in
Contemporary America* by Tricia Rose

TRICIA ROSE

✦

Black Noise

RAP MUSIC AND
BLACK CULTURE IN
CONTEMPORARY
AMERICA

✦

WESLEYAN UNIVERSITY PRESS

Published by University Press of New England

Hanover & London

WESLEYAN UNIVERSITY PRESS
Published by University Press of New England, Hanover, NH 03755
© 1994 by Tricia Rose
All rights reserved
Printed in the United States of America 5 4
CIP data appear at the end of the book

Copyright information follows for the lyrics quoted in this volume, and permission to reprint them is gratefully acknowledged:

"The Message," courtesy of Sugar Hill Music.

"Youthful Expression," by A. Shaheed, J. Davis, M. Gaye, and J. Nicks. Copyright 1989 ZOMBA ENTERPRISES INC./JAZZ MERCHANT MUSIC (Administered by ZOMBA ENTERPRISES INC.) and JOBETE MUSIC. Reprinted by Permission of CPP/BELWIN, INC., Miami, Florida. International Copyright Secured. Made in U.S.A. All Rights Reserved.

"Talking All That Jazz," written by Glenn Bolton. © T-Girl Music Publishing, Inc. (BMI). All Rights Reserved. Used with Permission.

"Get Up Everybody (Get Up)." © 1988 Next Plateau Music, Inc./Sons of Koss.

"Music and Politics," written by Michael Franti and Charlie Hunter. Copyright © 1992 PolyGram International Publishing, Inc., and Beatnigs Music. Used by Permission. All Rights Reserved.

"Paid in Full," written by Eric Barrier and William Griffin. Copyright © 1987 Songs of PolyGram International, Inc., and Robert Hill Music. Used by permission. All Rights Reserved.

"The Devil Made Me Do It," written by Oscar Jackson. © T-Boy Music Publishing, Inc. (ASCAP)/ Scarface Music (ASCAP). All Rights Reserved. Used with Permission.

"Night of the Living Baseheads" and "Prophets of Rage," by Carlton Ridenhour, Eric Sadler and Hank Shocklee; copyright 1988 "Def American Songs, Inc. (BMI)."

"Fuck Tha Police" (O. Jackson/L. Patterson/A. Young). Ruthless Attack Muzick (ASCAP). Used by permission.

"Endangered Species (Tales from the Darkside)" and "The Nigga Ya Love to Hate" (Ice Cube, Eric Sadler). © 1990 WB MUSIC CORP., GANGSTA BOOGIE MUSIC, WARNER-TAMERLANE PUBLISHING CORP., YOUR MOTHER'S MUSIC. All rights on behalf of GANGSTA BOOGIE MUSIC administered by WB MUSIC CORP. All rights on behalf of YOUR MOTHER'S MUSIC administered by WARNER-TAMERLANE PUBLISHING CORP. All Rights Reserved. Used By Permission.

"Necessary" and "Stop the Violence" (copyright 1988) and "Who Protects Us from You" (copyright 1989), by L. Parker. Copyright ©ZOMBA ENTERPRISES INC./BDP MUSIC (administered by ZOMBA ENTERPRISES INC.) and JOBETE MUSIC. Reprinted by Permission of CPP-BELWIN, INC., Miami, Florida. International copyright secured. Made in U.S.A. All Rights Reserved.

"Tramp," by Lowell Fulsom and Jimmy McCracklin. © 1966 POWERFORCE MUSIC 50%/ BUDGET MUSIC 50%. All rights administered by CAREERS-BMG MUSIC PUBLISHING, INC. (BMI). All rights reserved. Used by Permission.

"Paper Thin," written by MC Lyte. Courtesy of First Priority Music.

"Ladies First," written by Dana Owens/Simone Johnson/Mark James/Anthony Peaks/Shane Faber. © T-Boy Music Publishing, Inc./Queen Latifah Music/Forty-Five King Music/Forked Tongue Music (all ASCAP). All Rights Reserved. Used with Permission.

"Shake Your Thang (It's Your Thing)," by O'Kelly Isley, Rudolph Isley and Ronald Isley. © 1969, 1988 EMI APRIL MUSIC INC. and BOVINA MUSIC. All rights controlled and administered by EMI APRIL MUSIC INC. All Rights Reserved. International Copyright Secured. Used by Permission.

(Acknowledgments continued on p. 239)

For my parents
George & Jeanne Rose
&
for the hip hop community

Contents

✦

Acknowledgments

✦

I owe mad thanks to the hip hop community, all the rappers, musicians, and industry folks who talked to me, introduced me to others, and shared their time and knowledge generously. Some of the more exuberant folks called to share local news from other hip hop communities or sent newsclippings about the latest rap controversy, style innovation, or tour stop. Others listened patiently as I ranted and raved about the latest misinterpretation of a rap song or incident. Still others tipped me to new underground groups or offered aesthetic critiques and video production secrets. Some went into a deep head nod with me at the sound of a great hip hop beat. For all this and more, much respect due to: DJ Red Alert, Harry Allen, Elizabeth Alexander, Phat Andy, Kevin Bray, Michael Franti (from Disposable Heroes of Hiphoprisy), dream hampton, Gina Harrell, Harmony, Laura Hynes, Kid (from Kid-N-Play), Ron Kriedman, Queen Latifah, Crazy Legs, Emir Lewis, Felix Mickens, Nicole Moore, Chris Rose, Eric & Karen Sadler, Salt (from Salt 'N' Pepa), Chuck Stone, Wiggles, and many more too numerous to mention here.

Others pored over drafts of chapters and encouraged me to keep pushing forward. Along these lines I am grateful to Susan McClary, Robert Walser, Herman Gray, Reebee Garofalo, and Tommy Lott, who all read various drafts of the book in detail and gave sage and spirited comments. Very special thanks go to Robin D. G. Kelley for his generosity, critical dialogue, and friendship; to Jeffrey Decker, who has been a wonderful friend and intellectual colleague from jump; to Glenn Decker for his flawless research assistance and patience; and to Barron Claiborne, Sue Kwon, and Lisa Leone for allowing me to use their photographs. Also, thanks to Ninety-Nine for her poetic contribution.

For research support and institutional guidance at various stages of this project I would like to thank the Dorothy Danforth-Compton Foundation, Dean Bernard Bruce, Professor Mari Jo Buhle, the Williams College Bolin Doctoral Fellowship Program, and the Rutgers University American Studies Program faculty and staff.

There are three people whose contributions are almost impossible to isolate because they are part of the force field that brought this book into existence. It is difficult to imagine what would have come of this project were it not for the friendship, spiritual riches, and intellectual brilliance of George Lipsitz, Greg Tate, and Arthur Jafa. George's vision, commitment to students, great sense of humor, and unwavering support guided me through some of the most difficult stages. Many late phone dialogues with Greg and AJ provided me with the inspiration to move the project in its most dynamic directions. Greg not only shared his ideas and contacts, he listened carefully and critically. AJ donated the title of the book from his vast storehouse of truly innovative ideas and made pivotal intellectual contributions. He has taught me more in three years than I have learned in twenty-odd years of formal education, about black life, black culture, and the human spirit. I look forward to sharing this intellectual hothouse with him for years to come.

Finally, I would like to celebrate my parents, Jeanne J. Rose and George N. Rose. It is impossible to imagine how this project would have been realized without the passion, confidence, tenacity, faith, and love that have served as guiding principles in their extraordinary parenting against the odds.

T.R.

November 1993
New York City

Introduction

✦

In 1979, a Bronx minister delivered a wedding sermon for a good friend of mine from junior high school. He organized his sermon around Chic's current hit song "Good Times." "These," he told my friend and his new wife, "are the good times, the times when you feel abundant love for your new partner, generosity and optimism about the future." He continued on in this vein for a few minutes. "But," he growled darkly, "what of those bad times to come, and believe me they will come—will you be there for each other then? What about those dark times, those dark times when good times are only a memory? Will you stand by each other all the way through good and bad all the way until death do you part?" The minister knew that for this 18-year-old couple and their friends, Chic's song would be the perfect hook, the ideal medium for conveying his beliefs about life's pleasures, commitments, and pitfalls to such a young congregation. "Good Times," which narrated the pleasures of summer parties, rollerskating, good friends, and carefree thoughts to a profoundly funky baseline, was not only a big disco hit in its own right but also the musical backdrop for "Rapper's Delight," rap's first major commercial breakthrough that took place the same year.

My teenage years coincided with the years in which hip hop culture began taking shape in New York City. The reception for my friend's wedding was held at the Stardust Ballroom, a Bronx club that had already begun featuring local aspiring rappers and DJ talent. Summer nights often featured boom boxes with homemade tapes of disco beats and unpolished raps. In addition to the college-bound set, several of my friends were planning to go into music, and a couple were writers—graffiti writers, that is. Leaving New York shortly thereafter to attend college myself, I kept my eye on rap's developments, albeit from a distance.

While lecturing and teaching on hip hop, I am frequently asked how

I got into rap. Several audience members have said that I don't fit the image of a b-girl, but when it comes to hip hop I seem to have the passion of one. Basically, they say that I don't look as if I learned about hip hop in school but I know it like I been studying it. I suppose I learned about hip hop the way most kids from the Bronx did at that time; it was the language and sound of our peer group. But this does not explain how I got here from there.

In 1985 I decided that if I could work on rap music and hip hop culture, then more school wouldn't be such a bad idea. Rap's sound, power, and style had been one of my greatest fascinations. So much so that, after many a day's work at a local housing authority in Connecticut, I would go to the library and trace rap's appearances on the billboard black music charts. I couldn't believe that this music that seemed so local, so particular could capture the attention of so many people around the country. A year later, when I arrived at the American Studies Program at Brown University, I was fully committed to writing my doctoral thesis on rap music. Even though most of the faculty thought it was a quirky idea, they didn't discourage it. What worried them was that rap would disappear before I finished my research, I wouldn't have enough material to write about, and I might be unmarketable as a job candidate.

The theoretical issues that dominated my academic coursework are crucial to understanding the processes of culture making in a capitalist and fully commodified society and, therefore, to understanding rap music. These structures of knowledge clearly serve as one foundation of this project. However, I have not relied solely on these theoretical tools; I have merged multiple ways of knowing, of understanding, of interpreting culture and practice in *Black Noise*. I hope that this polyvocal approach will encourage other students of culture to deal head-on with the deeply contradictory and multilayered voices and themes expressed in popular culture; to use theoretical ideas in enabling and creative ways; and to try to occupy as many subject positions as possible. The future of insightful cultural inquiry lies in those modes of analyses that can account for and at the same time critique the raging contradictions that comprise daily life. When a comfortable fit between theoretical concerns and the limits of an oppositional practice is revealed, the reason may not be because the practice itself has failed to work in oppositional ways but, instead, that the theory could not in some way account for the conditions that shaped the practice and its practioners. The script that has emerged, then is a complex fusion of the cultural theories that I still believe can help to explain the complex territory that rap navigates and an interpretation of the voices and spiritual power that sustain rap and African-American people.

The specific composition of my identities and my relationships to rap music means that this script is in many ways as polyvocal as its subject matter. As an African-American woman of biracial parentage with second-generation immigrant parents, I have often found myself on both sides of a contentious social and racial divide. This is, of course, further complicated by my specific concerns. Speaking from my positions as a pro-black, biracial, ex–working-class, New York–based feminist, left cultural critic adds even greater complexity to the way I negotiate and analyze the social world.

However, I also believe that my peculiarly situated identities have been immensely productive in my efforts to produce a blueprint for understanding contemporary black popular expression. I do not think one need share all of or any of these identities to work on rap; but they have helped me to construct this project—one that attempts to explore rap's tensions and contradictions and to theorize about its core organizing principles. For example, at some points in this excursion, I am most seriously concerned with the nature of black female expression; at other points, I focus on public displays of black masculinity (that affirm black masculinity in a terrain that is hostile to black men, but that also have had the effect of pushing black female expressions to the margins of public discourse). In other places, I focus on the class-based nature of the oppression that hip hop artists and fans face and yet find competing evidence to make racially based arguments regarding the discursive and ideological power of racist domination. I feel certain that much of rap's critical force grows out of the cultural potency that racially segregated conditions foster. However, the same segregated conditions, whether by choice or by design, have been instrumental in confining and oppressing African Americans.

I make no claims to offer a complete history of rap music, nor have I attempted to explain every facet of rap's effects on contemporary American culture and cultures around the world. Instead, I describe, theorize, and critique elements of rap, including rap's lyrics, music, culture, and style, as well as the social context within which rap music takes place. I offer explanations for what I believe to be some of the most narratively compelling elements that have emerged inside rap music. This has meant ignoring some of the most highly publicized issues in rap music, as media attention on rap music has been based on extremist tendencies within rap, rather than the day-to-day cultural forces that enter into hip hop's vast dialogue.

Black Noise examines the complex and contradictory relationships between forces of racial and sexual domination, black cultural priorities, and popular resistance in contemporary rap music. What are the terms of the ideological, cultural, and sexual struggles that take place in rap? How are these struggles taken up by black youth? Because popular forms contain significant cultural traditions and cannot be fully severed from the sociohistorical moment in which they take place, then what are the sociohistorical conditions that help to explain the specificity of rap's development? How do women rappers revise sexist discourse? How does rap sustain and transform long-standing black cultural forms and traditions? How does new technology change the nature of black cultural production? How is technology shaped by black cultural priorities?

Like hip hop itself, I draw on a wide range of sources, ways of reading, texts, and experiences. In addition to relying on black cultural theory, urban history, personal experiences, black feminism, and theories that explore working-class oppositional practices, I have listened attentively to a large majority of rap albums available, transcribed over five dozen songs,[1] taped and viewed hundreds of rap music videos, researched rap samples, attended over thirty rap concerts and conferences, and carefully followed the coverage of rap music in popular music magazines, newspapers, and scholarly publications. Although this may seem sufficient to answer the questions I present, it is not. The sampling controversy, how rap records are made, how black teens became technological innovators, and the insurance company policies for booking rap shows cannot be explored by relying on the music itself. So, in addition, I have interviewed and spoken with several people who are involved in rap music, including rappers, music industry representatives, dancers, lawyers, and music producers. Because these interviews are excerpted primarily as supporting evidence and to flesh out relationships between oppression and cultural resistance, only a small part of these conversations has been referred to directly. Yet, these conversations were crucial in helping me to understand some of what is at stake in rap music and in my exploration of the hidden politics of popular pleasure.

It is my firm belief that this project—which grounds black cultural signs and codes in black culture and examines the polyvocal languages of rap as the "black noise" of the late twentieth century—will foster the development of more globally focused projects. Some of these might center on the pleasure that hip hop style and rap music affords suburban white teenagers in small, relatively homogeneous midwestern towns, or the rich hip hop hybrids nurtured in Mexican and Puerto Rican communities in Los Angeles and New York, the Chinese and Japanese breakdancers with whom I spoke in a downtown Hong Kong mall and in

1. Most rappers write their own lyrics. I nonetheless have been careful to use examples from songs that are at least partially written by the rapper. Most examples cited here are copyrighted by the rapper himself or herself.

Tokyo in 1984. The French North African immigrant hip hop scene in Paris or the German, British, and Brazilian rap scenes could each fill its own book. I believe these projects will follow and hope that my book will play its part in bringing them to life.

In rap, relationships between black cultural practice, social and economic conditions, technology, sexual and racial politics, and the institutional policing of the popular terrain are complex and in constant motion. Therefore, *Black Noise* is in no way an all-inclusive analysis of every facet of rap's impact on the popular terrain. Instead, it is a selective intervention that explores many, but by no means all, of the extraordinary social, cultural, and political implications of hip hop culture. I have chosen four main areas of inquiry: (1) the history of rap and hip hop in relationship to the New York postindustrial urban terrain; (2) rap's musical and technological interventions; (3) rap's racial politics, institutional critiques, and media and institutional responses; and (4) rap's sexual politics, particularly female rappers' critiques of men and the feminist debates that surround women rappers.

Chapter 1 is a general discussion of the relationship between rap's socially marginalized position and its heavily commercially mediated voices about life in urban America for young black people. It explores the process of rap's commercial marketing, music video production, and the context for its reception. Chapter 2 is a broad sweeping exploration of hip hop (i.e., graffiti, breakdancing, and rap) and considers some primary factors that contributed to its emergence and tracks hip hop's shifting relationship to dominant culture. Striking a balance between Afrodiasporic influences and historically specific structural forces, Chapter 2 grounds rap music in hip hop culture and Afrodiasporic practices at the same time as it demonstrates the ways in which the 1970s urban landscape in New York and broader mass communication, technological, and economic transformations contributed significantly to hip hop's articulation.

Chapter 3 examines rap's technological interventions and the relationship between black oral and musical traditions and technology in rap music production. Rap's process of techno-black cultural syncretism revises and expands black cultural priorities and the use of technological instruments (e.g., sampling equipment). This syncretic process is especially apparent in the relationship between orality and technology in rap and its production of orally derived communal narratives via sampling equipment. This chapter explores these revisions and expansions and then relates them to larger debates over creativity and the industrial effects on musical structures, particularly musical repetition.

Chapter 4 is an extended examination of rap's lyrical transcripts, with specific reference to the relationship between these transcripts and the discursive and institutional territory within which they operate. Using James Scott's interpretation of hidden and public transcripts in popular practices as a framework, the first section is devoted to the ways in which rappers critique the police, the media, and the government and other contradictory moments of discursive and ideological insubordination in rap. The second section unpacks the complex relationship between hidden facets of the institutional policing of rappers and rap fans (e.g., large-venue insurance coverage), media coverage of rap concerts, the social construction of rap-related violence, and the effects of such policing on the content and reception of rap music. Overall, Chapter 4 demonstrates the struggle between rappers' counterdominant public speech acts and the exercise of institutional and discursive power against them.

Chapter 5 also explores the relationship between speech and discursive power, but in this case women rappers' dialogues on sexual politics are the chosen terrain. This chapter examines the ways in which black women rappers work within and against dominant sexual and racial narratives and within and against male rappers' discourse, rather than in complete opposition to them. Three central themes in the works of black female rappers, heterosexual courtship, the centrality of the female voice in women's rap, and black female displays of physical and sexual freedom, are contextualized in two ways. First, in dialogue with male rappers' sexual discourses and second, in dialogue with larger social discourses, particularly feminism.

Trying to speak across different audiences has its pitfalls. At some point in the conversation, each of us feels a bit out of place, unfamiliar with some references. Rappers probably know this better than anyone; their combinations of ever-changing black urban slang with musical, television, film, cartoon, gang culture, karate, and multigenre musical references can't possibly guarantee a posse of listeners with maximum competency in every case. Even the serious hip hop junkie runs the risk of being confused and feeling left out. However, the most receptive listeners are always rewarded. What is at first unfamiliar and perhaps unintelligible is increasingly absorbed, and new ways of seeing and hearing become second nature. This is the sort of creative and dynamic engagement that empowers rap music. I hope that *Black Noise* rewards receptive readers similarly.

Black Noise

◆

CHAPTER ONE

Voices from the Margins
Rap Music and Contemporary Black Cultural Production

✦

Public Enemy's "Can't Truss It" opens with rapper Flavor Flav shouting "Confusion!" over a heavy and energetic bass line. The subsequent lyrics suggest that Flavor Flav is referring to lead rapper Chuck D's story about the legacy of slavery, that it has produced extreme cultural confusion. He could just as easily be describing the history of rap. Rap music is a confusing and noisy element of contemporary American popular culture that continues to draw a great deal of attention to itself. On the one hand, music and cultural critics praise rap's role as an educational tool, point out that black women rappers are rare examples of aggressive pro-women lyricists in popular music, and defend rap's ghetto stories as real-life reflections that should draw attention to the burning problems of racism and economic oppression, rather than to questions of obscenity. On the other hand, news media attention on rap seems fixated on instances of violence at rap concerts, rap producers' illegal use of musical samples, gangsta raps' lurid fantasies of cop killing and female dismemberment, and black nationalist rappers' suggestions that white people are the devil's disciples. These celebratory and inflammatory aspects in rap and the media coverage of them bring to the fore several long-standing debates about popular music and culture. Some of the more contentious disputes revolve around the following questions: Can violent images incite violent action, can music set the stage for political mobilization, do sexually explicit lyrics contribute to the moral "breakdown" of society, and finally, is this really *music* anyway?

And, if these debates about rap music are not confusing enough, rappers engage them in contradictory ways. Some rappers defend the work of gangster rappers and at the same time consider it a negative influence on black youths. Female rappers openly criticize male rappers' sexist work and simultaneously defend the 2 Live Crew's right to sell misogynist music. Rappers who criticize America for its perpetuation of racial and economic discrimination also share conservative ideas about personal responsibility, call for self-improvement strategies in the black community that focus heavily on personal behavior as the cause and solution for crime, drugs, and community instability.

Rap music brings together a tangle of some of the most complex social, cultural, and political issues in contemporary American society. Rap's contradictory articulations are not signs of absent intellectual clarity; they are a common feature of community and popular cultural dialogues that always offer more than one cultural, social, or political viewpoint. These unusually abundant polyvocal conversations seem irrational when they are severed from the social contexts where everyday struggles over resources, pleasure, and meanings take place.

Rap music is a black cultural expression that prioritizes black voices from the margins of urban America. Rap music is a form of rhymed storytelling accompanied by highly rhythmic, electronically based music. It began in the mid-1970s in the South Bronx in New York City as a part of hip hop, an African-American and Afro-Caribbean youth culture composed of graffiti, breakdancing, and rap music. From the outset, rap music has articulated the pleasures and problems of black urban life in contemporary America. Rappers speak with the voice of personal experience, taking on the identity of the observer or narrator. Male rappers often speak from the perspective of a young man who wants social status in a locally meaningful way. They rap about how to avoid gang pressures and still earn local respect, how to deal with the loss of several friends to gun fights and drug overdoses, and they tell grandiose and sometimes violent tales that are powered by male sexual power over women. Female rappers sometimes tell stories from the perspective of a young woman who is skeptical of male protestations of love or a girl who has been involved with a drug dealer and cannot sever herself from his dangerous life-style. Some raps speak to the failures of black men to provide security and attack men where their manhood seems most vulnerable: the pocket. Some tales are one sister telling another to rid herself from the abuse of a lover.

Like all contemporary voices, the rapper's voice is imbedded in powerful and dominant technological, industrial, and ideological institutions. Rappers tell long, involved, and sometimes abstract stories with catchy and memorable phrases and beats that lend themselves to black sound bite packaging, storing critical fragments in fast-paced electrified rhythms. Rap tales are told in elaborate and ever-changing black slang and refer to black cultural figures and rituals, mainstream film, video and television characters, and little-known black heroes. For rap's language wizards, all images, sounds, ideas, and icons are ripe for recontextual-ization, pun, mockery, and celebration. Kool Moe Dee boasts that each of his rhymes is like a dissertation, Kid-N-Play have quoted Jerry Lee Lewis's famous phrase "great balls of fire," Big Daddy Kane brags that he's raw like sushi (and that his object of love has his nose open like a jar of Vicks), Ice Cube refers to his ghetto stories as "tales from the darkside," clearly referencing the television horror show with the same name. Das Efx's raps include Elmer Fud's characteristic "OOOH I'm steamin'!" in full character voice along with a string of almost surreal collagelike references to Bugs Bunny and other television characters. At the same time, the stories, ideas, and thoughts articulated in rap lyrics invoke and revise stylistic and thematic elements that are deeply wedded to a number of black cultural storytelling forms, most promi-nently toasting and the blues. Ice-T and Big Daddy Kane pay explicit homage to Rudy Ray Moore as "Dolomite," Roxanne Shante toasts Millie Jackson, and black folk wisdom and folktales are given new lives and meanings in contemporary culture.

Rap's stories continue to articulate the shifting terms of black mar-ginality in contemporary American culture. Even as rappers achieve what appears to be central status in commercial culture, they are far more vulnerable to censorship efforts than highly visible white rock art-ists, and they continue to experience the brunt of the plantationlike system faced by most artists in the music and sports industries. Even as they struggle with the tension between fame and rap's gravitational pull toward local urban narratives, for the most part, rappers continue to craft stories that represent the creative fantasies, perspectives, and experiences of racial marginality in America.

Rap went relatively unnoticed by mainstream music and popular cul-ture industries until independent music entrepreneur Sylvia Robinson released "Rappers Delight" in 1979. Over the next five years rap music was "discovered" by the music industry, the print media, the fashion in-dustry, and the film industry, each of which hurried to cash in on what was assumed to be a passing fad. During the same years, Run DMC (who recorded the first gold rap record *Run DMC* in 1984), Whodini, and the Fat Boys became the most commercially successful symbols of rap music's sounds and style.

By 1987, rap music had survived several death knells, Hollywood mockery, and radio bans and continued to spawn new artists, such as Public Enemy, Eric B. & Rakim, and L.L. Cool J. At the same time, women rappers, such as MC Lyte and Salt 'N' Pepa, encouraged by Roxanne Shante's early successes, made inroads into rap's emerging commercial audience. Between 1987 and 1990 a number of critical musical and industry changes took place. Public Enemy became rap's first superstar group, and media attention to its black nationalist political articulations intensified. The success of De La Soul's playful Afrocentricity, tongue in cheek spoof of rap's aggressive masculinity and manipulation of America's television culture encouraged the Native Tongues wing of rap that opened the door to such future groups as A Tribe Called Quest, Queen Latifah, Brand Nubian, and Black Sheep. Ice-T put the Los Angeles gangsta rap style on the national map, which encouraged the emergence of NWA, Ice Cube, Too Short, and others.

At the industry level, the effects of rap's infiltration were widespread. Black filmmaker Spike Lee's commercially successful use of b-boys, b-girls, hip hop music, and style in the contemporary urban terrain as primary themes in *She's Gotta Have It* and *Do the Right Thing* fired up Hollywood's new wave of black male ghetto films, most notably, *Colors*, *New Jack City*, *Boyz in the Hood*, *Juice* and *Menace II Society*. By 1989, MTV began playing rap music on a relatively regular basis, and multi-million unit rap sales by the Beastie Boys, Tone Loc, M.C. Hammer and Vanilla Ice convinced music industry executives that rap music, for all of its "blackness" in attitude, style, speech, music, and thematics, was a substantial success with white teenagers.

Rap's black cultural address and its focus on marginal identities may appear to be in opposition to its crossover appeal for people from different racial or ethnic groups and social positions. How can this black public dialogue speak to the thousands of young white suburban boys and girls who are critical to the record sales successes of many of rap's more prominent stars? How can I suggest that rap is committed culturally and emotionally to the pulse, pleasures, and problems of black urban life in the face of such diverse constituencies?

To suggest that rap is a black idiom that prioritizes black culture and that articulates the problems of black urban life does not deny the pleasure and participation of others. In fact, many black musics before rap (e.g., the blues, jazz, early rock 'n' roll) have also become American popular musics precisely because of extensive white participation; white America has always had an intense interest in black culture. Consequently, the fact that a significant number of white teenagers have become rap fans is quite consistent with the history of black music in America and should not be equated with a shift in rap's discursive or stylistic focus away from black pleasure and black fans. However, extensive white participation in black culture has also always involved white appropriation and attempts at ideological recuperation of black cultural resistance. Black culture in the United States has always had elements that have been at least bifocal—speaking to both a black audience and a larger predominantly white context. Rap music shares this history of interaction with many previous black oral and music traditions.

Like generations of white teenagers before them, white teenage rap fans are listening in on black culture, fascinated by its differences, drawn in by mainstream social constructions of black culture as a forbidden narrative, as a symbol of rebellion. Kathy Ogren's study of jazz in the 1920s shows the extensive efforts made by white entertainers and fans to imitate jazz music, dance styles, and language as well as the alarm such fascination caused on the part of state and local authority figures. Lewis Erenberg's study of the development of the cabaret illustrates the centrality of jazz music to the fears over blackness associated with the burgeoning urban nightlife culture. There are similar and abundant cases for rock 'n' roll as well.[1]

Fascination with African-American culture is not new, nor can the dynamics and politics of pleasure across cultural "boundaries" in segregated societies be overlooked. Jazz, rock 'n' roll, soul, and R&B each have large devoted white audience members, many of whom share traits with Norman Mailer's "white negroes," young white listeners trying to perfect a model of correct white hipness, coolness, and style by adopting the latest black style and image. Young white listeners' genuine pleasure and commitment to black music are necessarily affected by dominant racial discourses regarding African Americans, the politics of racial segregation, and cultural difference in the United States. Given the racially discriminatory context within which cultural syncretism takes place, some rappers have equated white participation with a process of dilution and subsequent theft of black culture. Although the terms dilution and theft do not capture the complexity of cultural incorporation and syncretism, this interpretation has more than a grain of truth in it. There is abundant evidence that white artists imitating black styles have greater economic opportunity and access to larger audiences than black innovators. Historical accounts of the genres often position these subsequently better known artists as the central figures, erasing or marginalizing the artists and contexts within which the genre developed. The process of incorporation and marginalization of black practitioners has also fostered the development of black forms and practices that are less and less accessible, forms that require greater knowledge of black language and styles in order to participate. Be Bop, with its insider language and its "willfully harsh, anti-assimilationist sound" is a clear example of this response to the continuation of plantation system logic in American culture.[2] In addition to the sheer pleasure black musicians derive from developing a new and exciting style, these black cultural reactions to American culture suggest a reclaiming of the definition of blackness and an attempt to retain aesthetic control over black cultural forms. In the 1980s, this re-claiming of blackness in the popular realm is complicated by access to new reproduction technologies and revised corporate relations in the music industry.

In a number of ways, rap has followed the patterns of other black popular musics, in that at the outset it was heavily rejected by black and white middle-class listeners; the assumption was that it would be a short-lived fad; the mainstream record industry and radio stations rejected it; its marketing was pioneered by independent entrepreneurs and independent labels; and once a smidgen of commercial viability was established the major labels attempted to dominate production and distribution. These rap-related patterns were augmented by more general music industry consolidation in the late 1970s that provided the major music corporations with greater control over the market. By 1990 virtually all major record chain store distribution is controlled by six major record companies: CBS, Polygram, Warner, BMG, Capitol-EMI, and MCA.[3]

However, music industry consolidation and control over distribution is complicated by three factors: the expansion of local cable access, sophisticated and accessible mixing, production, and copying equipment, and a new relationship between major and independent record labels. In previous eras when independent labels sustained the emergence of new genres against industry rejection, the eventual absorption of these genres by larger companies signalled the dissolution of the independent labels. In the early 1980s, after rap spurred the growth of new independent labels, the major labels moved in and attempted to dominate the market but could not consolidate their efforts. Artists signed to independent labels, particularly Tommy Boy, Profile, and Def Jam continued to flourish, whereas acts signed directly to the six majors could not produce comparable sales. It became apparent that the independent labels had a much greater understanding of the cultural logic of hip hop and rap music, a logic that permeated decisions ranging from signing acts to promotional methods. Instead of competing with smaller, more street-savvy labels for new rap acts, the major labels developed a new strategy: buy the independent labels, allow them to function relatively autonomously, and provide them with production resources and access to major retail distribution.[4] Since the emergence of Public Enemy and their substantial cross-genre success in the late 1980s, rappers have generally been signed to independent labels (occasionally black owned and sometimes their own labels) and marketed and distributed by one of the six major companies. In this arrangement, the six majors reap the benefits of a genre that can be marketed with little up-front capital investment, and the artists are usually pleased to have access to the large record and CD chain stores that would otherwise never consider carrying their work.

In the 1980s, the trickle-down effect of technological advances in electronics brought significantly expanded access to mixing, dubbing, and copying equipment for consumers and black market retailers. Clearly, these advances provided aspiring musicians with greater access to recording and copying equipment at less expense. They also substantially improved the market for illegal dubbing of popular music for street corner sale at reduced cost. (Illegally recorded cassette tapes cost approximately $5.00, one-half the cost of label issues.) These lower quality tapes are usually sold in poorer, densely populated communities where reduced cost is a critical sales factor. Rap music is a particularly popular genre for bootleg tapes in urban centers.[5]

Even though actual sales demographics for rap music are not available, increasing sales figures for rap musicians (several prominent rap artists have sales over 500,000 units per album), suggest that white teenage rap consumers have grown steadily since the emergence of Public Enemy in 1988.[6] Middle-class white teenage rap consumers appear to be an increasingly significant audience. This can be inferred from location sales via market surveys and Soundscan, a new electronic scan system installed primarily in large, mostly suburban music chain stores. It is quite possible, however, that the percentage of white rap consumers in relation to overall sales is being disproportionately represented, because bootleg street sales coupled with limited chain music store outlets in poor communities makes it very difficult to assess the demographics for actual sales of rap music to urban black and Hispanic consumers. In addition to inconsistent sales figures, black teen rap consumers may also have a higher "pass-along rate," that is, the rate at which one purchased product is shared among consumers. In my conversations with James Bernard, an editor at *The Source* (a major hip hop culture magazine with a predominantly black teen readership), *The Source's* pass-along rate is approximately 1 purchase for every 11–15 readers. According to Bernard, this rate is at least three to four times higher than the average magazine industry pass-along rate. It is conceivable, then, that a similar pass-along rate exists among rap music CD and cassette consumption, especially among consumers with less disposable income.

Cable television exploded during the 1980s and had a significant effect on the music industry and on rap music. Launched in August 1981 by Warner Communications and the American Express Company, MTV became the fastest growing cable channel and as Garofalo points out, "soon became the most effective way for a record to get national exposure."[7] Using its rock format and white teen audience as an explanation for its almost complete refusal to play videos by black artists (once pressure was brought to bear they added Michael Jackson and Prince), MTV finally jumped on the rap music bandwagon. It was not until 1989, with the piloting of "Yo! MTV Raps" that any black artists began to appear on MTV regularly. Since then, as Jamie Malanowski reports, "'Yo MTV Raps' [has become] one of MTV's most popular shows, is dirt cheap to produce and has almost single-handedly dispelled the giant tastemaking network's reputation for not playing black artists."[8]

Since 1989, MTV has discovered that black artists in several genres are marketable to white suburban teenagers and has dramatically revised its formatting to include daily rap shows, Street Block (dance music), and the rotation of several black artists outside of specialized-genre rotation periods. However, MTV's previous exclusion of black artists throughout the mid-1980s, inspired other cable stations to program black music videos. Black Entertainment Television (BET), the most notable alternative to MTV, continues to air a wide variety of music videos by black artists as one of its programming mainstays. And local and syndicated shows (e.g., "Pump It Up!" based in Los Angeles and "Video Music Box" based in New York), continue to play rap music videos, particularly lower budget, and aggressively black nationalist rap videos deemed too angry or too antiwhite for MTV.

MTV's success has created an environment in which the reception and marketing of music is almost synonymous with the production of music videos. Fan discussions of popular songs and the stories they tell are often accompanied by a reading of the song's interpretation in music video. Music video is a collaboration in the production of popular music; it revises meanings, provides preferred interpretations of lyrics, creates a stylistic and physical context for reception; and valorizes the iconic presence of the artist. Can we really imagine, nonetheless understand, the significance of Michael Jackson's presence as a popular cultural icon without interpreting his music video narratives? The same holds true for Madonna, Janet Jackson, U2, Whitney Houston, Nirvana, and Guns N Roses among others. The visualization of music has far-reaching effects on musical cultures and popular culture generally, not the least of which is the increase in visual interpretations of sexist power relationships, the mode of visual storytelling, the increased focus on how a singer looks rather than how he or she sounds, the need to craft an image to accompany one's music, and ever-greater pressure to abide by corporate genre-formatting rules.

The significance of music video as a partner in the creation or reception of popular music is even greater in the case of rap music. Because the vast majority of rap music (except by the occasional superstar) has been virtually frozen out of black radio programming—black radio representatives claim that it scares off high-quality advertising—and because of its limited access to large performance venues, music video has been a crucial outlet for rap artist audiences and performer visibility. Rap music videos have animated hip hop cultural style and aesthetics and have facilitated a cross-neighborhood, cross-country (transnational?) dialogue in a social environment that is highly segregated by class and race.

The emergence of rap music video has also opened up a previously nonexistent creative arena for black visual artists. Rap music video has provided a creative and commercially viable arena where black film, video, set design, costume, and technical staff and trainees can get the crucial experience and connections to get a foot in the world of video and film production. Before music video production for black musicians, these training grounds, however exploitative, were virtually inaccessible to black technicians. The explosion of music video production, especially black music video, has generated a pool of skilled young black workers in the behind-the-scenes nonunion crews (union membership is overwhelmingly white and male), who are beginning to have an impact on current black film production.

Shooting in the Ghetto: locating rap music video production

Rap video has also developed its own style and its own genre conventions. These conventions visualize hip hop style and usually affirm

© Lisa Leone

rap's primary thematic concerns: identity and location. Over most of its brief history (rap video production began in earnest in the mid-to-late 1980s), rap video themes have repeatedly converged around the depiction of the local neighborhood and the local posse, crew, or support system. Nothing is more central to rap's music video narratives than situating the rapper in his or her milieu and among one's crew or posse. Unlike heavy metal videos, for example, which often use dramatic live concert footage and the concert stage as the core location, rap music videos are set on buses, subways, in abandoned buildings, and almost always in black urban inner-city locations. This usually involves ample shots of favorite street corners, intersections, playgrounds, parking lots, school yards, roofs, and childhood friends. When I asked seasoned music video director Kevin Bray what comprised the three most important themes in rap video, his immediate response was, "Posse, posse, and posse. . . . They'll say, 'I want my shit to be in my hood. Yeah, we got this dope old parking lot where I used to hang out when I was a kid.'"[9] The hood is not a generic designation; videos featuring South Central Los Angeles rappers such as Ice Cube, Ice-T, and NWA very often capture the regional specificity of spatial, ethnic, temperate, and psychological facets of black marginality in Los Angeles, whereas Naughty by Nature's videos feature the ghetto specificity of East Orange, New Jersey.[10]

Rappers' emphasis on posses and neighborhoods has brought the ghetto back into the public consciousness. It satisfies poor young black people's profound need to have their territories acknowledged, recognized, and celebrated. These are the street corners and neighborhoods that usually serve as lurid backdrops for street crimes on the nightly news. Few local people are given an opportunity to speak, and their points of view are always contained by expert testimony. In rap videos, young mostly male residents speak for themselves and for the community, they speak when and how they wish about subjects of their choosing. These local turf scenes are not isolated voices; they are voices from a variety of social margins that are in dialogue with one another. As Bray points out, "If you have an artist from Detroit, the reason they want to shoot at least one video on their home turf is to make a connection with, say, an East Coast New York rapper. It's the dialogue. It's the dialogue between them about where they're from."[11]

However, the return of the ghetto as a central black popular narrative has also fulfilled national fantasies about the violence and danger that purportedly consume the poorest and most economically fragile communities of color. Some conservative critics such as George Will have affirmed the "reality" of some popular cultural ghetto narratives and used this praise as a springboard to call for more police presence and military invasionlike policies.[12] In other cases, such as that of white rapper Vanilla Ice, the ghetto is a source of fabricated white authenticity. Controversy surrounding Ice, one of rap music's most commercially successful artists, highlights the significance of "ghetto blackness" as a model of "authenticity" and hipness in rap music. During the winter of 1989, Vanilla Ice summoned the wrath of the hip hop community not only by successfully marketing himself as a white rapper but also by "validating" his success with stories about his close ties to black poor neighborhoods, publicly sporting his battle scars from the black inner city. According to *Village Voice* columnist Rob Tannenbaum, Robert Van Winkle (aka Vanilla Ice) told Stephen Holden of the *New York Times* that "he 'grew up in the ghetto,' comes from a broken home, hung out mainly with blacks while attending the same Miami high school as Luther Campbell of 2 Live Crew, and was nearly killed in a gang fight." Yet, in a copyrighted, front page story in the Dallas *Morning News*, Ken P. Perkins charges, among other things, that Mr. Van Winkle is instead a middle-class kid from

Dallas, Texas.[13] Vanilla Ice's desire to be a "white negro" (or, as some black and white hip hop fans say, a Wigger—a white nigger), to "be black" in order to validate his status as a rapper hints strongly at the degree to which ghetto-blackness is a critical code in rap music. Vanilla Ice not only pretended to be from the ghetto, but he also pretended to have produced the music for his mega-hit "Ice, Ice Baby." In keeping with his pretenses, he only partially credited—and paid no royalties to—black friend and producer Mario Johnson, aka Chocolate(!), who actually wrote the music for "Ice, Ice Baby" and a few other cuts from Vanilla's fifteen times platinum record *To the Extreme*. After a lengthy court battle, Chocolate is finally getting paid in full.[14]

Convergent forces are behind this resurgence of black ghetto symbolism and representation. Most important, the ghetto *exists* for millions of young black and other people of color—it is a profoundly significant social location. Using the ghetto as a source of identity—as rapper Trech would say, if you're not from the ghetto, don't ever come to the ghetto—undermines the stigma of poverty and social marginality. At the same time, the ghetto badman posture-performance is a protective shell against real unyielding and harsh social policies and physical environments. Experience also dictates that public attention is more easily drawn to acts, images, and threats of black male violence than to any other form of racial address. The ghetto produces a variety of meanings for diverse audiences, but this should not be interpreted to mean that intragroup black meanings and uses are less important than larger social receptions. Too often, white voyeuristic pleasure of black cultural imagery or such imagery's role in the performance of ghetto crisis for the news media, are interpreted as their primary value. Even though rappers are aware of the diversity of their audiences and the context for reception, their use of the ghetto and its symbolic significances is primarily directed at other black hip hop fans. If white teen and adult viewers were the preferred audience, then it wouldn't matter which ghetto corner framed images of Trech from rap group Naughty by Nature, especially as most white popular cultural depictions of ghetto life are drained of relevant detail, texture, and complexity. Quite to the contrary, rap's ghetto imagery is too often intensely specific and locally significant, making its preferred viewer someone who can read ghettocentricity with ghetto sensitivity.

The fact that rappers' creative desires or location requests are frequently represented in music videos should not lead one to believe that rappers control the music video process. Music video production is a complex and highly mediated process dictated by the record company in what is sometimes a contentious dialogue with the artists' management, the chosen video director, and video producer. Even though the vast majority of the music video production budget is advanced from the artists' royalties (rap video budgets can range from a low $5,000 to an unusual $100,000 with an average video costing about $40,000), the artist has very little final decision-making control over the video process. Generally speaking, once the single is chosen, a group of music video directors are solicited by the record company, management, and artist to submit video ideas or treatments, and an estimated budget range is projected. After listening to the rapper's work, the video directors draft narrative treatments that usually draw on the rap artists' desires, strengths, lyrical focus, and the feel of the music while attempting to incorporate his or her own visual and technical strengths and preferred visual styles. Once a director is selected, the treatment and budget are refined, negotiated, and the video is cast and produced.[15]

In the first few years of rap video production, the record companies were less concerned about music video's creative process, leaving artists and directors more creative decision-making power. As rappers developed more financial viability, record companies became increasingly invasive at the editing stage, going even so far as to make demands about shot selection and sequencing. This intervention has been facilitated by record companies' increasing sophistication about the video production process. Recently, record companies have begun hiring ex-freelance video producers as video commissioners whose familiarity with the production process aids the record company in channeling and constraining directors, producers, and artist decisions. For veteran music video director Charles Stone, these commercial constraints define music video, in the final analysis, as a commercial product: "Commercial expectations are always an undercurrent. Questions like, does the artist look good, is the artist's image being represented—are always a part of your decision-making process. You have to learn how to protect yourself from excessive meddling, but some negotiation with record companies and artist management always takes place."[16]

With rap's genre and stylistic conventions and artists' desires flanking one side of the creative process and the record company's fiscal and artist management's marketing concerns shoring up the other, music video directors are left with a tight space within which to exercise their creativity. Still, video directors find imaginative ways to engage the musical and lyrical texts and enter into dialogue with the rappers' work. For Bray and other directors, the best videos have the capacity to offer new interpretations after multiple viewings, they have the spontaneity and intertextuality of the music, and most importantly, as Bray describes, the best videos are "sublime visual interpretations of the lyrics which work as another instrument in the musical arrangement; the music video is a visual instrument." Sometimes this visual instrumentation is a thematic improvisation on the historical point of reference suggested by the musical samples. So, a cool jazz horn sample might evoke a contemporary refashioning of a jazz club or cool jazz coloring or art direction. Stone often relies on text and animation to produce creative interpretations of musical works. "Using word overlay," Stone says, "is particularly compatible with rap's use of language. Both are candid and aggressive uses of words, and both play with words' multiple meanings." His selective and unconventional use of animation often makes rappers seem larger than life and can visually emphasize the superheroic powers suggested by rappers' lyrical delivery and performance.

Satisfying the record companies, artists, and managers is only half the battle; MTV, the most powerful video outlet, has its own standards and guidelines for airing videos. These guidelines, according to several frustrated directors, producers, and video commissioners, are inconsistent and unwritten. The most consistent rule is the "absolutely not" list (that some people claim has been subverted by powerful artists and record companies). The "absolutely not" list includes certain acts of violence, some kinds of nudity and sex, profanity and epithets (e.g., "nigger" or "bitch" no matter how these words are being used). The list of censored words and actions expands regularly.

Independent video producer Gina Harrell notes that the process of establishing airing boundaries takes place on a case-by-case basis. MTV is frequently sent a rough cut for approval as part of the editing process to determine if they will *consider* airing the video, and often several changes, such as word reversals, scene cuts, and lyrical rewrites, must be made to accommodate their standards: "Afterwards, you wind up with very little to work with. There is so much censorship now, and from the other end, the record company's video commissioners are much more exacting about what they want the end result to be. It has extended the editing process and raised production costs. Basically, there are too many cooks in the kitchen." There is, not surprisingly, special concern over violence: "The cop issue has really affected rap music video. You can't shoot anybody in a video, you can hold up a gun, but you can't show who you're pointing at. So you can hold up a gun in one frame and then cut to the person being shot in the next frame, but you can't have a person shooting at another person in the same frame."[17] Even so, many artists refuse to operate in a self-censoring fashion and continue to push on these fluid boundaries by shooting footage that they expect will be censored.

MTV's sex policies are equally vague. Although MTV has aired such a video as Wrecks-N-Effect's "Rumpshaker," whose concept is a series of closeup and sometimes magnified distortions of black women's bikini-clad gyrating behinds and breasts, it refused to allow A Tribe Called Quest to say the word *prophylactic* in the lyrical soundtrack for the video "Bonita Applebum," a romantic and uncharacteristically emotionally honest portrayal of teen desire and courtship. MTV denied Stone's request to show condoms in the video, even though the song's mild references to sex and his video treatment were cast in safe sex language. Given the power of cultural conservatives to "strike the fear of god" in music industry corporations, most video producers and directors are bracing themselves for further restrictions.

Rap music and video have been wrongfully characterized as thoroughly sexist but rightfully lambasted for their sexism. I am thoroughly frustrated but not surprised by the apparent need for some rappers to craft elaborate and creative stories about the abuse and domination of young black women. Perhaps these stories serve to protect young men from the reality of female rejection; maybe and more likely, tales of sexual domination falsely relieve their lack of self-worth and limited access to economic and social markers for heterosexual masculine power. Certainly, they reflect the deep-seated sexism that pervades the structure of American culture. Still, I have grown weary of rappers' stock retorts to charges of sexism in rap: "There are 'bitches' or 'golddiggers' out there, and that's who this rap is about," or "This is just a story, I don't *mean anything* by it." I have also grown impatient with the cowardly silence of rappers who I know find this aspect of rap troubling.

On the other hand, given the selective way in which the subject of sexism occupies public dialogue, I am highly skeptical of the timing and strategic deployment of outrage regarding rap's sexism. Some responses to sexism in rap music adopt a tone that suggests that rappers have infected an otherwise sexism-free society. These reactions to rap's sexism deny the existence of a vast array of accepted sexist social practices that make up adolescent male gender role modeling that results in social norms for adult male behaviors that are equally sexist, even though they are usually expressed with less profanity. Few popular analyses of rap's sexism seem willing to confront the fact that sexual and institutional control over and abuse of women is a crucial component of developing a heterosexual masculine identity. In some instances, the music has become a scapegoat that diverts attention away from the more entrenched problem of redefining the terms of heterosexual masculinity.

Rap's sexist lyrics are also part of a rampant and viciously normalized sexism that dominates the corporate culture of the music business. Not only do women face gross pay inequities, but also they face extraordinary day-to-day sexual harassment. Male executives expect to have sexual and social access to women as one of many job perks, and many women, especially black women, cannot establish authority with male coworkers or artists in the business unless they are backed up by male superiors. Independent video producers do not have this institutional backup and, therefore, face exceptionally oppressive work conditions. Harrell has left more than one position because of recurrent, explicit pressure to sleep with her superiors and finds the video shoots an even more unpredictably offensive and frustrating terrain:

For instance, during a meeting with Def Jam executives on a video shoot, a very famous rapper started lifting up my pants leg trying to rub my leg. I slapped his hand away several times. Later on he stood onstage sticking his tongue out at me in a sexually provocative way—everyone was aware of what he was doing, no one said a word. This happens quite a bit in the music business. Several years ago I had begun producing videos for a video director who made it clear that I could not continue to work with him unless I slept with him. I think that women are afraid to respond legally or aggressively, not only because many of us fear professional recriminations, but also because so many of us were molested when we were children. Those experiences complicate our ability to defend ourselves.[18]

These instances are not exceptions to the rule—they are the rule, even for women near the very top of the corporate ladder. As Carmen Ashhurst-Watson, president of Rush Communications (a multimedia offshoot of Def Jam Records) relates: "The things that Anita Hill said she heard from Clarence Thomas over a four-year period, I might hear in a morning."[19]

Mass media outlets need to be challenged into opening dialogue about pervasive and oppressive sexual conditions in society and into facilitating more frank discussion about sexist gender practices and courtship rituals. The terms of sexual identities, sexual oppression, and their relationship to a variety of forms of social violence need unpacking and closer examination. Basically, we need more discussions about sex, sexism, and violence, not less.

MTV and the media access it affords is a complex and ever-changing facet of mass-mediated and corporation-controlled communication and culture. To refuse to participate in the manipulative process of gaining access to video, recording materials, and performing venues is to almost guarantee a negligible audience and marginal cultural impact. To participate in and try to manipulate the terms of mass-mediated culture is a double-edged sword that cuts both ways—it provides communication channels within and among largely disparate groups and requires compromise that often affirms the very structures much of rap's philosophy seems determined to undermine. MTV's acceptance and gatekeeping of rap music has dramatically increased rap artists' visibility to black, white, Asian, and Latino teenagers, but it has also inspired antirap censorship groups and fuels the media's fixation on rap and violence.

Commercial marketing of rap music represents a complex and contradictory aspect of the nature of popular expression in a corporation-dominated information society. Rap music and hip hop style have become common ad campaign hooks for McDonald's, Burger King, Coke, Pepsi, several athletic shoe companies, clothing chain stores, MTV, anti-drug campaigns, and other global corporate efforts ad nauseam. Rap music has grown into a multimillion dollar record, magazine, and video industry with multiplatinum world renowned rappers, disc jockeys, and entertainers. Dominating the black music charts, rap music and rap music cousins, such as Hip House, New Jack Swing (a dance style of R&B with rap music rhythms and drum beats), have been trendsetters for popular music in the U.S. and around the world. Rap's musical and visual style have had a profound impact on all contemporary popular music. Rock artists have begun using sampling styles and techniques developed by rappers; highly visible artists, such as Madonna, Janet Jackson, and New Kids on the Block wear hip hop fashions, use hip hop dances in their stage shows and rap lyrics and slang words in their recordings.

Yet, rap music is also Black American TV, a public and highly accessible place, where black meanings and perspectives—even as they are manipulated by corporate concerns—can be shared and validated among black people. Rap is dependent on technology and mass reproduction and distribution. As Andrew Ross has observed, popular music is capable of transmitting, disseminating, and rendering "visible 'black' meanings, *precisely because of*, and not in spite of, its industrial forms of production, distribution, and consumption."[20] Such tensions between rap's highly personal, conversational intimacy and the massive institutional and technological apparatuses on which rap's global voice depends are critical to hip hop, black culture, and popular cultures around

© suekwon

the world in the late twentieth century. Inside of these commercial constraints, rap offers alternative interpretations of key social events such as the Gulf War, The Los Angeles uprising, police brutality, censorship efforts, and community-based education. It is the central cultural vehicle for open social reflection on poverty, fear of adulthood, the desire for absent fathers, frustrations about black male sexism, female sexual desires, daily rituals of life as an unemployed teen hustler, safe sex, raw anger, violence, and childhood memories. It is also the home of innovative uses of style and language, hilariously funny carnivalesque and chitlin-circuit-inspired dramatic skits, and ribald storytelling. In short, it is black America's most dynamic contemporary popular cultural, intellectual, and spiritual vessel.

Rap's ability to draw the attention of the nation, to attract crowds around the world in places where English is rarely spoken are fascinating elements of rap's social power. Unfortunately, some of this power is linked to U.S.-based cultural imperialism, in that rappers benefit from the disproportionate exposure of U.S. artists around the world facilitated by music industry marketing muscle. However, rap also draws international audiences because it is a powerful conglomeration of voices from the margins of American society speaking about the terms of that position. Rap music, like many powerful black cultural forms before it, resonates for people from vast and diverse backgrounds. The cries of pain, anger, sexual desire, and pleasure that rappers articulate speak to hip hop's vast fan base for different reasons. For some, rappers offer symbolic prowess, a sense of black energy and creativity in the face of omnipresent oppressive forces; others listen to rap with an ear toward the hidden voices of the oppressed, hoping to understand America's large, angry, and "unintelligible" population. Some listen to the music's powerful and life-affirming rhythms, its phat beats and growling bass lines, revelling in its energy, seeking strength from its cathartic and electric presence. Rap's global industry-orchestrated (but not industry-created) presence illustrates the power of the language of rap and the salience of the stories of oppression and creative resistance its music and lyrics tell. The drawing power of rap is precisely its musical and narrative commitment to black youth and cultural resistance, and nothing in rap's commercial position and cross-cultural appeal contradicts this fact. Rap's margin(ality) is represented in the contradictory reaction rap receives in mainstream American media and popular culture. It is at once part of the dominant text and, yet, always on the margins of this text; relying on and commenting on the text's center and always aware of its proximity to the border.

Rap music and hip hop culture are cultural, political, and commercial forms, and for many young people they are the primary cultural, sonic, and linguistic windows on the world. After the Los Angeles riots, author Mike Davis attended an Inglewood Crip and Blood gang truce meeting in which gang members voiced empassioned testimonials and called for unity and political action. Describing their speeches, Davis said: "These guys were very eloquent, and they spoke in a rap rhythm and with rap eloquence, which I think kind of shook up the white television crews." Later, he noted that the gang truce and the political struggles articulated in that meeting were "translated into the [hip hop] musical culture." Hip hop, Davis concluded, "is the fundamental matrix of self-expression for this whole generation."[21]

CHAPTER TWO

"All Aboard the Night Train"

Flow, Layering, and Rupture in Postindustrial New York

◆

> Got a bum education, double-digit inflation
> Can't take the train to the job, there's a strike at the station
> Don't push me cause I'm close to the edge
> I'm tryin' not to lose my head
> It's like a jungle sometimes it makes me wonder
> How I keep from going under.
> —"The Message"[1]

Life on the margins of postindustrial urban America is inscribed in hip hop style, sound, lyrics, and thematics.[2] Situated at the "crossroads of lack and desire," hip hop emerges from the deindustrialization meltdown where social alienation, prophetic imagination, and yearning intersect.[3] Hip hop is a cultural form that attempts to negotiate the experiences of marginalization, brutally truncated opportunity, and oppression within the cultural imperatives of African-American and Caribbean history, identity, and community. It is the tension between the cultural fractures produced by postindustrial oppression and the binding ties of black cultural expressivity that sets the critical frame for the development of hip hop.[4]

The dynamic tensions and contradictions shaping hip hop culture can confound efforts at interpretation by even the most skilled critics and observers. Some analysts see hip hop as a quintessentially postmodern practice, and others view it as a present-day successor to premodern oral traditions. Some celebrate its critique of consumer capitalism, and others condemn it for its complicity with commercialism. To one enthusiastic group of critics, hip hop combines elements of speech and song, of dance and display, to call into being through performance new identities and subject positions. Yet, to another equally vociferous group, hip hop merely displays in phantasmagorical form the cultural logic of late capitalism. I intend to demonstrate the importance of locating hip hop culture within the context of deindustrialization, to show how both postmodern and premodern interpretive frames fail to do justice to its complexities, and how hip hop's primary properties of flow, layering, and rupture simultaneously reflect and contest the social roles open to urban inner-city youths at the end of the twentieth century.

Worked out on the rusting urban core as a playground, hip hop transforms stray technological parts intended for cultural and industrial trash heaps into sources of pleasure and power. These transformations have become a basis for digital imagination all over the world. Its earliest practitioners came of age at the tail end of the Great Society, in the twilight of America's short-lived federal commitment to black civil rights and during the predawn of the Reagan-Bush era.[5] In hip hop, these abandoned parts, people, and social institutions were welded and then spliced together, not only as sources of survival but as sources of pleasure.

Hip hop replicates and reimagines the experiences of urban life and symbolically appropriates urban space through sampling, attitude, dance, style, and sound effects. Talk of subways, crews and posses, urban noise, economic stagnation, static and crossed signals leap out of hip hop lyrics, sounds, and themes. Graffiti artists spraypainted murals and (name) "tags" on trains, trucks, and playgrounds, claiming territories and inscribing their otherwise contained identities on public property.[6] Early breakdancers' elaborate technologically inspired street corner dances involving head spins on concrete sidewalks made the streets theatrically friendly and served as makeshift youth centers. The dancers' electric robotic mimicry and identity-transforming characterizations foreshadowed the fluid and shocking effect of morphing, a visual effect made famous in *Terminator* 2.[7] DJs who initiated spontaneous street parties by attaching customized, makeshift turntables and speakers to street light electrical sources revised the use of central thoroughfares, made "open-air" community centers in neighborhoods where there were none. Rappers seized and used microphones as if amplification was a lifegiving source. Hip hop gives voice to the tensions and contradictions in the public urban landscape during a period of substantial transformation in New York and attempts to seize the shifting urban terrain, to make it work on behalf of the dispossessed.

Hip hop's attempts to negotiate new economic and technological conditions as well as new patterns of race, class, and gender oppression in urban America by appropriating subway facades, public streets, language, style, and sampling technology are only part of the story. Hip hop music and culture also relies on a variety of Afro-Caribbean and Afro-American musical, oral, visual, and dance forms and practices in the face of a larger society that rarely recognizes the Afrodiasporic significance of such practices. It is, in fact, the dynamic and often contentious relationship between the two—larger social and political forces and black cultural priorities—that centrally shape and define hip hop.

In their work on the blues, Houston A. Baker and Hazel Carby describe the ways in which various themes and sounds in blues music articulate race-, gender-, and class-related experiences in southern rural black life, as well as the effects of industrialization and black northern and urban migration. Similarly, George Lipsitz's work on rock 'n' roll illustrates how post–WW II labor-related migration patterns, urbanization, municipal policies, and war-related technology critically shaped the sounds and themes in early rock 'n' roll and the cultural integrations that made it possible.[8] He also illustrates how rock 'n' roll depended heavily on black musical structures, slang, and performance rituals in producing its own lexicon.

Examining how musical forms are shaped by social forces is important, because it brings into focus how significantly technology and economics contribute to the development of cultural forms. It also illuminates both the historically specific aspects of musical expressions (e.g., rock 'n' roll as a post–WW II phenomena) and the stylistic links between musical forms across historical periods (e.g., mapping the relationship between rock 'n' roll and blues music). In line with this, Andre Craddock-Willis situates four major black musical forms: the blues, jazz, rhythm and blues, and rap as expressions that emerge in relation to significant historical conditions and the relationship between black Americans and the larger political and social character of America. Linking jazz to de facto racial segregation, rhythm and blues to the nagging inequality that fueled the civil rights movement, Willis locates these musical genres as cultural forms that articulate in part community reactions to specific social and political contexts. Yet, he also alludes to the points of continuity between these and other black forms and practices, such as the cultural traditions, styles, and approaches to sound, motion, and rhythm that link jazz to blues and blues to rap.[9]

Willis, however, misapplies this useful formulation when he attends to rap music and its relationship to contemporary American society. For him, rap's distinguishing characteristic is its status as a postmodern form whose contradictory articulations are a by-product of the postmodern condition. In describing rap music as "an expression of the complexity of post-modern African-American life," Willis argues that rap's contradictory stance toward capitalism, its raging sexism, and other "non progressive" elements are unresolved postmodern contradictions that, once they have been sorted out, will permit rap to take its place "on the historical continuum of Black musical expression." Willis perceives rap's contradictory positions to be postmodern contradictions, rather than an expression of long-standing social and political inequalities and beliefs. He situates rap's "bad" facets as points of discontinuity with previous black cultural forms and its "good" facets as points of continuity, going so far as to suggest that once these good and evil forces are worked out and good has prevailed, rap will be able to "take its place at the altar" of emancipatory black cultural production.[10]

There are at least three major, yet familiar, problems with this formulation. First, it vigorously erases the contradictory stance toward capitalism, raging sexism, and other "non progressive" elements that have *always* been part and parcel of jazz, the blues, and R&B, as well as any number of other nonblack cultural forms. Early toasts are as vulgar and jazz and blues lyrics are as sexist as any contemporary rap lyrics; the desire for commodities as articulated in some blues and R&B lyrics rivals rap's frequent obsession with conspicuous consumption. One must have rather deeply rose-tinted lenses to miss the abundant and persistent existence of these "non progressive" elements throughout many cultural expressions.

Second, it necessarily refuses to understand these contradictions as *central* to hip hop and to popular cultural articulations in general. Hip hop's liberatory, visionary, and politically progressive elements are deeply linked to those regressive elements that Willis believes "sells the tradition short." This aspect of hip hop's contradictions is not unique to postmodernity, it is a central aspect of popular expression and popular thought. In other words, cultural forms contain cultural ideas and ways of thinking that are already a part of social life. In fact, it is these contradictions that make the culture coherent and relevant to the society in which it operates. It is the contradictory nature of pleasure and social resistance in the popular realm that must be confronted, theorized, and understood, instead of erasing or rigidly rejecting those practices that ruin our quest for untainted politically progressive cultural expressions.[11]

Finally, his identification of rap as a postmodern form is not consistent with his previous formulations of jazz, blues, and R&B as forms that are rooted in economic relations, power relationships, and social struggle. To be consistent with his historical linking of jazz to de facto segregation and R&B to the "de-humanization" that fueled the civil rights movement, he should have linked rap *and* hip hop more directly to the processes of urban deindustrialization in the 1970s, the post-industrial urban landscape in the 1980s, and their impact on African-American urban communities.

Expanding Willis's frame to include hip hop, I would like to retain his central formulation; that is, the necessary tension between the historical specificity of hip hop's emergence and the points of continuity between hip hop and several Afrodiasporic forms, traditions, and practices. Hip hop's development in relationship to New York cultural politics in the 1970s is not unlike the relationship between other major cultural expressions and the broader social contexts within which they emerged. Hip hop shares the experimental and innovative qualities that characterized rock 'n' roll, the blues, and many other musically based cultural forms that have developed at the junctures of major social transitions. Yet, the emergence of hip hop's styles and sounds cannot be considered mere by-products of these broad sweeping forces. Hip hop is propelled by Afrodiasporic traditions. Stylistic continuities in dance, vocal articulations, and instrumentation between rap, breakdancing, urban blues, be bop, and rock 'n' roll move within and between these historical junctions and larger social forces, creating Afrodiasporic narratives that manage and stabilize these transitions.[12]

In an attempt to rescue rap from its identity as postindustrial commercial product and situate it in the history of respected black cultural practices, many historical accounts of rap's roots consider it a direct extension of African-American oral, poetic, and protest traditions, to which it is clearly and substantially indebted. This accounting, which builds important bridges between rap's use of boasting, signifying, preaching, and earlier related black oral traditions produces at least three problematic effects. First, it reconstructs rap music as a singular oral poetic form that appears to have developed autonomously (e.g., outside hip hop culture) in the 1970s; quite to the contrary, as music historian Reebee Garofalo points out, "rap music must be understood as one cultural element within a larger social movement known as hip hop."[13] Second, it substantially marginalizes the significance of rap's *music*. Rap's musical elements and its use of music technology are a crucial aspect of the development of the form and are absolutely critical to the evolution of hip hop generally. Third, it renders invisible the crucial role of the postindustrial city on the shape and direction of rap and hip hop. Clearly, rap's oral and protest roots, its use of toasting, signifying, boasting, and black folklore are vitally important; however these influences are only one facet of the context for rap's emergence. Rap's primary context for development is hip hop culture, the Afrodiasporic traditions it extends and revises, *and* the New York urban terrain in the 1970s.

Situating the emergence of rap music inside hip hop is not simply a matter of historical accuracy. If the specificity of rap music is to be fully understood, the coherence of hip hop style and how rap developed inside of it is crucial. The hip hop context helps to show how rap is separate and distinct from other related black forms such as toasting and signifying and how its musical collages, which have discrete qualities that differ from jazz, R&B, disco, and soul, developed. It also provides a richer understanding of the intertextual relationships between graffiti, rap, and breakdancing. Although rap is clearly a form of protest, naming it protest music is not sufficient motivation for the emergence of rap music or hip hop. Being angry and poor were not new or unusual phenomena for many African Americans in the 1970s. Furthermore, as a great deal of the history of black cultural practices has been disproportionately explored via male subjects, the oral and protest roots models for rap's development refer to a male-centered scholarly tradition that inadvertently contributes to a contemporary analysis that further marginalizes women producers.[14] Women, although fewer in number than their male counterparts, were integral members in hip hop culture several years before "Rapper's Delight" brought rapping to dominant American popular music. Gender politics were an important facet of hip hop's development. Finally, and most important for my purposes, an examination of how and why hip hop arises helps us to understand the logic of rap's development and links the intertextual and dialogic qualities in rap to the diverse cultural and social context within which it emerges.

The chief questions under consideration are: What is hip hop culture, and what contributed to its emergence? What are some of the defining aesthetic and stylistic characteristics of hip hop? What is it about the postindustrial city in general and the social and political terrain in the 1970s in New York City specifically that contributed to the emergence and early reception of hip hop? Even as today's rappers revise and redirect rap music, most understand themselves as working out of a tradition of style, attitude, and form that has critical and primary roots in New York City in the 1970s. Substantial postindustrial shifts in economic conditions, access to housing, demographics, and communication networks were crucial to the formation of the conditions that nurtured the cultural hybrids and sociopolitical tenor of hip hop's lyrics and music.

Yet, hip hop has styles and themes that share striking similarities with many past and contiguous Afrodiasporic musical and cultural expressions. These themes and styles, for the most part, are revised and reinterpreted, using contemporary cultural and technological elements. Hip hop's central forms—graffiti, breakdancing, and rap music—developed in relation to one another and in relation to the larger society. The remainder of this chapter is devoted to offering a more in-depth understanding of the similarities between hip hop and other cultural forms and of the specificity of hip hop style as it has been shaped by market forces, dominant cultural ideas, and the postindustrial urban context.

The Urban Context

Postindustrial conditions in urban centers across America reflect a complex set of global forces that continue to shape the contemporary urban metropolis. The growth of multinational telecommunications networks, global economic competition, a major technological revolution, the formation of new international divisions of labor, the increasing power of finance relative to production, and new migration patterns from Third World industrializing nations have all contributed to the economic and social restructuring of urban America. These global forces have had a direct and sustained impact on urban job opportunity structures, have exacerbated long-standing racial and gender-based forms of discrimination, and have contributed to increasing multinational corporate control of market conditions and national economic health.[15] Large-scale restructuring of the workplace and job market has had its effect upon most facets of everyday life. It has placed additional pressures on local community-based networks and whittled down already limited prospects for social mobility.

In the 1970s, cities across the country were gradually losing federal funding for social services, information service corporations were beginning to replace industrial factories, and corporate developers were buying up real estate to be converted into luxury housing, leaving working-class residents with limited affordable housing, a shrinking job market and diminishing social services. The poorest neighborhoods and the least powerful groups were the least protected and had the smallest safety nets. By the 1980s, the privileged elites displayed unabashed greed as their strategies to reclaim and rebuild downtown business and tourist zones with municipal and federal subsidies exacerbated the already widening gap between classes and races.

Given New York's status as hub city for international capital and information services, it is not surprising that these larger structural changes and their effects were quickly and intensely felt there.[16] As John Mollenkopf notes, "during the 1970s, the U.S. system of cities crossed a watershed. New York led other old, industrial metropolitan areas into population and employment decline."[17] The federal funds that might have offset this process had been diminishing throughout the 1970s. In 1975, President Ford's unequivocal veto to requests for a federal bail out to prevent New York from filing for bankruptcy made New York a national symbol for the fate of older cities under his administration. The New York *Daily News* legendary headline "Ford to New York: Drop Dead" captured the substance and temperament of Ford's veto and sent a sharp message to cities around the country.[18] Virtually bankrupt and in a critical state of disrepair, New York City and New York State administrators finally negotiated a federal loan, albeit one accompanied by an elaborate package of service cuts and that carried harsh repayment terms. "Before the crisis ended," Daniel Walkowitz notes, "60,000 city employees went off the payroll, and social and public services suffered drastic cuts. The city had avoided default only after the teachers' union allowed its pension fund to become collateral for city loans."[19] These deep social service cuts were part of a larger trend in unequal wealth distribution and was accompanied by a housing crisis that continued well into the 1980s. Between 1978 and 1986, the people in the bottom 20 percent of the income scale experienced an absolute decline in income, whereas the top 20 percent experienced most of the economic growth. Blacks and Hispanics disproportionately occupied this bottom fifth. During this same period, 30 percent of New York's Hispanic households (40 percent for Puerto Ricans) and 25 percent of black households lived at or below the poverty line. Since this period, low-income housing has continued to disappear and blacks and Hispanics are still much more likely to live in overcrowded, dilapidated, and seriously undermaintained spaces.[20] It is not surprising that these serious trends have contributed to New York's large and chronically homeless population.

In addition to housing problems, New York and many large urban centers faced other major economic and demographic forces that sustained and exacerbated significant structural inequalities. Even though urban America has always been socially and economically divided, these divisions have taken on a new dimension. At the same time that racial succession and immigration patterns were reshaping the city's population and labor force, shifts in the occupational structure away from a high-wage, high-employment economy grounded in manufacturing, trucking, warehousing, and wholesale trade and toward a low-wage, low-employment economy geared toward producer services generated new forms of inequality. As Daniel Walkowitz suggests, New York became "sharply divided between an affluent, technocratic, professional, white-collar group managing the financial and commercial life of an international city and an unemployed and underemployed service sector which is substantially black and Hispanic." Earlier divisions in the city were predominantly ethnic and economic. Today, "racial and gender divisions and the growing predominance of white-collar work on the one hand and worklessness on the other hand have made New York's labor market resemble that of a Third World city."[21] As Mollenkopf and Castells point out, blue-collar white ethnics who were the single largest social stratum in the 1950s are vastly diminished today. In their place, three new groups have emerged as the dominant stratum. The largest group of the three are white male professionals and managers, followed by female and black or Latino clerical and service workers, and finally, Latino and Asian manufacturing workers. "New York," Mollenkopf concludes, "has been transformed from a relatively well-off white blue-collar city into a more economically divided, multi-racial white collar city." This "disorganized periphery" of civil service and manufacturing workers contributes to the consolidation of power among white-collar professional corporate managers, creating the massive inequalities displayed in New York.[22]

The commercial imperatives of corporate America have also undermined the process of transmitting and sharing local knowledge in the urban metropolis. Ben Bagdikian's study *The Media Monopoly* reveals that monopolistic tendencies in commercial enterprises seriously constrain access to a diverse flow of information. For example, urban renewal relocation efforts not only dispersed central-city populations to the suburbs, but also they replaced the commerce of the street with the needs of the metropolitan market. Advertisers geared newspaper articles and television broadcasts toward the purchasing power of suburban buyers, creating a dual "crisis of representation" in terms of whose lives and images were represented physically in the paper and whose interests got represented in the corridors of power.[23] These media outlet and advertising shifts have been accompanied by a massive telecommunications revolution in the information-processing industry. Once the domain of the government, information processing and communication technology now lie at the heart of corporate America. As a result of government deregulation in communications via the breakup of AT&T in 1982, communication industries have consolidated and internationalized. Today, telecommunications industries are global data-transmittal corporations with significant control over radio, television, cable, telephone, computer, and other electronic transmittal systems. Telecommunication expansion, coupled with corporate consolidation has dismantled local community networks and has irrevocably changed the means and character of communication.[24] Since the mid-1980s, these expansions and consolidations have been accompanied by a tidal wave of widely available communications products that have revolutionized business and personal communications. Facsimile machines, satellite-networked beepers, cordless phones, electronic mail networks, cable television expansions, VCRs, compact discs, video cameras and games, and personal computers have dramatically transformed the speed and character of speech, written, and visual communication.

Postindustrial conditions had a profound effect on black and Hispanic communities.[25] Shrinking federal funds and affordable housing, shifts in the occupational structure away from blue-collar manufacturing and toward corporate and information services, along with frayed local communication patterns, meant that new immigrant populations and the city's poorest residents paid the highest price for deindustrialization and economic restructuring. These communities are more susceptible to slumlords, redevelopers, toxic waste dumps, drug rehabilitation centers, violent criminals, red-lining, and inadequate city services and transportation. It also meant that the city's ethnic and working-class–based forms of community aid and support were growing increasingly less effective against these new conditions.

In the case of the South Bronx, which has been frequently dubbed the "home of hip hop culture," these larger postindustrial conditions were exacerbated by disruptions considered an "unexpected side effect" of the larger politically motivated policies of "urban renewal." In the early 1970s, this renewal [sic] project involved massive relocations of economically fragile people of color from different areas in New York City into parts of the South Bronx. Subsequent ethnic and racial transition in the South Bronx was not a gradual process that might have allowed already taxed social and cultural institutions to respond self-protectively; instead, it was a brutal process of community destruction and relocation executed by municipal officials and under the direction of legendary planner Robert Moses.

Between the late 1930s and the late 1960s Moses, a very powerful city planner, executed a number of public works projects, highways, parks, and housing projects that significantly reshaped the profile of New York City. In 1959, city, state, and federal authorities began the implementation of his planned Cross-Bronx Expressway that cut directly through the center of the most heavily populated working-class areas in the Bronx. The Expressway was clearly designed to link New Jersey and Long Island, New York, communities and to facilitate suburban commutation into New York City. Although he could have modified his route slightly to bypass densely populated working-class ethnic residential communities, he elected a path that required the demolition of hundreds of residential and commercial buildings. In addition, throughout the 1960s and early 1970s, some 60,000 Bronx homes were razed. Designating these old blue-collar housing units as "slums," Moses's Title I Slum Clearance program forced the relocation of 170,000 people.[26] These "slums" were in fact densely populated stable neighborhoods, comprised mostly of working- and lower-middle class Jews, but they also contained solid Italian, German, Irish and black neighborhoods. Although the neighborhoods under attack had a substantial Jewish population, black and Puerto Rican residents were disproportionately affected. Thirty-seven percent of the relocated residents were nonwhite. This, coupled with the subsequent "white flight," devastated kin networks and neighborhood services. Marshall Berman, in *All That Is Solid Melts into Air*, reflects on the massive disruption Moses's project created:

Miles of streets alongside the road were choked with dust and fumes and deafening noise. . . . Apartment houses that had been settled and stable for over twenty years emptied out, often virtually overnight; large and impoverished black and Hispanic families, fleeing even worse slums, were moved wholesale, often under the auspices of the Welfare Department, which even paid inflated rents, spreading panic and accelerating flight. . . . Thus depopulated, economically depleted, emotionally shattered, the Bronx was ripe for all the dreaded spirals of urban blight.[27]

Between the late 1960s and mid-1970s, the vacancy rates in the southern section of the Bronx, where demolition was most devastating, skyrocketed. Nervous landlords sold their property as quickly as possible, often to professional slumlords, which accelerated the flight of white tenants into northern sections of the Bronx and into Westchester. Equally anxious shopkeepers sold their shops and established businesses elsewhere. The city administration, touting Moses's expressway as a sign of progress and modernization, was unwilling to admit the devastation that had occurred. Like many of his public works projects, Moses's Cross-Bronx Expressway supported the interests of the upper classes against the interests of the poor and intensified the development of the vast economic and social inequalities that characterize contemporary

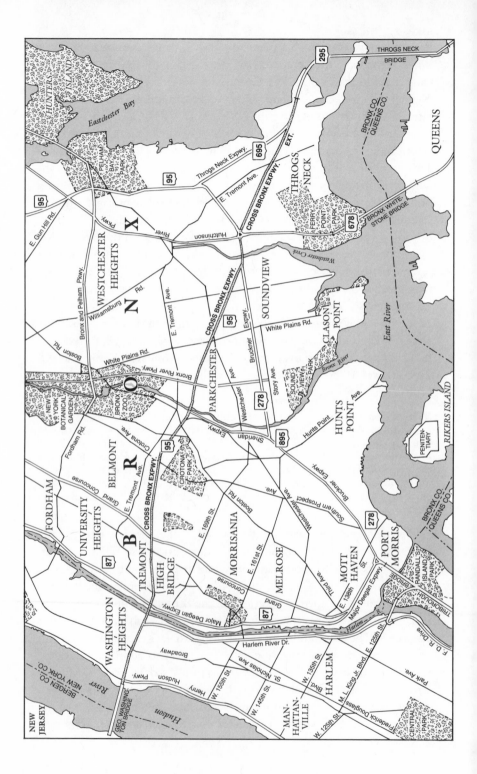

New York. The newly "relocated" black and Hispanic residents in the South Bronx were left with few city resources, fragmented leadership, and limited political power.

The disastrous effects of these city policies went relatively unnoticed in the media until 1977, when two critical events fixed New York and the South Bronx as national symbols of ruin and isolation. During the summer of 1977, an extensive power outage blacked out New York, and hundreds of stores were looted and vandalized. The poorest neighborhoods (the South Bronx, Bedford Stuyvesant, Brownsville, and Crown Heights areas in Brooklyn, the Jamaica area in Queens, and Harlem), where most of the looting took place, were depicted by the City's media organs as lawless zones where crime is sanctioned and chaos bubbles just below the surface. The 1965 blackout, according to the *New York Times* was "peaceful by contrast," suggesting that America's most racially tumultuous decade was no match for the despair and frustration articulated in the summer of 1977.[28] The blackout seemed to raise the federal stakes in maintaining urban social order. Three months later, President Carter made his "sobering" historic motorcade visit through the South Bronx, to "survey the devastation of the last five years" and announced an unspecified "commitment to cities." (Not to its inhabitants?) In the national imagination, the South Bronx became the primary "symbol of America's woes."[29]

Following this lead, images of abandoned buildings in the South Bronx became central popular cultural icons. Negative local color in popular film exploited the devastation facing the residents of the South Bronx and used their communities as a backdrop for social ruin and barbarism. As Michael Ventura astutely notes, these popular depictions (and I would add, the news coverage as well) rendered silent the people who struggled with and maintained life under difficult conditions: "In roughly six hours of footage—*Fort Apache*, *Wolfen* and *Koyaanisqatsi*—we haven't been introduced to one soul who actually lives in the South Bronx. We haven't heard one voice speaking its own language. We've merely watched a symbol of ruin: the South Bronx [as] last act before the end of the world."[30] Depictions of black and Hispanic neighborhoods were drained of life, energy, and vitality. The message was loud and clear: to be stuck here was to be lost. Yet, although these visions of loss and futility became defining characteristics, the youngest generation of South Bronx exiles were building creative and aggressive outlets for expression and identification. The new ethnic groups who made the South Bronx their home in the 1970s, while facing social isolation, economic fragility, truncated communication media, and shrinking social service organizations, began building their own cultural networks, which would prove to be resilient and responsive in the age of high technology. North American blacks, Jamaicans, Puerto Ricans, and other Caribbean people with roots in other postcolonial contexts reshaped their cultural identities and expressions in a hostile, technologically sophisticated, multiethnic, urban terrain. Although city leaders and the popular press had literally and figuratively condemned the South Bronx neighborhoods and their inhabitants, its youngest black and Hispanic residents answered back.

Hip Hop

Hip hop culture emerged as a source for youth of alternative identity formation and social status in a community whose older local support institutions had been all but demolished along with large sectors of its built environment. Alternative local identities were forged in fashions and language, street names, and most important, in establishing neighborhood crews or posses. Many hip hop fans, artists, musicians, and dancers continue to belong to an elaborate system of crews or posses. The crew, a local source of identity, group affiliation, and support system appears repeatedly in all of my interviews and virtually all rap lyrics and cassette dedications, music video performances, and media interviews with artists. Identity in hip hop is deeply rooted in the specific, the local experience, and one's attachment to and status in a local group or alternative family. These crews are new kinds of families forged with intercultural bonds that, like the social formation of gangs, provide insulation and support in a complex and unyielding environment and may serve as the basis for new social movements. The postindustrial city, which provided the context for creative development among hip hop's earliest innovators, shaped their cultural terrain, access to space, materials, and education. While graffiti artists' work was significantly aided by advances in spray paint technology, they used the urban transit system as their canvas. Rappers and DJs disseminated their work by copying it on tape-dubbing equipment and playing it on powerful, portable "ghetto blasters." At a time when budget cuts in school music programs drastically reduced access to traditional forms of instrumentation and composition, inner-city youths increasingly relied on recorded sound. Breakdancers used their bodies to mimic "transformers" and other futuristic robots in symbolic street battles. Early Puerto Rican, Afro-Caribbean, and black American hip hop artists transformed obsolete vocational skills from marginal occupations into the raw materials for creativity and resistance. Many of them were "trained" for jobs in fields that were shrinking or that no longer exist. Puerto Rican graffiti writer Futura graduated from a trade school specializing in the printing industry. However, as most of the jobs for which he was being trained had already been computerized, he found himself working at McDonald's after graduation. Similarly, African-American DJ Red Alert (who also has family from the Caribbean) reviewed blueprints for a drafting company until computer automation rendered his job obsolete. Jamaican DJ Kool Herc attended Alfred E. Smith auto mechanic trade school, and African-American Grandmaster Flash learned how to repair electronic equipment at Samuel Gompers vocational High School. (One could say Flash "fixed them alright.") Salt and Pepa (both with family roots in the West Indies) worked as phone telemarketing representatives at Sears while considering nursing school. Puerto Rican breakdancer Crazy Legs began breakdancing largely because his single mother couldn't afford Little League baseball fees.[31] All of these artists found themselves positioned with few resources in marginal economic circumstances, but each of them found ways to become famous as an entertainer by appropriating the most advanced technologies and emerging cultural forms. Hip hop artists used the tools of obsolete industrial technology to traverse contemporary crossroads of lack and desire in urban Afrodiasporic communities.

Stylistic continuities were sustained by internal cross-fertilization between rapping, breakdancing, and graffiti writing. Some graffiti writers, such as black American Phase 2, Haitian Jean-Michel Basquiat, Futura, and black American Fab Five Freddy produced rap records. Other writers drew murals that celebrated favorite rap songs (e.g., Futura's mural "The Breaks" was a whole car mural that paid homage to Kurtis Blows's rap of the same name). Breakdancers, DJs, and rappers wore graffiti-painted jackets and tee-shirts. DJ Kool Herc was a graffiti writer and dancer first before he began playing records. Hip hop events featured breakdancers, rappers, and DJs as triple-bill entertainment. Graffiti writers drew murals for DJ's stage platforms and designed posters and flyers to advertise hip hop events. Breakdancer Crazy Legs, founding member of the Rock Steady Crew, describes the communal atmosphere between writers, rappers, and breakers in the formative years of hip hop: "Summing it up, basically going to a jam back then was (about) watching people drink, (break) dance, compare graffiti art in their black books. These jams were thrown by the (hip hop) D.J. . . . it was about piecing while a jam was going on."[32] Of course, sharing ideas and styles is not always a peaceful process. Hip hop is very competitive and confrontational; these traits are both resistance to and preparation for a hostile world that denies and denigrates young people of color. Breakdancers often fought other breakdance crews out of jealousy; writers sometimes destroyed murals and rappers and DJ battles could break out in fights. Hip hop remains a never-ending battle for status, prestige, and group adoration, always in formation, always contested, and never fully achieved. Competitions among and cross-fertilization between breaking, graffiti writing, and rap music was fueled by shared local experiences and social position and similarities in approaches to sound, motion, communication, and style among hip hop's Afrodiasporic communities.

As in many African and Afrodiasporic cultural forms, hip hop's prolific self-naming is a form of reinvention and self-definition.[33] Rappers, DJs, graffiti artists, and breakdancers all take on hip hop names and identities that speak to their role, personal characteristics, expertise, or "claim to fame." DJ names often fuse technology with mastery and style: DJ Cut Creator, Jazzy Jeff, Spindarella, Terminator X Assault Technician, Wiz, and Grandmaster Flash. Many rappers have nicknames that suggest street smarts, coolness, power, and supremacy: L.L. Cool J. (Ladies Love Cool James), Kool Moe Dee, Queen Latifah, Dougie Fresh (and the Get Fresh Crew), D-Nice, Hurricane Gloria, Guru, MC Lyte, EPMD (Eric and Parrish Making Dollars), Ice-T, Ice Cube, Kid-N-Play, Boss, Eazy E, King Sun, and Sir Mix-a-Lot. Some names serve as self-mocking tags; others critique society, such as, Too Short, The Fat Boys, S1Ws (Security of the First World), The Lench Mob, NWA (Niggas with Attitude), and Special Ed. The hip hop identities for such breakdancers as Crazy Legs, Wiggles, Frosty Freeze, Boogaloo Shrimp, and Headspin highlight their status as experts known for special moves. Taking on new names and identities offers "prestige from below" in the face of limited access to legitimate forms of status attainment.

In addition to the centrality of naming, identity, and group affiliation, rappers, DJs, graffiti writers, and breakdancers claim turf and gain local status by developing new styles. As Hebdige's study on punk illustrates, style can be used as a gesture of refusal or as a form of oblique challenge to structures of domination.[34] Hip hop artists use style as a form of identity formation that plays on class distinctions and hierarchies by using commodities to claim the cultural terrain. Clothing and consumption rituals testify to the power of consumption as a means of cultural expression. Hip hop fashion is an especially rich example of this sort of appropriation and critique via style. Exceptionally large "chunk" gold and diamond jewelry (usually fake) mocks, yet affirms, the

Courtesy of Kid (of Kid-N-Play)

gold fetish in Western trade; fake Gucci and other designer emblems cup up and patch-stitched to jackets, pants, hats, wallets, and sneakers in custom shops, work as a form of sartorial warfare (especially when fake Gucci–covered b-boys and b-girls brush past Fifth Avenue ladies adorned by the "real thing.") Hip hop's late 1980s fashion rage—the large plastic (alarm?) clock worn around the neck over leisure/sweat suits—suggested a number of contradictory tensions between work, time, and leisure.[35] Early 1990s trends—super-oversized pants and urban warrior outer apparel, "hoodies," "snooties," "tims," and "triple fat" goose down coats, make clear the severity of the urban storms to be weathered and the saturation of disposable goods in the crafting of cultural expressions.[36] As an alternative means of status formation, hip hop style forges local identities for teenagers who understand their limited access to traditional avenues of social status attainment. Fab Five Freddy, an early rapper and graffiti writer, explains the link between style and identity in hip hop and its significance for gaining local status: "You make a new style. That's what life on the street is all about. What's at stake is honor and position on the street. That's what makes it so important, that's what makes it feel so good—that pressure on you to be the best. Or to try to be the best. To develop a new style nobody can deal with."[37] Styles "nobody can deal with" in graffiti, breaking, and rap music not only boost status, but also they articulate several shared approaches to sound and motion found in the Afrodiaspora. As Arthur Jafa has pointed out, stylistic continuities between breaking, graffiti style, rapping, and musical construction seem to center around three concepts: *flow, layering*, and *ruptures in line*.[38] In hip hop, visual, physical, musical, and lyrical lines are set in motion, broken abruptly with sharp angular breaks, yet they sustain motion and energy through fluidity and flow. In graffiti, long-winding, sweeping, and curving letters are broken and camouflaged by sudden breaks in line. Sharp, angular, broken letters are written in extreme italics, suggesting forward or backward motion. Letters are double and triple shadowed in such a way as to illustrate energy forces radiating from the center—suggesting circular motion—yet, the scripted words move horizontally.

Breakdancing moves highlight flow, layering, and ruptures in line. Popping and locking are moves in which the joints are snapped abruptly into angular positions. And, yet, these snapping movements take place one joint after the previous one—creating a semiliquid effect that moves the energy toward the fingertip or toe. In fact, two dancers may pass the popping energy force back and forth between each other via finger to finger contact, setting off a new wave. In this pattern, the line is both a series of angular breaks and yet sustains energy and motion through flow. Breakers double each other's moves, like line shadowing or layering in graffiti, intertwine their bodies into elaborate shapes, transforming the body into a new entity (like camouflage in graffiti's wild style), and then, one body part at a time reverts to a relaxed state. Abrupt, fractured yet graceful footwork leaves the eye one step behind the motion, creating a time-lapse effect that not only mimics graffiti's use of line shadowing but also creates spatial links between the moves that gives the foot series flow and fluidity.[39]

The music and vocal rapping in rap music also privileges flow, layering, and ruptures in line. Rappers speak of flow explicitly in lyrics, referring to an ability to move easily and powerfully through complex lyrics as well as of the flow in the music.[40] The flow and motion of the initial bass or drum line in rap music is abruptly ruptured by scratching (a process that highlights as it breaks the flow of the base rhythm), or the rhythmic flow is interrupted by other musical passages. Rappers stutter and alternatively race through passages, always moving within the beat or in response to it, often using the music as a partner in rhyme. These verbal moves highlight lyrical flow and points of rupture. Rappers layer meaning by using the same word to signify a variety of actions and objects; they call out to the DJ to "lay down a beat," which is expected to be interrupted, ruptured. DJs layer sounds literally one on top of the other, creating a dialogue between sampled sounds and words.

What is the significance of flow, layering, and rupture as demonstrated on the body and in hip hop's lyrical, musical, and visual works? Interpreting these concepts theoretically, one can argue that they create and sustain rhythmic motion, continuity, and circularity via flow; accumulate, reinforce, and embellish this continuity through layering; and manage threats to these narratives by building in ruptures that highlight the continuity as it momentarily challenges it. These effects at the level of style and aesthetics suggest affirmative ways in which profound social dislocation and rupture can be managed and perhaps contested in the cultural arena. Let us imagine these hip hop principles as a blueprint for social resistance and affirmation: create sustaining narratives, accumulate them, layer, embellish, and transform them. However, be also prepared for rupture, find pleasure in it, in fact, *plan on* social rupture. When these ruptures occur, use them in creative ways that will prepare you for a future in which survival will demand a sudden shift in ground tactics.

Although accumulation, flow, circularity, and planned ruptures exist across a wide range of Afrodiasporic cultural forms, they do not take place outside of capitalist commercial constraints. Hip hop's explicit focus on consumption has frequently been mischaracterized as a movement *into* the commodity market (e.g., hip hop is no longer "authentically" black, if it is for sale). Instead, hip hop's moment(s) of incorporation are a shift in the already existing relationship hip hop has always had to the commodity system. For example, the hip hop DJ produces, amplifies, and revises already recorded sounds, rappers use high-end microphones, and it would be naive to think that breakers, rappers, DJs and writers were never interested in monetary compensation for their work. Graffiti murals, breakdancing moves, and rap lyrics often appropriated and sometimes critiqued verbal and visual elements and physical movements from popular commercial culture, especially television, comic books, and karate movies. If anything, black style through hip hop has contributed to the continued Afro-Americanization of contemporary commercial culture. The contexts for creation in hip hop were never fully outside or in opposition to commodities; they involved struggles over public space and access to commodified materials, equipment, and products of economic viability. It is a common misperception among hip hop artists and cultural critics that during the early days, hip hop was motivated by pleasure rather than profit, as if the two were incompatible. The problem was not that they were uniformly uninterested in profit; rather, many of the earliest practitioners were unaware that they could profit from their pleasure. Once this link was made, hip hop artists began marketing themselves wholeheartedly. Just as graffiti writers hitched a ride on the subways and used its power to distribute their tags, rappers "hijacked" the market for their own purposes, riding the currents that were already out there, not just for wealth but for empowerment, and to assert their own identities. During the late 1970s and early 1980s, the market for hip hop was still based inside New York's black and Hispanic communities. So, although there is an element of truth to this common perception, what is more important about the shift in hip hop's orientation is not its movement from precommodity to commodity but the shift in control over the scope and direction of the profit-making process, out of the hands of local black and Hispanic entrepreneurs and into the hands of larger white-owned, multinational businesses.

Hebdige's work on the British punk movement identifies this shift as the moment of incorporation or recuperation by dominant culture and perceives it to be a critical element in the dynamics of the struggle over the meaning(s) of popular expression. "The process of recuperation," Hebdige argues, "takes two characteristic forms . . . one of conversion of subcultural signs (dress, music, etc.) into mass-produced objects and the 'labelling' and redefinition of deviant behavior by dominant groups—the police, media and judiciary." Hebdige astutely points out, however, that communication in a subordinate cultural form, even prior to the point of recuperation, usually takes place via commodities, "even if the meanings attached to those commodities are purposefully distorted or overthrown." And so, he concludes, "it is very difficult to sustain any absolute distinction between commercial exploitation on the one hand and creativity and originality on the other."[41]

Hebdige's observations regarding the process of incorporation and the tension between commercial exploitation and creativity as articulated in British punk is quite relevant to hip hop. Hip hop has always been articulated via commodities and engaged in the revision of meanings attached to them. Clearly, hip hop signs and meanings are converted, and behaviors are relabeled by dominant institutions. As the relatively brief history of hip hop that follows illustrates, graffiti, rap, and breakdancing were fundamentally transformed as they moved into new relations with dominant cultural institutions.[42] In 1994, rap music is one of the most heavily traded popular commodities in the market, yet it still defies total corporate control over the music, its local use and incorporation at the level of stable or exposed meanings.

Expanding on the formulation advanced by Lipsitz and others at the outset, in the brief history of hip hop that follows I attempt to demonstrate the necessary tension between the historical specificity of hip hop's emergence and the points of continuity between hip hop and several black forms and practices. It is also an overview of the early stages of hip hop and its relationship to popular cultural symbols and products and its revisions of black cultural practices. This necessarily includes hip hop's direct and sustained contact with dominant cultural institutions in the early to mid-1980s and the ways in which these practices emerge in relation to larger social conditions and relationships, including the systematic marginalization of women cultural producers. In each practice, gender power relations problematized and constrained the role of women hip hop artists, and dominant cultural institutions shaped hip hop's transformations.

GRAFFITI

Although graffiti as a social movement (i.e., writing names, symbols, and images on public facades) first emerged in New York during the late 1960s, it is not until almost a decade later that it began to develop elaborate styles and widespread visibility. Even though the vast majority of graffiti writers are black and Hispanic, the writer credited with inspiring the movement, Taki 183, is a Greek teenager named Demetrius who lived in the Washington Heights section of Manhattan. While working as a messenger, traveling by subway to all five boroughs of the city, Taki wrote his name all over the subway cars and stations. In 1971, a staff writer at the *New York Times* located Taki and published a story about his tagging that apparently "struck a responsive chord" among his peers. Martha Cooper and Henry Chalfant describe the effect Taki's notoriety had on his peers:

Kids were impressed by the public notoriety of a name appearing all over the city (and) realized that the pride they felt in seeing their name up in the neighborhood could expand a hundredfold if it traveled beyond the narrow confines of the block. The competition for fame began in earnest as hundreds of youngsters, emulating Taki 183, began to tag trains and public buildings all over town. "Getting up" became a vocation. Kids whose names appeared the most frequently or in the most inaccessible places became folk heroes.[43]

By the mid-1970s, graffiti took on new focus and complexity. No longer a matter of simple tagging, graffiti began to develop elaborate individual styles, themes, formats, and techniques, most of which were designed to increase visibility, individual identity, and status. Themes in the larger works included hip hop slang, characterizations of b-boys, rap lyrics, and hip hop fashion. Using logos and images borrowed from television, comic books, and cartoons, stylistic signatures, and increasingly difficult executions, writers expanded graffiti's palette. Bubble letters, angular machine letters, and the indecipherable wild style were used on larger spaces and with more colors and patterns. These stylistic developments were aided by advances in marker and spray paint technology; better spraying nozzles, marking fibers, paint adhesion, and texture enhanced the range of expression in graffiti writing.[44] Small-scale tagging developed into the top to bottom, a format that covered a section of a train car from the roof to the floor. This was followed by the top to bottom whole car and multiple car "pieces," an abbreviation for graffiti masterpieces.

The execution of a piece is the culmination of a great deal of time, labor, and risk. Writers work out elaborate designs and patterns in notebooks, test new markers and brands of spray paints and colors well in advance. Obtaining access to the subway cars for extended periods requires detailed knowledge of the train schedules and breaking into the train yards where out of service trains are stored. Writers stake out train yards for extended periods, memorizing the train schedule and wait for new trains to leave the paint shop. A freshly painted train would be followed all day and when it reached its designated storage yard (the "lay-up") at night, writers were ready to "bomb" it.

Writers climbed walls, went through holes in fences, vaulted high gates, and "ran the boards," (walked along the board that covers the electrified third rail) to gain access to the trains. Once inside the yards, the risks increased. Craig Castleman explains:

Trains frequently are moved in the yards, and an unwary writer could be hit by one. Trains stored in lay-ups are hazardous painting sites because in-service trains pass by them closely on either side, and the writer has to climb under the parked train or run to the far side of the tracks to escape being hit. Movement through tunnels is dangerous because the catwalks are high and narrow, it is dark and there are numerous open grates, abutments, and low hanging signs and light fixtures that threaten even the slowest moving writer.[45]

Some writers who have been seriously injured continued to write. In an exceptional case, master writer Kase 2 lost his arm in a yard accident and continued to execute highly respected multicar pieces.

Train facades are central to graffiti style for a number of reasons. First, graffiti murals depend on size, color, and constant movement for their visual impact. Although handball courts and other flat and stationary surfaces are suitable, they cannot replace the dynamic reception of subway facades. Unlike handball courts and building surfaces, trains pass through diverse neighborhoods, allowing communication between various black and Hispanic communities throughout the five boroughs and the larger New York population and disseminating graffiti writers' public performance. Second, graffiti artists are guerilla outlaws who thrive on risk as a facet of one's skill—the element of surprise and eluding authority among writers, the fact that it is sometimes considered criminal to purchase the permanent markers, spray paints, and other supplies necessary to write. Subway cars are stored in well-protected but dangerous yards that heighten the degree of difficulty in execution. An especially difficult and creative concept, coloration and style are all the more appreciated when they are executed under duress. Well-executed train work is a sign of mastering the expression.

Although (master) pieces are usually executed individually, writers belong to and work in crews. Group identity and individual development are equally central to graffiti writers practices. These crews meet regularly and work on ideas, share knowledge, and plan trips to the train yards and other desired locations together. Crew members, among other things, compete with other crews (and each other), photograph each other's work for study, protect each other, and trade book outlines for paint supplies. Pieces are often signed individually and then identified by crew. Craig Castleman identified hundreds of crews; prominent ones include: Three Yard Boys (3YB), The Burners (TB), The Spanish Five (TSF) Wild Styles, Destroy All Trains (DAT) and the Mad Transit Artists (MTA).[46]

Female graffiti writers participated alongside male writers rather than in separate groups or crews. In addition to risks associated with execution in yards and elsewhere, women writers had to combat sexism from their male peers. Two prominent female writers, Lady Pink, an Hispanic American born in Ecuador and Lady Heart, an African-American born in Queens, understood that their three o'clock in the morning trips to the train yards involved risking their safety as well as their reputations. In some cases, male graffiti writers spread rumors about female writers' sexual promiscuity to discourage female participation and discredit female writers' executions. So, unlike male writers, female writers had to protect their artistic reputations by protecting their sexual reputation. Lady Heart believes that, although it was sometimes an effective strategy, fear of family reprisals and the physical risks in train yards were much greater deterrents against female participation.[47]

Although both male and female writers chose to paint pieces involving social criticism and developed elaborate tags and characterizations, female writers often chose different colors and selected images that highlighted their female status as a means to greater recognizability. Many female writers used bright pinks, less black, more landscapes and flower scenes around the tags, and fewer "death and destruction" cartoon characters. However, female writers sustained the stylistic approaches to line, motion, and rupture. In this way, color selection and subject matter were forms of gender-based individualization inside the parameters of the expression that were not unlike male writer Dondi's use of a character in comic book artist Vaughn Bode's work, or graffiti writer Seen's use of Smurf characters.[48]

Although city officials had always rejected graffiti as a form of juvenile delinquency, antigraffiti discourse and policy took a dramatic turn in the mid- to late 1970s. No longer merely "an infuriating type of juvenile delinquency," as it was defined by municipal leaders in the late 1960s and early 1970s, the graffiti problem was reconstructed as a central reason for the decline in quality of life in a fiscally fragile and rusting New York. By the mid 1970s, graffiti emerged as a central example of the extent of urban decay and heightened already existing fears over a loss of control of the urban landscape. If the city could not stop these young outlaws from writing all over trains and walls, some political leaders feared, then what could the city manage?[49] Reconstructed as symbols of civic disorder, graffiti writers were understood as a psychic as well as material toll on New York, solidifying its image as a lawless, downtrodden urban jungle.

As the *New York Times* and municipal representatives searched for newer and more aggressive strategies to stamp out graffiti writing and symbolically reestablish control, graffiti writers were expanding and refining the form. In the mid-1970s, elaborate train facade murals and multicar pieces arrived on platforms most mornings. A simple name tag had developed into multiple train car skylines, Christmas greetings, abstract drawings likened to cubist art, romantic expressions, and political slogans all drawn with illustrations in dozens of colors, shades, styles, and elaborate lettering.

In 1977 the Transit Authority made an extensive effort to regain control. At the center of this effort was a new chemical many believed spelled disaster for graffiti writers: the buff. Although the buff did not end graffiti writing, it discouraged many writers and dramatically limited the life of the murals on the train facades. Steve Hager describes the chemical process and its effects:

Many writers dropped out in 1977, when the Transit Authority erected its "final solution" to the graffiti problem in a Coney Island train yard. At an annual cost of $400,000, the T.A. began operating a giant car wash that sprayed vast amounts of petroleum hydroxide on the sides of graffitied trains. The solvent spray was followed by a vigorous buffing. At first the writers called it "the Orange Crush," after Agent Orange, a defoliant used in Vietnam. Later it was simply known as "the buff." Fumes emanating from the cleaning station were so deadly that a nearby school closed after students complained of respiratory problems. . . . Even T.A. workers admitted that they couldn't stand downwind from the station without getting nauseous. Meanwhile the solvent was seeping into the underfloorings of the trains, causing considerable corrosion and damage to electrical parts.[50]

"The buff" was followed by $24 million worth of system-wide fencing that included barbed wire fences, ribbon wire (which ensnares and shreds the body or object that attempts to cross it), and for a brief stint, attack dogs.[51] By the early 1980s, the T.A. had regained control of the subway facades by preventing most of the work from reaching the public *intact*. Yet, this did not spell the end of graffiti art. Kase 2, Lee Quinones, Futura 2000, Rammelzee, Lady Pink, Dondi, Lady Heart, Seen, Zephyr, and many other writers continued to write. The buff did not erase the graffiti, it just discolored it, rendering the subways cars truly defaced and a profoundly depressing symbol of a city at war to silence its already discarded youths. Writing continued, albeit less often and new locations for graffiti and new means of dissemination developed.

The level of municipal hostility exhibited toward graffiti art was matched only by the SoHo art scene's embrace of it. Early interest in graffiti art among gallery owners and collectors in the mid 1970s was short-lived and inconsistent. However, in the late 1970s, new interest was sparked, in part as a result of the promotional efforts of Fab Five Freddy, who now appears as a rap host on MTV. Appearing in an article in the Scenes column in the *Village Voice* in February 1979, Fab Five Freddy offered graffiti mural services at $5 a square foot. Using his art school training and fluidity with art school language, Freddy became a broker for graffiti. Making a number of critical contacts between the "legitimate art world" and graffiti writers, Freddy led the way for future exhibits at the Fun Gallery, Bronx gallery Fashion Moda, and the Times Square Show throughout the early 1980s, coupled with the efforts of artists, collectors, and gallery owners (e.g., Stephan Eins, Sam Esses, Henry Chalfant, and Patti Astor) gave graffiti momentary institutional clout and provided mostly unemployed graffiti artists financial renumeration for their talents. Clearly, the downtown art scene, in providing the graffiti artists with fleeting legitimacy, was most interested in making an investment in their own "cutting-edge image." Few writers would make a living as gallery artists for long, and almost all writers were paraded about as the latest "naturally talented" street natives.[52] Once the art world had satisfied its craving for street art, writers continued to work, albeit not as much on the subways.

Graffiti is no longer a widely visible street form, a fact that has led to the assumption that the form is no longer practiced. However, recent research by Joe Austin demonstrates that graffiti writers continue to write, using strategies for display and performance that work around social constraints. According to Austin, writers paint murals, videotape and photograph them, and distribute the tapes and photos through graffiti fan magazines all over the country. Via videotape and fanzines, train murals are documented before they are painted over or deformed by "the buff," allowing the process of writing on the train surface to be shared.[53] Although many writers are still outlaws, their status as such is no longer a major source of public embarrassment for city officials. In fact, Transit Authority publicity campaigns in 1992 and 1993, such as "sub-talk," refer to their victory against graffiti as a sign of their role in the city's supposed improving health, all the while continuing to scrub and paint hundreds of train cars before they go into service to sustain these illusions. Although SoHo seems uninterested in graffiti art, businesses and community centers in the Barrio, Harlem, the Bronx, and Brooklyn still commission graffiti art for logos, building facades, and graffiti art is represented on tee-shirts, rap artists' clothing, and music video set designs.

BREAKDANCING

In the mid-1970s, dancing to disco music was a seamless and fluid affair. Disco dances, such as the Hustle, emphasized the continuity and circularity of the beat and worked to mask the breaks between steps. In disco music, the primary role of the DJ was to merge one song's conclusion into the next song's introduction as smoothly as possible, eliminating or masking the breaks between songs. At the height of disco's popularity, a new style of dance and musical pastiche emerged that used disco music to focus on the break points, to highlight and extend the breaks in and between songs. At these break points in the DJ's performance, the dancers would *breakdance*, executing moves that imitated the rupture in rhythmic continuity as it was highlighted in the musical break.[54]

Described as a "competitive, acrobatic and pantomimic dance with outrageous physical contortions, spins and backflips [which are] wedded to a fluid syncopated circling body rock," breakdancing is the physical manifestation of hip hop style.[55] Breaking, originally referring only to a particular group of dance moves executed during the break beat in a DJ's rap mixes, has since come to include a number of related movements and dances (e.g., electric boogie and up-rock) that take place at various points in the music.[56]

As the dance steps and routines developed, breaking began to center on the freeze, an improvised pose or movement that ruptured, or "broke the beat." Usually practiced in a circle formation, breaking involved the entry into the circle, the footwork, which was highlighted by the freeze, and the exit. Nelson George offers an insightful and rich description of the dance:

Each person's turn in the ring was very brief—ten to thirty seconds—but packed with action and meaning. It began with an entry, a hesitating walk that allowed him to get in step with the music for several beats and take his place "on stage." Next the dancer "got down" to the floor to do the footwork, a rapid, slashing, circular scan of the floor by sneakered feet, in which the hands support the body's weight while the head and torso revolve at a slower speed, a kind of syncopated sunken pirouette, also known as the helicopter. Acrobatic transitions such as head spins, hand spins, shoulder spins, flips and the swipe—a flip of the weight from hands to feet that also involves a twist in the body's direction—served as bridges between the footwork and the freeze. The final element was the exit, a spring back to verticality or a special movement that returned the dancer to the outside of the circle.[57]

To stop the time was only one part of the freeze. In the freeze, the dancer also took on an alternative identity and served as a challenge to competitors. Dancers would freeze-pose as animals, super heroes, business men, GQ models, elderly or injured people and as female pin-up models. The freeze pose embodied an element of surprise that served as a challenge to the next dancer to outdo the previous pose. As a moment of boasting or sounding on the dancers' competitors, freeze poses might include presenting one's behind to an opponent, holding one's nose or grabbing one's genitals to suggest bad odor or sexual domination.[58]

Breaking was practiced in hallways on concrete and sometime with cardboard pads. Streets were preferred practice spaces for a couple of reasons. Indoor community spaces in economically oppressed areas are rare, and those that are available are not usually big enough to accommodate large groups performing acrobatic dances. In addition, some indoor spaces had other drawbacks. One of the breakers with whom I spoke pointed out that the Police Athletic League, which did have gymnasium-size space, was avoided because it was used as a means of community surveillance for the police. Whenever local police were looking for a suspect, kids hanging out in the PAL were questioned.

Breakdancers practiced and performed in crews that dominated certain neighborhoods. During competitions, if one crew's boasting or sounding won over the crowd completely, the embarrassment it caused the other crew usually resulted in fighting. Bad blood between crews often remained long after the competition and dancers had to be careful in their travels around New York. Crazy Legs, known for inventing the "W" move as well as a special backspin, explained that during the Rock Steady Crew's heyday, they had to fight other crews just about every weekend.[59]

Although the Rock Steady Crew, a mostly Puerto Rican group, always had female breakers, such was not the case with all predominantly male breakdancing crews. Rock Steady's Daisy Castro, aka "Baby Love," attributes this absence to lack of exposure, social support, and male discouragement.[60] Female breakdance crews, such as the Dynamic Dolls, breakers such as Janet, aka "Headspin," Suzy Q, Rock Steady's Yvette, Chunky and Pappy were always part of the breakdance scene. Yet, few women regularly performed the break-specific moves, such as the headspin or the hand-glide; they were more likely to be seen executing the popping, locking, and electric boogie moves.

Although this absence has in some cases to do with relative ease of execution of specific moves for female bodies, most girls were heavily discouraged from performing break moves because they were perceived by some male peers as "unsafe" or "unfeminine." Female breakdancers sometimes executed moves in conventionally feminine ways, to high-

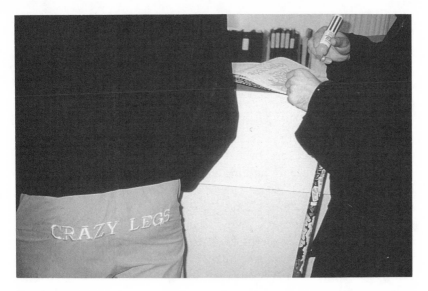

© suekwon

light individuality and perhaps to deflect male criticism. Again, women who performed these moves were often considered masculine and undesirable or sexually "available." Although these sexist attitudes regarding the acceptable limits of female physical expression are widespread, they are not absolute. In my interview with Crazy Legs and Wiggles, two Rock Steady Crew dancers, Crazy Legs had no objections to any female dancers executing any moves, whereas Wiggles would "respect" a female breaker but was not as comfortable with females exhibiting the level of physical exertion breaking required.[61]

Breaking combines themes and physical moves found in contemporary popular culture with moves and styles commonly found in Afrodiaspora dances. Breakdancing shares "families of resemblance" with a number of African-American dances. It shares moves and combinations with the lindy-hop, the Charleston, the cakewalk, the jitterbug, the flashdancing in Harlem in the 1940s, double dutch, and black fraternity and sorority stepping. Breaking has also frequently been associated with the Afro-Brazilian martial arts dance Capoiera, particularly for the striking similarities between their spinning and cartwheel-like moves. Yet, breakers also borrow and revise popularized Asian martial arts moves by watching "karate" movies in Times Square. Recent hip hop dance moves, such as the Popeye, the Cabbage Patch, or the Moonwalk, imitate and are named after popular cultural images and characters. Sociologist Herman Gray, referring to another hip hop dance, the Running

Man, points out that it may also mime the common experience of young black men being chased by the police. The "lockitup" is a Newark, New Jersey–based dance inspired by car-jacking, an armed form of auto theft. According to Marcus Reeves, its moves are said to "act out the procedures of 'poppin' (stealing) a car. While the dancer mimics the car theft ritual, the crowd urges him or her with chants of "lockitup!"[62]

Much like graffiti, breakdancing developed a contradictory relationship to dominant culture. In January 1980, one of the first published articles on breakdancing covered a group of breakdancers who were detained by the police for fighting and causing a disturbance in a Washington Heights area subway station. Once the police were convinced that it was, in fact, "just a dance," the breakers were let go. As unsanctioned public dance and public occupation of space, particularly by black and Puerto Rican youths, breakdancing continued to draw the attention of the police. Over the following five years, articles in the *New York Times, Washington Post*, and the *Los Angeles Times* continued to cite examples of the police arresting breakdancers for "disturbing the peace" and "attracting undesirable crowds" in the malls.[63]

At the same time, breakdancing became the latest popular dance craze in the United States, Europe, and Japan. Not only were breakdance crews forming, but dance schools began hiring breakdancers to teach breakdancing lessons, geared to "hip" middle-class whites.[64] Like SoHo's response to graffiti, breakdancers were hired by popular downtown dance clubs for private parties to provide entertainment for their leisured clientele. Crazy Legs recollects this period of notoriety and exploitation and his reaction to it:

We got ripped off by so many people. When it came down to Roxy's, they gave me a 50-person guest list every week, but I realize now that they were making crazy dollars. Packed. We weren't making no money. But the bottom line was, they were giving me and Bam (Afrika Bambaataa) and all these other people such a great guest list because all these white people were coming in. . . . We were pretty much on display, and we didn't even know it. We just thought it was great because we was like "Wow, now we got a great floor to dance on, and go party, and we have juice, and we have ghetto status and things like that . . ." Now I realize we were on display. People were paying $8 and $7 whatever it cost . . . to watch us. And we weren't getting anything from the door.[65]

By 1986, when commercial outlets seemed to have exhausted breakdancing as a "fad," breakdancers as mainstream press copy all but disappeared. Yet, the form is still heavily practiced, particularly alongside rap artists and other dance music genres. Dancers in hip hop clubs still perform in circles, inventing steps in response to rap's rhythms. Although rappers' dancers are no longer named *breakers*, the moves are extensions and revisions of breakers' stock moves and with approaches to motion, line, and rupture that refer to and affirm the stylistic approaches of graffiti writers, rap DJs, and the early breakers. The Public Broadcasting System's 1991 dance special "Everybody Dance Now!" demonstrated the stylistic continuities between the moves executed by early breakers and more recent rock, soul, and dance performers such as Janet and Michael Jackson, Madonna, C&C Music Factory, New Kids on the Block, New Edition, The Fly Girls on Fox Television's Comedy Show *In Living Color*, and MC Hammer—illustrating the centrality of hip hop dance style in contemporary popular entertainment.

RAP MUSIC

Rapping, the last element to emerge in hip hop, has become its most prominent facet. In the earliest stages, DJs were the central figures in hip hop; they supplied the break beats for breakdancers and the soundtrack for graffiti crew socializing. Early DJs would connect their turntables and speakers to any available electrical source, including street lights, turning public parks and streets into impromptu parties and community centers.

Although makeshift stereo outfits in public settings are not unique to rap, two innovations that have been credited to Jamaican immigrant DJ Kool Herc separated rap music from other popular musics and set the stage for further innovation. Kool Herc was known for his massive stereo system speakers (which he named the Herculords) and his practice of extending obscure instrumental breaks that created an endless collage of peak dance beats named b-beats or break-beats. This collage of break-beats stood in sharp contrast to Eurodisco's unbroken dance beat that dominated the dance scene in the mid- to late 1970s. Kool Herc's range of sampled b-beats was as diverse as contemporary rap music, drawing on, among others, New Orleans jazz, Isaac Hayes, Bob James, and Rare Earth. Within a few years, Afrika Bambaataa, DJ and founder of the Zulu Nation, would also use beats from European disco bands such as Kraftwerk, rock, and soul in his performances. I emphasize the significance of rap's earliest DJs' use of rock, because popular press on rap music has often referred to Run DMC's use of samples from rock band Aerosmith's "Walk This Way" in 1986 as a crossover strategy and a departure from earlier sample selections among rap DJs. The bulk of the press coverage on Run DMC regarding their "forays into rock" also suggested that by using rock music, rap was maturing (e.g., moving beyond the "ghetto") and expanding its repertoire. To the contrary, the success of Run DMC's "Walk This Way" brought these strategies

Courtesy of Kid (of Kid-N-Play)

of intertextuality into the commercial spotlight and into the hands of white teen consumers. Not only had rock samples always been reimbedded in rap music, but also Run DMC recorded live rock guitar on *King of Rock* several years earlier.[66] Beats selected by hip hop producers and DJs have always come from and continue to come from an extraordinary range of musics. As Prince Be Softly of P.M. Dawn says, "my music is based in hip-hop, but I pull everything from dance-hall to country to rock together. I can take a Led Zeppelin drum loop, put a Lou Donaldson horn on it, add a Joni Mitchell guitar, then get a Crosby Stills and Nash vocal riff."[67]

Kool Herc's Herculords, modeled after the Jamaican sound systems that produced dub and dance-hall music, were more powerful than the average DJ's speakers and were surprisingly free of distortion, even when played outdoors.[68] They produced powerful bass frequencies and also played clear treble tones. Herc's break-beats, played on the Herculords, inspired breakdancers' freestyle moves and sparked a new generation of hip hop DJs. While working the turntables, Kool Herc also began reciting prison-style rhymes (much like those found on The Last Poet's *Hustler's Convention*), using an echo chamber for added effect. Herc's rhymes also drew heavily from the style of black radio personalities, the latest and most significant being DJ Hollywood, a mid-1970s disco DJ who had developed a substantial word-of-mouth following around the club scene in New York and eventually in other cities via homemade cassettes.

Like the graffiti and breakdance crews, DJs battled for territories. Four main Bronx DJs emerged: Kool Herc's territory was the west Bronx, Afrika Bambaataa dominated the Bronx River East, DJ Breakout's territory was the northernmost section of the Bronx, and Grandmaster Flash controlled the southern and central sections.[69] These territories were established by local DJ battles, club gigs, and the circulation of live performance tapes. DJs' performances, recorded by the DJ himself and audience members, were copied, traded, and played on large portable stereo cassette players (or "ghetto blasters"), disseminating the DJ's sounds. These tapes traveled far beyond the Bronx; Black and Puerto Rican army recruits sold and traded these tapes in military stations around the country and around the world.[70]

Grandmaster Flash is credited with perfecting and making famous the third critical rap music innovation: scratching. Although Grand Wizard Theodore (only 13 years old at the time) is considered its inventor, Theodore did not sustain a substantial enough following to advance and perfect scratching. Scratching is a turntable technique that involves playing the record back and forth with your hand by scratching the needle against and then with the groove. Using two turntables, one record is scratched in rhythm or against the rhythm of another record while the second record played. This innovation extended Kool Herc's use of the turntables as talking instruments, and exposed the cultural rather than structural parameters of accepted turntable use.

Flash also developed the backspin and extended Kool Herc's use of break beats.[71] Backspinning allows the DJ to "repeat phrases and beats from a record by rapidly spinning it backwards." Employing exquisite timing, these phrases could be repeated in varying rhythmic patterns, creating the effect of a record skipping irregularly or a controlled stutter effect, building intense crowd anticipation. Break beats were particularly good for building new compositions. Making the transition to recordings and anticipating the range of sounds and complexity of collage now associated with sampling technology, Flash's 1981 "The Adventures of Grandmaster Flash on the Wheels of Steel" lays the groundwork for the explosive and swirling effects created by Public Enemy producers, the Bomb Squad, seven years later. In an attempt to capture the virtuosity of Flash's techniques and the vast range of his carefully selected samples, I have included a lengthy and poetic description of his performance of the "The Adventures of Grandmaster Flash on the Wheels of Steel." Nelson George describes the Grandmaster's wizardry:

It begins with "you say one for the trouble," the opening phrase of Spoonie Gee's "Monster Jam," broken down to "you say" repeated seven times, setting the tone for a record that uses the music and vocals of Queen's "Another One Bites the Dust," the Sugar Hill Gang's "8th Wonder," and Chic's "Good Times" as musical pawns that Flash manipulates at whim. He repeats "Flash is bad" from Blondie's "Rapture" three times, turning singer Deborah Harry's dispassion into total adoration. While playing "Another One Bites the Dust," Flash places a record on the second turntable, then shoves the needle and the record against each other. The result is a rumbling, gruff imitation of the song's bass line. As the guitar feedback on "Dust" builds, so does Flash's rumble, until we're grooving on "Good Times." Next, "Freedom" explodes between pauses in Chic's "Good Times" bass line. His bass thumps, and then the Furious Five chant, "Grandmaster cuts faster." Bass. "Grandmaster." Bass. "Cut." Bass. "Cuts . . . cuts . . . faster." But the cold crusher comes toward the end when, during "8th Wonder" Flash places a wheezing sound of needle on vinyl in the spaces separating a series of claps.[72]

Using multiple samples as dialogue, commentary, percussive rhythms, and counterpoint, Flash achieved a level of musical collage and climax with two turntables that remains difficult to attain on advanced sampling equipment ten years later.

The new style of DJ performance attracted large excited crowds, but it also began to draw the crowd's attention away from dancing and toward watching the DJ perform.[73] It is at this point that rappers were added to the DJs' shows to redirect the crowd's attention. Flash asked two friends, Cowboy and Melle Mel (both would later become lead rappers along with Kid Creole for Flash and the Furious Five) to perform some boasts during one of his shows. Soon thereafter, Flash began to attach an open mike to his equipment inspiring spontaneous audience member participation. Steve Hager's description of their intertextuality, fluidity, and rhythmic complexity indicates a wide range of verbal skills not generally associated with early rappers: "Relying on an inventive use of slang, the percussive effect of short words, and unexpected internal rhymes, Mel and Creole began composing elaborate rap routines, intricately weaving their voices through a musical track mixed by Flash. They would trade solos, chant, and sing harmony. It was a vocal style that effectively merged the aggressive rhythms of James Brown with the language and imagery of *Hustler's Convention*."[74] Many early rappers were inspired by the intensity of Melle Mel's voice and his conviction. Kid, from rap group Kid-N-Play, attributed some of this intensity to the fact that Mel was rapping for a living rather than a hobby: "For Melle Mel, rapping was his job. Melle Mel made a living rapping each weekend at a party or whatever. So he's rapping to survive. As such, his subject matter is gonna reflect that. I go on record as saying Melle Mel is king of all rappers. He's the reason I became a rapper and I think he's the reason a lot of people became rappers. That's how pervasive his influence was."[75] Melle Mel's gritty dark voice was immortalized on Flash and Furious Five's 1982 "The Message," voted best pop song of 1982. The power of rappers' voices and their role as storytellers ensured that rapping would become the central expression in hip hop culture.

The rappers who could fix the crowd's attention had impressive verbal dexterity and performance skills. They spoke with authority, conviction, confidence, and power, shouting playful ditties reminiscent of 1950s black radio disc jockeys. The most frequent style of rap was a variation on the toast, a boastful, bragging, form of oral storytelling sometimes explicitly political and often aggressive, violent, and sexist in content. Musical and oral predecessors to rap music encompass a variety of vernacular artists including the Last Poets, a group of late 1960s to early 1970s black militant storytellers whose poetry was accompanied by conga drum rhythms, poet, and singer Gil Scott Heron, Malcolm X, the Black Panthers, the 1950s radio jocks, particularly Douglas "Jocko" Henderson, soul rapper Millie Jackson, the classic Blues women, and countless other performers. "Blaxsploitation" films such as Melvin Van Peebles' *Sweet Sweetback's Baadasss Song*, Donald Goines's gangsta fiction, and "pimp narratives" that explore the ins and outs of ghetto red-light districts are also especially important in rap. Regardless of thematics, pleasure and mastery in toasting and rapping are matters of control over the language, the capacity to outdo competition, the craft of the story, mastery of rhythm, and the ability to rivet the crowd's attention.[76]

Rap relies heavily on oral performance, but it is equally dependent on technology and its effects on the sound and quality of vocal reproduction. A rapper's delivery is dependent on the use and mastery of technology. The iconic focus of the rapper is the microphone; rappers are dependent on advanced technology to amplify their voices, so that they can be heard over the massive beats that surround the lyrics. Eric B. & Rakim's "Microphone Fiend" describes the centrality of the microphone in rap performance:

> I was a microphone fiend before I became a teen.
> I melted microphones instead of cones of ice cream
> Music-oriented so when hip hop was originated
> Fitted like pieces of puzzles, complicated.[77]

As rapping moved center stage, rappers and DJs began to form neighborhood crews who hosted block parties school dances and social clubs. Like breakdance crew competitions, rappers and DJs battled for local supremacy in intense verbal and musical duels. These early duels were not merely a matter of encouraging crowd reaction with simple ditties such as "Yell, ho!" and "Somebody Scream." (Although these ditties have important sentimental value.) These parties and competitions lasted for several hours and required that the performers had a well-stocked arsenal of rhymes and stories, physical stamina, and expertise. Local independent record producers realized that these battles began to draw consistently huge crowds and approached the rappers and DJs about producing records. While a number of small releases were under way, Sylvia Robinson of Sugar Hill records created the Sugar Hill Gang whose 1979 debut single "Rapper's Delight" brought rap into the commercial spotlight. By early 1980, "Rapper's Delight" had sold several million copies and rose to the top of the pop charts.[78]

"Rapper's Delight" changed everything; most important, it solidified rap's commercial status. DJs had been charging fees for parties and relying on records and equipment for performance, but the commercial potential at which "Rapper's Delight" only hinted significantly raised the economic stakes. Like rock 'n' roll's transition into mainstream commercial markets, rap was fueled by small independent labels and a system of exploitation in which artists had no choice but to submit to draconian contracts that turned almost all creative rights and profits over to the record company if they wanted their music to be widely available. Black-owned and white-owned labels alike paid small flat fees to rappers, demanded rigid and lengthy production contracts (such as five completed records in seven years), made unreasonable demands, and received almost all of the money. Salt from the female rap group Salt 'N' Pepa said that before they signed with Next Plateau Records they were paid $20 apiece per show. When she challenged her manager about their arrangement he threatened her and eventually beat her up for asking too many business questions.[79]

"Rapper's Delight" has also been cited by rappers from all over the country as their first encounter with hip hop's sound and style. In fact, the commercial success of "Rapper's Delight" had the contradictory effect of sustaining and spawning new facets of rap music in New York and elsewhere and at the same time reorienting rap toward more elaborate and restraining commercial needs and expectations. Within the next three years Kurtis Blow's "The Breaks," Spoonie Gee's "Love Rap," The Treacherous Three's "Feel The Heartbeat," Afrika Bambaataa and the Soul Sonic Force's "Planet Rock," Sequence's "Funk You Up," and Grandmaster Flash and the Furious Five's "The Message" were commercially marketed and successful rap singles that made and continue to make more money for Sugar Hill records and other small labels than they do for the artists.[80]

Although Salt 'N' Pepa have been cited as the first major female rappers, some of the earliest rap groups, such as the Funky Four Plus One More had female members, and there were a few all-female groups, such as Sequence. In keeping with young women's experiences in graffiti and breaking, strong social sanctions against their participation limited female ranks. Those who pushed through found that "answer records," (rap battles between the sexes records) were the most likely to get airplay and club response. The first "queen of rap," Roxanne Shante, wrote and recorded a scathing rap in response to UTFO's "Roxanne Roxanne," a rap that accused a girl named Roxanne of being conceited for spurning sexual advances made by UTFO. Roxanne Shante's "Roxanne's Revenge" was a caustic and frustrated response that struck a responsive chord among b-girls and b-boys.[81] Rapped in a sassy high-pitched girl's voice (Shante was 13 years old at the time), Shante told UTFO: "Like corn on the cob you're always trying to rob / You need to be out there lookin' for a job." And the chorus, "Why you have make a record 'bout me? The R/O/X/A/N/N/E?" has become a classic line in hip hop.[82]

Although black and Latino women have been a small but integral presence in graffiti, rapping, and breaking, with the exception of Sha Rock, who was one of the innovators of the beat box, they have been virtually absent from the area of music production. Although there have been female DJs and producers, such as Jazzy Joyce, Gail 'sky' King, and Spindarella, they are not major players in the use of sampling technology nor have they made a significant impact in rap music production and engineering. There are several factors that I believe have contributed to this. First, women in general are not encouraged in and often actively discouraged from learning about and using mechanical equipment. This takes place informally in socialization and formally in gender-segregated vocational tracking in public school curriculum. Given rap music's early reliance on stereo equipment, participating in rap music production requires mechanical and technical skills that women are much less likely to have developed.

Second, because rap music's approaches to sound reproduction developed informally, the primary means for gathering information is shared local knowledge. As Red Alert explained to me, his pre–hip hop interest and familiarity with electronic equipment were sustained by access to his neighbor Otis who owned elaborate stereo equipment configurations. Red Alert says that he spent almost all of his free time at Otis's house, listening, learning, and asking questions. For social, sexual, and cultural reasons young women would be much less likely to be permitted or feel comfortable spending such extended time in a male neighbor's home.

Even under less intimate circumstances, young women were not especially welcome in male social spaces where technological knowledge is shared. Today's studios are extremely male-dominated spaces where technological discourse merges with a culture of male bonding that inordinately problematizes female apprenticeship. Both of these factors have had a serious impact on the contributions of women in contemporary rap music production. Keep in mind, though, that the exclusion of women from musical production in rap is not to be understood as specific to rap or contemporary music, it is instead the continuation of the pervasive marginalization of women from music throughout European and American history.

One of the ways around these deterrents is to create female-centered studio spaces. I have always imagined that rap's most financially successful female rappers would build a rap music production studio that hired and trained female technicians and interns, a space in which young women of color would have the kind of cultural and social access to technology and musical equipment that has, for the most part, been a male dominion. It would also quickly become a profitable and creative space for a wide range of musicians committed to supporting women's musical creativity and forging new collaborative environments.

Unlike breakdancing and graffiti, rap music had and continues to have a much more expansive institutional context within which to operate. Music is more easily commodified than graffiti, and music can be consumed away from the performance context. This is not to suggest that rap's incorporation has been less contradictory or complicated. Quite to the contrary; because of rap music's commercial power, the sanctions against as well as the defenses for rap have been more intense, and thus resistance has been more contradictory.

Throughout the late 1980s, rap music's commercial status increased dramatically, rappers began exploring more themes with greater intertextual references and complexity, and hip hop crews from urban ghettos in several major cities began telling stories that spoke not only of the specifics of life in Houston's fifth ward for example but also of the general bridges between the fifth ward and Miami's Overtown or Boston's Roxbury. In the same time period, Run DMC's mid- to late 1980s popularity among white teens prompted the *New York Times* to declare that rap had finally reached the mainstream.[83] At the same time, Eric B. & Rakim, Public Enemy, KRS One, L.L. Cool J. MC Lyte and De La Soul also emerged as major figures in rap's directional shifts.[84]

During the late 1980s Los Angeles rappers from Compton and Watts, two areas severely paralyzed by the postindustrial economic redistribution developed a West Coast style of rap that narrates experiences and fantasies specific to life as a poor young, black, male subject in Los Angeles. Ice Cube, Dr. Dre, Ice-T, Ezy-E, Compton's Most Wanted, W.C. and the MAAD Circle, Snoop Doggy Dog, South Central Cartel, and others have defined the gangsta rap style. The Los Angeles school of gangsta rap has spawned other regionally specific hardcore rappers, such as New Jersey's Naughty by Nature, Bronx-based Tim Dog, Onyx and Redman, and a new group of female gangsta rappers, such as Boss (two black women from Detroit), New York-based Puerto Rican rapper Hurrican Gloria, and Nikki D.

Mexican, Cuban, and other Spanish-speaking rappers, such as Kid Frost, Mellow Man Ace and El General, began developing bilingual raps and made lyrical bridges between Chicano and black styles. Such groups as Los Angeles-based Cypress Hill, which has black and Hispanic members, serve as an explicit bridge between black and Hispanic communities that builds on long-standing hybrids produced by blacks and Puerto Ricans in New York. Since 1990, in addition to gangsta raps, sexual boasting, Afrocentric and protest raps, rap music features groups that explore the southern black experience, that specialize in the explicit recontextualization of jazz samples, live instrumentation in rap performance and recording, introspective raps, raps that combine acoustic folk guitar with rap's traditional dance beats and even New Age/Soul rap fusions.[85]

These transformations and hybrids reflect the initial spirit of rap and hip hop as an experimental and collective space where contemporary issues and ancestral forces are worked through simultaneously. Hybrids in rap's subject matter, not unlike its use of musical collage, and the influx of new, regional, and ethnic styles have not yet displaced the three points of stylistic continuity to which I referred much earlier: approaches to flow, ruptures in line and layering can still be found in the vast majority of rap's lyrical and music construction. The same is true of the critiques of the postindustrial urban America context and the cultural and social conditions that it has produced. Today, the South Bronx and South Central are poorer and more economically marginalized than they were ten years ago.

Hip hop emerges from complex cultural exchanges and larger social and political conditions of disillusionment and alienation. Graffiti and rap were especially aggressive public displays of counterpresence and voice. Each asserted the right to write[86]—to inscribe one's identity on an environment that seemed Teflon resistant to its young people of color;

an environment that made legitimate avenues for material and social participation inaccessible. In this context, hip hop produced a number of double effects. First, themes in rap and graffiti articulated free play and unchecked public displays; yet, the settings for these expressions always suggested existing confinement.[87] Second, like the consciousness-raising sessions in the early stages of the women's rights movement and black power movement of the 1960s and 1970s, hip hop produced internal and external dialogues that affirmed the experiences and identities of the participants and at the same time offered critiques of larger society that were directed to both the hip hop community and society in general.

Out of a broader discursive climate in which the perspectives and experiences of younger Hispanic, Afro-Caribbeans and African-Americans had been provided little social space, hip hop developed as part of a cross-cultural communication network. Trains carried graffiti tags through the five boroughs; flyers posted in black and Hispanic neighborhoods brought teenagers from all over New York to parks and clubs in the Bronx and eventually to events throughout the metropolitan area. And, characteristic of communication in the age of high-tech telecommunications, stories with cultural and narrative resonance continued to spread at a rapid pace. It was not long before similarly marginalized black and Hispanic communities in other cities picked up on the tenor and energy in New York hip hop. Within a decade, Los Angeles County (especially Compton), Oakland, Detroit, Chicago, Houston, Atlanta, Miami, Newark and Trenton, Roxbury, and Philadelphia, have developed local hip hop scenes that link various regional postindustrial urban experiences of alienation, unemployment, police harassment, social, and economic isolation to their local and specific experience via hip hop's language, style, and attitude.[88] Regional differentiation in hip hop has been solidifying and will continue to do so. In some cases these differences are established by references to local streets and events, neighborhoods and leisure activities; in other cases regional differences can be discerned by their preferences for dance steps, clothing, musical samples, and vocal accents. Like Chicago and Mississippi blues, these emerging regional identities in hip hop affirm the specificity and local character of cultural forms, as well as the larger forces that define hip hop and Afrodiasporic cultures. In every region, hip hop articulates a sense of entitlement and takes pleasure in aggressive insubordination.

Few answers to questions as broadly defined as, "what motivated the emergence of hip hop" could comprehensively account for all the factors that contribute to the multiple, related, and sometimes coincidental events that bring cultural forms into being. Keeping this in mind, this exploration has been organized around limited aspects of the relationship between cultural forms and the contexts within which they emerge. More specifically, it has attended to the ways in which artistic practice is shaped by cultural traditions, related current and previous practice, *and* by the ways in which practice is shaped by technology, economic forces, and race, gender, and class relations. These relationships between form, context, and cultural priority demonstrate that hip hop shares a number of traits with, and yet revises, long-standing Afrodiasporic practices; that male dominance in hip hop is, in part, a by-product of sexism and the active process of women's marginalization in cultural production; that hip hop's form is fundamentally linked to technological changes and social, urban space parameters; that hip hop's anger is produced by contemporary racism, gender, and class oppression; and finally, that a great deal of pleasure in hip hop is derived from subverting these forces and affirming Afrodiasporic histories and identities.

Developing a style nobody can deal with—a style that cannot be easily understood or erased, a style that has the reflexivity to create counterdominant narratives against a mobile and shifting enemy—may be one of the most effective ways to fortify communities of resistance and *simultaneously* reserve the right to communal pleasure. With few economic assets and abundant cultural and aesthetic resources, Afrodiasporic youth have designated the street as the arena for competition, and style as the prestige-awarding event. In the postindustrial urban context of dwindling low-income housing, a trickle of meaningless jobs for young people, mounting police brutality, and increasingly draconian depictions of young inner city residents, hip hop style *is* black urban renewal.

CHAPTER THREE

Soul Sonic Forces
Technology, Orality, and Black Cultural Practice in Rap Music

◆

Rap music has inspired me because I know that when Chuck D tells you to "bring the noise," he's telling you that it's hard. And when you hear the tribal beat and the drums, they are the same drums of the African past that draws the community to war. The drum beats are just faster, because the condition is accelerating so they've got to beat faster. And when your feet are jumping, dancing . . . it's the spirit attempting to escape the entrapment. When you feel that the children have gone mad, if you don't feel it, and when you look at the dances you don't see it and when you listen to the music and you don't hear a call, then you missed the jam.   —Sister Souljah[1]

"The sound" I tell them, that's the final answer to any question in music—the sound.
—Max Roach[2]

In the spring of 1989, I was speaking animatedly with an ethnomusicology professor about rap music and the aims of this project. He found some of my ideas engaging and decided to introduce me and describe my project to the chairman of his music department. At the end of his summary the department head rose from his seat and announced casually, "Well, you must be writing on rap's social impact and political lyrics, because there is nothing to the music." My surprised expression and verbal hesitation gave him time to explain his position. He explained to me that although the music was quite simple and repetitive, the stories told in the lyrics had social value. He pointed out rap's role as a social steam valve, a means for the expression of social anger. "But," he concluded, referring to the music, "they ride down the street at 2:00 A.M. with it blasting from car speakers, and (they) wake up my wife and kids. What's the point in that?" I immediately flashed on a history lesson in which I learned that slaves were prohibited from playing African drums, because, as a vehicle for coded communication, they inspired fear in slaveholders. I suggested that perhaps the music was more complicated than it seemed to him, that a number of innovative approaches to sound and rhythm were being explored in rap music. He listened but seemed closed to such possibilities. Having had some experience with these sorts of "what I don't know can't penetrate me" exchanges, I knew it would be prudent to disengage from this brewing disagreement before it became a long and unpleasant exchange. The ethnomusicology professor who had introduced me ushered us out of the chairman's office.

For the music chairman, automobiles with massive speakers blaring bass and drum heavy beats looped continuously served as an explanation for the insignificance of the music and diminished rap's lyrical and political salience as well. The music was "nothing" to him on the grounds of its apparent "simplicity" and "repetitiveness." Rap music was also "noise" to him, unintelligible yet aggressive sound that disrupted his familial domain ("they wake up my wife and kids") and his sonic territory. His legitimate and important question, "What is the point of that?" was offered rhetorically to justify his outright dismissal of the music, rather than presented seriously to initiate at least a hypothetical inquiry into a musical form that for him seemed at once to be everywhere and yet going nowhere. Let us take his question seriously: What is the point of rap's volume, looped drum beats, and bass frequencies? What meanings can be derived from the sound rap musicians have created? How is the context for its consumption connected to both its *black cultural priorities* and its *sociological* effects? His dismissive question is a productive point of entry into understanding rap's sonic power and presence. Rap's distinctive bass-heavy, enveloping sound does not rest outside of its musical and social power. Emotional power and presence in rap are profoundly linked to sonic force and one's receptivity to it. As Sistah Souljah reminds her audience at Abyssinian Baptist Church: "When you feel the children have gone mad, if you don't feel it . . . when you listen to the music and you don't hear a call, then you missed the jam."

Rap's black sonic forces are very much an outgrowth of black cultural traditions, the postindustrial transformation of urban life, and the contemporary technological terrain. Many of its musical practitioners were trained to repair and maintain new technologies for the privileged but have instead used these technologies as primary tools for alternative cultural expression. This advanced technology has not been straightforwardly adopted; it has been significantly revised in ways that are in keeping with long-standing black cultural priorities, particularly regarding approaches to sound organization. These revisions, especially the use of digital samplers, have not gone unnoticed by the music industry, the legal system, and other institutions responsible for defining, validating, and policing musical production and distribution. Sampling technology and rap producers' commercially profitable use of sampled sounds have seriously challenged the current scope of copyright laws (which are based on notated compositions) and raised larger, more complex questions regarding fair use of musical property and the boundaries of ownership of musical phrases.

Rap's use of sampling technology, looped rhythmic lines, coupled with its significant commercial presence also raises questions about the relationship between industrial imperatives and their impact on cultural production. Is rap's use of repetition in rhythm and sound organization (via looping and sampling) a by-product of the parameters of industrial production (for example, formulas that streamline the sale of music such as commercial radio's four-minute song cap or rap's reuse of previously recorded music). Or, are there cultural explanations for the musical structures in rap's use of electronic equipment?

At the same time as rap music has dramatically changed the intended use of sampling technology, it has also remained critically linked to black poetic traditions and the oral forms that underwrite them. These oral traditions and practices clearly inform the prolific use of collage, intertextuality, boasting, toasting, and signifying in rap's lyrical style and organization. Rap's oral articulations are heavily informed by technological processes, not only in the way such oral traditions are formulated, composed, and disseminated, but also in the way orally based approaches to narrative are embedded in the use of the technology itself. In this contentious environment, these black techno-interventions are often dismissed as nonmusical effects or rendered invisible. These hybrids between black music, black oral forms, and technology that are at the core of rap's sonic and oral power are an architectural blueprint for the redirection of seemingly intractable social ideas, technologies, and ways of organizing sounds along a course that affirms the histories and communal narratives of Afro-diasporic people.

*   *   *

> The organizing principle which makes the black style is rhythm. It is the most perceptible and the least material thing. —Leopold Sedar Senghor[3]

> Rhythm. Rap music is so powerful because of rhythm. —Harmony[4]

Rap's rhythms—"the most perceptible, yet least material elements"—are its most powerful effect. Rap's primary force is sonic, and the distinctive, systematic use of rhythm and sound, especially the use of repetition and musical breaks, are part of a rich history of New World black traditions and practices. Rap music centers on the quality and nature of rhythm and sound, the lowest, "fattest beats" being the most significant and emotionally charged. As rapper Guru has said, "If the beat was a princess, I'd marry it."[5] Many of the popular "Jeep beats" feature dark, strong, prominent, and riveting bass lines.[6] These musical lines dominate production—even at the expense of the rapper's vocal presence. The arrangement and selection of sounds rap musicians have invented via samples, turntables, tape machines, and sound systems are at once deconstructive (in that they actually take apart recorded musical compositions) and recuperative (because they recontextualize these elements creating new meanings for cultural sounds that have been relegated to commercial wastebins). Rap music revises black cultural priorities via new and sophisticated technological means. "Noise" on the one hand and communal countermemory on the other, rap music conjures and razes in one stroke.

These revisions do not take place in a cultural and political vacuum, they are played out on a cultural and commercial terrain that embraces black cultural products and simultaneously denies their complexity and coherence. This denial is partly fueled by a mainstream cultural adherence to the traditional paradigms of Western classical music as the highest legitimate standard for musical creation, a standard that at this point should seem, at best, only marginally relevant in the contemporary popular music realm (a space all but overrun by Afrodiasporic sounds and multicultural hybrids of them). Instead, and perhaps because of, the blackening of the popular taste, Western classical music continues to serve as the primary intellectual and legal standard and point of reference for "real" musical complexity and composition. For these reasons, a comparative look at these two musical and cultural forces is of the utmost importance if we are to make sense of rap's music and the responses to it.

Rhythmic Repetition, Industrial Forces, and Black Practice

Unlike the complexity of Western classical music, which is primarily represented in its melodic and harmonic structures, the complexity of rap music, like many Afrodiasporic musics, is in the rhythmic and percussive density and organization.[7] "Harmony" versus "rhythm" is an oft-sited reduction of the primary distinctions between Western classical and African and African-derived musics. Still, these terms represent significant differences in sound organization and perhaps even disparate approaches to ways of perception, as it were. The outstanding technical feature of the Western classical music tradition is tonal functional harmony. Tonal functional harmony is based on clear, definite pitches and logical relations between them; on the forward drive toward resolution of a musical sequence that leads to a final resolution: the final perfect cadence. The development of tonal harmony critically confined the range of possible tones to twelve tones within each octave arranged in only one of two possible ways, major or minor. It also restricted the rhythmic complexity of European music. In place of freedom with respect to accent and measure, European music focused rhythmic activity onto strong and weak beats in order to prepare and resolve harmonic dissonance. Furthermore, as Christopher Small has argued, Western classical tonal harmony is structurally less tolerant of "acoustically illogical and unclear sounds, sound not susceptible to total control." Other critical features of classical music, such as the notion system and the written score—the medium through which the act of composition takes place— separate the composer from both the audience and the performer and sets limits on composition and performance.[8] This classical music tradition, like all major musical and cultural developments, emerged as part of a larger historical shift in European consciousness:

[We see] changes in European consciousness that we call the Renaissance having its effect in music, with the personal, humanistic viewpoint substituted for the theocratic, universalistic viewpoint of the Middle Ages, expressed in technical terms by a great interest in chords and their effects in juxtaposition, and specifically in the perfect cadence and the suspended dissonance, rather than in polyphony and the independent life of the individual voice.[9]

Rhythm and polyrhythmic layering is to African and African-derived musics what harmony and the harmonic triad is to Western classical music. Dense configurations of independent, but closely related, rhythms, harmonic and nonharmonic percussive sounds, especially drum sounds, are critical priorities in many African and Afrodiasporic musical practices. The voice is also an important expressive instrument. A wide range of vocal sounds intimately connected to tonal speech patterns, "strong differences between the various registers of the voice, even emphasizing the *breaks* between them," are deliberately cultivated in African and African-influenced musics.[10] Treatment, or "versioning," is highly valued. Consequently, the instrument is not simply an object or vehicle for displaying one's talents, it is a "colleague in the creation." And, most important for this discussion, African melodic phrases "tend to be short and repetition is common; in fact, repetition is one of the characteristics of African music." Christopher Small elaborates:

A call-and-response sequence may go on for several hours, with apparently monotonous repetition of the same short phrase sung by a leader and answered by the chorus, but in fact subtle variations are going on all the time, not only in the melodic lines themselves but also in their relation to the complex cross-rhythms in the accompanying drumming or hand clapping. . . . The repetitions of African music have a function in time which is the reverse of (Western classical) music—to dissolve the past and the future into one eternal present, in which the passing of time is no longer noticed.[11]

Rhythmic complexity, repetition with subtle variations, the significance of the drum, melodic interest in the bass frequencies, and breaks in pitch and time (e.g., suspensions of the beat for a bar or two) are also consistently recognized features of African-American musical practices. In describing black New World approaches to rhythm, Ben Sidran refers to Rudi Blesh's notion of "suspended rhythm" and Andre Hodier's description of "swing" as rhythmic tension over stated or implied meter.[12] Time suspension via rhythmic breaks—points at which the bass lines are isolated and suspended—are important clues in explaining sources of pleasure in black musics.

Approaches to sound, rhythm, and repetition in rap music exhibit virtually all of these traits. Rap music techniques, particularly the use of sampling technology, involve the repetition and reconfiguration of rhythmic elements in ways that illustrate a heightened attention to rhythmic patterns and movement between such patterns via breaks and points of musical rupture. Multiple rhythmic forces are set in motion and then suspended, selectively. Rap producers construct loops of sounds and then build in critical moments, where the established rhythm is manipulated and suspended. Then, rhythmic lines reemerge at key relief points. One of the clearest examples of this practice is demonstrated in "Rock Dis Funky Joint" by the Poor Righteous Teachers. The music and the vocal rapping style of Culture Freedom has multiple and complicated time suspensions and rhythmic ruptures of the musical and lyrical passages.[13] Busta Rhymes from Leaders of the New School, reggae rapper Shabba Ranks, British rapper Monie Love, Treach from Naughty by Nature, B-Real from Cypress Hill, and Das Efx are known especially for using their voices as percussive instruments, bending words, racing through phrases, pausing and stuttering through complicated verbal rhythms.

These features are not merely stylistic effects, they are aural manifestations of philosophical approaches to social environments. James A. Snead, working along the same lines as Small, offers a philosophical explanation for the meaning and significance of repetition and rupture in black culture. As we shall see, musical elements that reflect worldviews, these "rhythmic instinctions," are critical in understanding the mean-

© Lisa Leone

ing of time, motion, and repetition in black culture and are of critical
importance to understanding the manipulation of technology in rap.

*   *   *

The rhythmic instinction to yield to travel beyond existing forces of life. Basically, that's
tribal and if you wanna get the rhythm, then you have to join a tribe.
—A Tribe Called Quest [14]

The outstanding fact of late-twentieth-century European culture is its ongoing
reconciliation with black culture. The mystery may be that it took so long to discern the
elements of black culture already there in latent form, and to realize that the separation
between the cultures was perhaps all along not one of nature, but of force.
—James A. Snead [15]

Snead suggests that the vast body of literature devoted to mapping
the cultural differences between European- and African-derived cultures, which has characterized differences between European and black
cultures as a part of "nature," are in fact differences in force; differences
in cultural responses to the inevitability of repetition. Snead argues that
repetition is an important and telling element in culture, a means by
which a sense of continuity, security, and identification are maintained.
This sense of security can be understood as, in fact, a kind of "coverage," both as insurance against sudden ruptures and as a way of hiding

and masking undesired or unpleasant facts or conditions. Snead argues quite convincingly that all cultures provide coverage against loss of identity, repression, assimilation, or attack. Where they "differ among one another primarily [is] in the tenacity with which the 'cover-up' is maintained . . . grafting leeway to those ruptures in the illusion of growth which most often occur in the déjà vus of exact repetition." He suggests that when we view repetition in cultural forms we are not viewing the same thing repeated, but its transformation, "repetition is not just a formal ploy, but often the willed grafting onto culture of an essentially philosophical insight about the shape of time and history. . . . One may readily classify cultural forms based on whether they tend to admit or cover up these repeating constituencies within them." [16]

Snead claims that European culture "secrets" repetition, categorizing it as progression or regression, assigning accumulation and growth or stagnation to motion, whereas black cultures highlight the observance of repetition, perceiving it as circulation, equilibrium. In a fashion resembling Small, Snead argues that Western classical music uses rhythm mainly as "an aid in the construction of a sense of progression to a harmonic cadence (and) *repetition has been suppressed* in favor of the fulfillment of the goal of harmonic resolution." Similarly, musicologist Susan McClary points out that "tonal music" (referring to the Western classical tradition) is "narratively conceived at least to the extent that the original key area—the tonic—also serves as the final goal. Tonal structures are organized teleologically, with the illusion of unitiary identity promised at the end of each piece." [17]

To the contrary, Snead claims that black cultures highlight the observance of repetition, perceiving it as circulation and equilibrium, rather than as a regulated force that facilitates the achievement of a final harmonic goal. Drawing on examples in literature, religion, philosophy, and music, Snead elaborates on the uses and manifestations of repetition in black culture. [18] For our purposes, his analysis of the meaning of repetition in black music is most relevant, specifically his description of rhythmic repetition and its relationship to the "cut":

In black culture, repetition means that the thing circulates, there in an equilibrium. . . . In European culture, repetition must be seen to be not just circulation and flow, but accumulation and growth. In black culture, the thing (the ritual, the dance, the beat) is there for you to pick up when you come back to get it." If there is a goal . . . it is always deferred; it continually "cuts" back to the start, in the musical meaning of a "cut" as an abrupt, seemingly unmotivated break (an accidental da capo) with a series already in progress and a willed return to a prior series. . . . Black culture, in the "cut," "builds" accidents into its coverage, almost as if to control their unpredictability. [19]

Deliberately "repetitive" in force, black musics (especially those genres associated with dance) use the "cut" to emphasize the repetitive nature of the music by "skipping back to another beginning which we have already heard," making room for accidents and ruptures inside the music itself. In this formulation, repetition and rupture work within and against each other, building multiple circular musical lines that are broken and then absorbed or managed in the reestablishment of rhythmic lines.

Rap music uses repetition and rupture in new and complex ways, building on long-standing black cultural forces. Advances in technology have facilitated an increase in the scope of break beat deconstruction and reconstruction and have made complex uses of repetition more accessible. Now, the desired bass line or drum kick can be copied into a sampler, along with other desired sounds, and programmed to loop in any desired tempo or order. Rap music relies on the loop, on the circularity of rhythm and on the "cut" or the "break beat" that systematically ruptures equilibrium. Yet, in rap, the "break beat" itself is looped—repositioned as repetition, as equilibrium inside the rupture. Rap music highlights points of rupture as it equalizes them.

Snead calls James Brown "an example of a brilliant American practitioner of the 'cut'" and describes the relationship between established rhythmic patterns and the hiatus of the cut in Brown's work as a rupture that affirms the rhythmic pattern while it interrupts it. "The ensuing rupture," Snead claims, "does not cause dissolution of the rhythm; quite to the contrary, it strengthens it." Snead's reading of James Brown as a brilliant practitioner of the "cut" is a prophetic one. Published in 1981, a number of years before hip hop producers had communally declared James Brown's discography the foundation of the break beat, Snead could not have known that Brown's exclamations, "hit me!" "take it to the bridge!" rapid horn and drum accents and bass lines would soon become the most widely used breaks in rap music.

Snead's approach presumes that music is fundamentally related to the social world, that music, like other cultural creations, fulfills and denies social needs, that music *embodies assumptions* regarding social power, hierarchy, pleasure, and worldview. This link between music and larger social forces, although not widely held in the field of musicology, is also critical to the work of Susan McClary, Christopher Small, and French political economist Jacques Attali. McClary, Small, and Attali demystify the naturalized, normalized status of nineteenth-century classical musical structures and conventions, positing an understanding of music's role as a way of perceiving the world and suggesting that every musical code is rooted in the social formations and technologies of its age.[20] These historically and culturally grounded interpretations of technological "advances" shed light on naturalized aesthetic parameters as they are embodied in equipment, illustrating the significance of culture in the development of technology.

Grounding music as a cultural discourse dismantles the causal link between rap's sonic force and the technological means for its expression. Rap producers' strategic use of electronic reproduction technology, particularly sampling equipment, affirms stylistic priorities in the organization and selection of sounds found in many black diasporic musical expressions. Although rap music is shaped by and articulated through advanced reproduction equipment, its stylistic priorities are not merely by-products of such equipment.

On the question of repetition as a cultural force, Attali and Snead part company. For Attali and other cultural theorists, repetition is primarily considered a manifestation of mass culture, a characteristic of culture in the age of reproduction. The advent of recording technology signaled the emergence of a society of mass production and repetition. Repetition is, therefore, equated with industrial standardization and represents a move toward a single totalitarian code. At the point of mass production and industrial standardization, Attali claims, music becomes an industry and "its consumption ceases to be collective."[21] Similarly, Adorno describes the "break" in pre-swing jazz as "nothing other than a disguised cadence" and explains that, "the cult of the machine which is represented by unabated jazz beats involves a self-renunciation that cannot but take root in the form of a fluctuating uneasiness somewhere in the personality of the obedient."[22] "In mass culture," Fredric Jameson claims, "repetition effectively volatizes the original object—so that the student of mass culture has no primary object of study."[23]

Repetition does, in fact, function as part of a system of mass production that structures and confines creative articulation; along these lines Adorno, Jameson, and Attali offer vital criticisms of the logic of massified culture in late capitalist societies. Yet, repetition cannot be reduced to a repressive, industrial force. Nor is it sufficient to understand repetition solely as a by-product of the needs of industrialization. I do not mean to suggest that any of the cultural theorists would claim that repetition was nonexistent in preindustrial society. However, their focus on repetition as an industrial condition encourages mischaracterizations of the black popular cultural phenomenon, particularly those forms that privilege repetition and are prominently positioned in the commodity system.

If we assume that industrial production sets the terms for repetition inside mass-produced music, then how can alternative uses and manifestations of repetition that are articulated *inside* the commodity market be rendered perceptible? Rap music's use of rhythmic lines constructed with sampled loops of sound are particularly vulnerable to misreadings or erasures along these lines. Working inside the commodity market and with industrial technology, rap music uses rhythmic forces that are informed by mass reproduction technology, but it uses it in ways that affirm black cultural priorities that sometimes work against market forces. Yet, none of this is visible if all mass-produced repetition is understood primarily as a manifestation of mass culture. If rap can be so overwhelmingly mischaracterized, then what other musical and cultural practices have been collapsed into the logic of industrial repetition, labeled examples of "cultlike" obedience? Adorno's massive misreading of the jazz break, beside betraying a severe case of black cultural illiteracy, is another obvious example of the pitfalls of reading musical structures in the popular realm as by-products of industrial forces.

Adorno, Jameson, and Attali, by constructing repetition as if it were a singular force, strongly suggest that mass production sets the terms for repetition and that any other cultural forms of repetition, once practiced inside systems of mass production, are subsumed by the larger logic of industrialization. Consequently, no other mass-produced or mass-consumed forms that privilege forms of repetition are accessible or relevant once inside this larger logic of industrial repetition.

Positioning repetition in late capitalist markets as a consequence of that market, marginalizes or erases alternative uses of and relationships to repetition that might suggest collective resistance to that system. Repetition, then, is all too easily vilified, collapsed into the logic of the commodity system and is employed as a means by which to effectively erase the multiplicity of cultures and traditions present in contemporary Western societies. I am not suggesting that black culture supersedes the effects of commodification. Nor am I suggesting that black cultural priorities lie outside of (or completely in opposition to) mass cultural industries. Quite to the contrary, this is a call for readings of commodification that can accommodate multiple histories and approaches to sound organization. I am mostly concerned, here, with facile and all-too-frequent readings of repetition that apply and naturalize dominant cultural principles and consequently colonize and silence black approaches, which, in the case of American popular music especially, have significant and problematic, dare I say racist, implications.[24]

Give me a (Break) Beat!: Sampling and Repetition in Rap Production

You see, you misunderstood
A sample is just a tactic,
A portion of my method, a tool.
In fact it's only of importance
When I make it a priority.
And what we sample is loved by the majority.
—Stetsasonic [25]

In rap, sampling remains a tactical priority. More precisely, samplers are the quintessential rap production tool. Although rappers did not invent drum machines or sampling, they have revolutionized their use. Prior to rap music's redefinition of the role samplers play in musical creativity, samplers were used almost exclusively as time- and moneysaving devices for producers, engineers, and composers. Samplers were used as short cuts; sometimes a horn section, a bass drum, or background vocals would be lifted from a recording easily and quickly, limiting the expense and effort to locate and compensate studio musicians. Although famous rock musicians have used recognizable samples from other prominent musicians as part of their album material, for the most part, samples were used to "flesh out" or accent a musical piece, not to build a new one.[26] In fact, prior to rap, the most desirable use of a sample was to mask the sample and its origin; to bury its identity. Rap producers have inverted this logic, using samples as a point of reference, as a means by which the process of repetition and recontextualization can be highlighted and privileged.

Samplers are computers that can digitally duplicate any existing sounds and play them back in any key or pitch, in any order, sequence and loop them endlessly. They also have a preprogrammed library of digital sounds, sounds that have not been "lifted" from other previously recorded materials but may also be arranged in any fashion. Harry Allen explains: "Record the sound of these pages turning as your TV plays the 'One Life to Live' theme in the background. Or record your boss yelling. Or a piece of Kool and the Gang, whatever, for up to 63 seconds. Loop it, so it plays end-on-end forever, or hook the S900 (sampler) up to a keyboard and play whatever you recorded in a scale."[27]

Samplers allow rap musicians to expand on one of rap's earliest and most central musical characteristics: the break beat. Dubbed the "best part of a great record" by Grandmaster Flash, one of rap's pioneering DJs, the break beat is a section where "the band breaks down, the rhythm section is isolated, basically where the bass guitar and drummer take solos."[28] These break beats are points of rupture in their former

© suekwon

contexts, points at which the thematic elements of a musical piece are suspended and the underlying rhythms brought center stage. In the early stages of rap, these break beats formed the core of rap DJs' mixing strategies. Playing the turntables like instruments, these DJs extended the most rhythmically compelling elements in a song, creating a new line composed only of the most climactic point in the "original." The effect is a precursor to the way today's rappers use the "looping" capacity on digital samplers.

WORKING IN THE RED

To make the noise that characterizes rap's most creative producers and musicians requires approaching sound and sound manipulation in ways that are unconcerned with the intended or standard use of the samplers. Rap producer Eric (Vietnam) Sadler explains:

Turn it all the way up so it's totally distorted and pan it over to the right so you really can't even hear it. Pan it over to the right means put the sound only in the right side speaker, and turn it so you can't barely even hear it—it's just like a noise in the side. Now, engineers . . . they live by certain rules. They're like, "You can't do that. You don't want a distorted sound, it's not right, it's not correct." With Hank (Shocklee) and Chuck (D) its like, "Fuck that it's not correct, just do this shit." And engineers won't do it. So if you start engineering yourself and learning these things yourself—[get] the meter goin' like this [he moves his hand into an imaginary red zone] and you hear the shit cracklin,' that's the sound we're lookin' for.[29]

Using the machines in ways that have not been intended, by pushing on established boundaries of music engineering, rap producers have developed an art out of recording with the sound meters well into the distortion zone. When necessary, they deliberately *work in the red*. If recording in the red will produce the heavy dark growling sound desired, rap producers record in the red. If a sampler must be detuned in order to produce a sought-after low-frequency hum, then the sampler is detuned. Rap musicians are not the only musicians to push on the limits of high-tech inventions.[30] Yet, the decisions they have made and the directions their creative impulses have taken echo Afrodiasporic musical priorities. Rap production resonates with black cultural priorities in the age of digital reproduction.

Volume, density, and quality of low-sound frequencies are critical features in rap production. Caribbean musics, especially Jamaica's talk over and dub, share a number of similarities with rap's sound. Each feature heavily amplified prominently featured drum and bass guitar tracks. Both insist on privileging repetition as the basis of rhythm and rhythm as the central musical force.[31] As writers Mark Dery and Bob Doerschuk point out, rappers' production philosophy reflects this emphasis on bass and drum sounds: "To preserve the urgency of rap at its rawest, while keeping the doors of innovation open, a different philosophy of production and engineering has had to evolve . . . a new generation of technicians is defining the art of rap recording. Old habits learned in MOR, hard rock and R&B do not apply. Like rap itself, the new rules are direct: keep it hot, keep the drums up front and boost that bass."[32] Rap producers use particular digital sound machines because of the types of sounds they produce, especially in the lower frequencies. Boosting the bass is not merely a question of loudness—it is a question of the quality of lower-register sounds at high volumes. The Roland TR-808 is a rap drum machine of choice because of its "fat sonic boom," because of the way it processes bass frequencies. Kurtis Blow explains: "The 808 is great because you can *detune* it and get this low-frequency hum. It's a car speaker destroyer. That's what we try to do as rap producers—break car speakers and house speakers and boom boxes. And the 808 does it. It's African music!"[33] Not only have rap producers selected the machines that allow for greater range of low-frequency resonance, they have also forced sound engineers to revise their mixing strategies to accommodate rap's stylistic priorities.[34] Gary Clugston, rap engineer at INS Recording in New York, explains how rap producers arrange sounds, first pushing the drums to the foreground and at the center of the piece and then using effects to manipulate the bass sounds: "If you're using a drum sample in a rock record, you want it to sit in the mix with everything else. In rap, you do whatever you can to make it stand out—by adding effects, EQ, bottom—and make it sound dirty." "So strong is this fixation with the bass," claim Dery and Doerschuk, "that producers and engineers had to adapt their usual mixing formulas to make room for the rumble." Steve Ett, engineer and co-owner of Chung House of Metal, a popular studio among rap's most prominent producers elaborates: "I always put that super-loud long sustaining 808 bass drum on track 2. I don't put anything on 1 or 3. If you put the bass drum on 2 and the snare on 3, the bass drum *leakage* is tremendous. It's the only bass drum in the world I'll do that with. . . . For me, rap is a matter of pumping the shit out of the low end. The bass drum is the loudest thing on the record. You definitely hear the vocals but they're very low compared to the bass drum."[35] Ett programs the 808 bass drum knowing that it will have to leak in order to get the desired rumble. This leakage means that the bass will take up more space than is "normally" intended and bleed into other deliberately emptied tracks, which gives the bass a heavier, grittier, less fixed sound. In traditional recording techniques, leakage is a problem to be avoided, it means the sounds on the tracks are not clearly separated, therefore making them less fixed in their articulation. Rock and heavy metal, among other musical genres, have used distortion and other effects that also require manipulation of traditional recording techniques. Like the use of distortion, if rap's desired sounds require leakage, then leakage is a managed part of a process of achieving desired sounds, rather than a problem of losing control of fixed pitches.

Hank Shocklee prefers the E-mu SP-1200 for its versatility and associates the TR-808 more closely with house music, a dance music cousin of rap.[36] Most important about his description of these machines is his explanation of how each sampler performs the same technical functions in significantly different ways. Each sampler creates a different feel, thus allowing greater articulation of different rhythmic qualities and musical priorities:

[The 1200] allows you to do everything with a sample. You can cut it off, you can truncate it really tight, you can run a loop in it, you can cut off certain drum pads. The limitation is that it sounds white, because it's rigid. The Akai Linn [MPC-60] allows you to create more of a feel; that's what Teddy Riley uses to get his swing beats. For an R&B producer, the Linn is the best, because it's a slicker machine. For house records, you want to use the TR-808, because it has that charging feel, like a locomotive coming at you. But every rap producer will tell you that the 1200 is still the ultimate drum machine.[37]

Shocklee prefers the 1200 because it allows him greater cutting and splicing mobility, even though the process of cutting on a 1200 is "stiff." His production work employs the "cut" extensively, demonstrating its capacity to suspend and propel time and motion.[38] Sounding "white" is his reductivist short-hand description for the equipment whose technological parameters adhere most stringently to the Western classical legacy of restricted rhythm in composition. Eric Sadler claims that the TR-808 is still very popular in rap production because of a digital preprogrammed drum sound called the 808 drum boom: "It's not like a regular kick drum. It's this big giant basketball that you hear on just about every record now . . . Boom . . . Boom. Big and heavy, just like a reggae sort of feel." Sadler adds that the engineering boards themselves are critical to the feel and sound of rap music, to the process of sound reproduction: "One of the reasons I'm here (in this studio) is because this board here is bullshit. It's old, it's disgusting, a lot of stuff doesn't work, there are fuses out . . . to get an old sound. The other room, I use that for something else. All sweet and crispy clear, it's like the Star Wars room. This room is the Titanic room."[39] Sadler's reference to the Titanic studio can be read as an interesting revision of one of the most well-known black folk toasts "The Titanic." In it, Shine, the black boiler room operator on the *Titanic*, tries to warn the white passengers that the ship is about to sink, but his warnings go unheeded. The Captain claims that his water pumps will keep back the water, even though Shine can clearly see they are failing to do so. After a number of warnings, Shine finally jumps over board saving his own life, saying, "your shittin' is good your shittin' is fine, but here's one time you white folks ain't gonna shit on Shine." Sadler's dubbing that studio the Titanic is his way of saying that it is old and obsolete, suggesting that he chooses the faulty, obsolete equipment deliberately because it allows him to construct his own historical, sonic narratives. The latest, slickest equipment in the Star Wars room denies him access to those sounds and that history. In the hip hop version of "The Titanic," Sadler, like Shine, ignores the white man's definition of technical use and value ("these new valves are better"), but in this case, he does so by staying with his ship, by holding on to the equipment that has been deemed obsolete but best suits his needs. Refusing to follow dominant conceptions of the value of new technology against their better judgement, Shine and Sadler "save" their own lives and narratives respectively.

These samplers, drum machines, and engineering boards are selected and manipulated by rap producers partially because they allow them to manage repetition and rupture with break beats and looping and cutting techniques and because of the *quality* of sounds they reproduce. Shock-lee and Sadler's comments are important to this discussion, because they illuminate cultural parameters as they are articulated in advanced electronic equipment. The equipment has to be altered to accommodate rap's use of low-frequency sounds, mixing techniques revised to create the arrangements of and relationships between drum sounds. And second, they make clear that rap producers actively and aggressively deploy strategies that revise and manipulate musical technologies so that they will articulate black cultural priorities.

Selecting drum samples also involve matters of sonic preference. Rap's heavy use of sampled live soul and funk drummers adds a desired textural dimension uncommon in other genres and that programmed drum machines cannot duplicate. These soul and funk drummers, recorded under very different circumstances, carry performative resonances that cannot be easily recreated. Bill Stephney, co-owner, with Hank Shocklee, of S.O.U.L. Records, explains why rappers favor particular sources for samples: "They (rap producers) hate digital drums. They like their snares to sound as if they've been recorded in a large live room, with natural skins and lots of reverb. They've tried recording with live drums. But you really cannot replicate those sounds. Maybe it's the way engineers mike, maybe it's the lack of baffles in the room. Who knows? But that's why these kids have to go back to the old records."[40] The quality of sound found in these 1960s and 1970s soul and funk records are as important to hip hop's sound as the machines that deconstruct and reformulate them.[41] Rap's sample-heavy sound is digitally reproduced but cannot be digitally created. In other words, the sound of a James Brown or Parliament drum kick or bass line and the equipment that processed it then, as well as the equipment that processes it now, are all central to the way a rap records feels; central to rap's sonic force. This is not to say that live drummers are not featured on rap records, many are; neither is this to say that rap producers do not draw on a wide range of genres, including rap's own previously recorded beats and rhymes. For example, rap's sampling excursions into jazz and rock are increasing all the time. Still, soul and funk drum kicks—live or recorded—are almost always the musical glue that binds these samples together, giving the likes of Miles Davis, Ron Carter, Louis Armstrong, and Roy Ayers a distinct difference and a hip hop frame. For example, A Tribe Called Quest's "Verses from the Abstract" features Ron Carter on bass but the hip hop drum lines completely recontextualize Carter's jazz sound; similar recontextualizations of jazz samples can be found on a host of rap albums, such as Guru's *Jazzamatazz* and Pete Rock and C.L. Smooth's *Mecca and the Soul Brother*.[42]

Sampling, as it is used by many of hip hop's premiere producers, is not merely a shortcut used to "copy" musical passages. If this were so, then producers would spare the legal costs of clearing usage of other artists' recorded material by programming or replaying very similar musical sequences. Furthermore, as Prince Be Softly of P.M. Dawn points out, finding musical samples can be more time-consuming: "Sampling artistry is a very misunderstood form of music. A lot of people still think sampling is thievery but it can take more time to find the right sample than to make up a riff. I'm a songwriter just like Tracy Chapman or Eric B. and Rakim."[43] The decision to adopt samples of live drum sounds involves quality-of-sound issues and a desire to increase the range of sound possibilities. A few years after rap's recording history began, pioneering rap producer and DJ Marley Marl discovered that real drum sounds could be used in place of simulated drum sounds:

One day in '81 or '82 we was doin' this remix. I wanted to sample a voice from off this song with an Emulator and accidentally, a snare went through. At first I was like, "That's the wrong thing," but the snare was soundin' good. I kept running the track back and hitting the Emulator. Then I looked at the engineer and said, "You know what this means?! I could take any drum sound from any old record, put it in here are get the old drummer sound on some shit. No more of that dull DMX shit." That day I went out and bought a sampler.[44]

For Marley Marl and other rap producers the sampler is a means to an end, not an end in itself. Nor is it necessarily a short cut to music production, although some rap producers use samplers and samples in uncreative ways. For the most part, sampling, not unlike versioning practices in Caribbean musics, is about paying homage, an invocation of another's voice to help you to say what you want to say.[45] It is also a means of archival research, a process of musical and cultural archeology. According to Daddy-O, rap producer for Stetsasonic; "Sampling's not a lazy man's way. We learn a lot from sampling; it's like school for us. When we sample a portion of a song and repeat it over and over we can better understand the matrix of the song. I don't know how they made those old funk and soul records. We don't know how they miked the drums. But we can learn from their records."[46] In addition, samples are not strung together in a linear fashion one after the other and then looped. Instead, as Bill Stephney points out, numerous tracks are often programmed simultaneously, sampled on top of one another to create a dense multilayered effect: "These kids will have six tracks of drum programs all at the same time. This is where sampling gets kind of crazy. You may get a kid who puts a kick from one record on one track, a kick from another record on another track, a Linn kick on a third track, and a TR-808 kick on a fourth—all to make one kick!"[47] Once constructed, these looped beats are not set in stone, they are merged with lyrics and reconstructed among other beats, sounds, and melodies. Sadler describes the architectural blueprint for Ice Cube's dense and edgy "The Nigger You Love to Hate": "The original loop [for it] was [from] Steve Arington's 'Weak in the Knees.' It was funky but basic all the way through. Cube heard it, liked it, put his vocals on it. . . . Then we stripped it apart like a car and put it back together totally again. . . . erasing musical parts under the choruses and other parts. Every time we got back to the original song, it would drop down. So we would have to build. That's why the song just kept going up. We kept having to find other parts." One of the most dense and cacophonous raps to date, "Night of the Living Baseheads," used nearly forty-five different samples in addition to the basic rhythm tracks and original music on twenty-four tracks. Sadler explains: "Not 48 tracks [which is common in music production today], but 24. You got stuff darting in and out absolutely everywhere. It's like somebody throwing rice at you. You have to grab every little piece and put it in the right place like in a puzzle. Very complicated. All those little snippets and pieces that go in, along with the regular drums that you gotta drop out in order to make room for it."[48]

Rap production involves a wide range of strategies for manipulating rhythm, bass frequencies, repetition, and musical breaks. Rap's engineering and mixing strategies address ways to manage and prioritize high-volume and low-frequency sounds. Selected samplers carry preferred "sonic booms" and aid rap producers in setting multiple rhythmic forces in motion and in recontextualizing and highlighting break beats. These strategies for achieving desired sounds are not random stylistic effects, they are manifestations of approaches to time, motion, and repetition found in many New World black cultural expressions.

BLACK PRACTICES: HIDING IN THE SPOTLIGHT

The world of organized sound is a boundless palette. On that palette you have classical European music, you have Charlie Parker . . . the music of the East, African music. . . . the Middle East, electronic music. Some people think that what they are doing way over here in one corner is the end of all organized sound. That's like saying the Earth is the end of the universe. —Max Roach[49]

Because few rappers are formally trained musicians, rarely compose elaborate melodic phrases, and do not frequently play "real" instruments, rap has been accused of not being music at all. David Samuels's

New Republic cover story on rap music entitled, "The Real Face of Rap: The 'black music' that isn't either," reduces rap's history to a commercial ploy to attract white teenagers and suggests that "rap's *hour* as an innovative popular music has come and gone." J. D. Considine's article in *Musician* magazine, "Fear of a Rap Planet," cites a number of examples of antirap media coverage regarding rap's lyrics but notes that the most common criticism about rap is not, in fact, related to its racial politics. Instead, he argues, most criticism of rap has to do with rap's status as music. Basically, many rock musicians do not consider rap as *music*. Considine, attempting to convince *Musician* readers that rap *is* music, claims that "even a seemingly simple rap record . . . reveals unexpected complexity if you know where to look." During the same month in 1992, Jon Parales published an article entitled "On Rap, Symbolism and Fear" in the *New York Times* that was devoted to mainstream white fears of rap because of its violent imagery and black teen audience. All of the response letters published two weeks later were in rather aggressive opposition to Parales's piece. However, rap's lyrics and angry audience were not addressed in these letters; rather, the fact that Parales presumed that rap is *music* was the source of the respondents' frustration. Writers claimed that, "loud, pounding rhythm with shouted lyrics and no melody do not constitute music," and "music began with rhythm, progressed to melody . . . reached its developmental culmination with harmony. Rap, despite its modern trappings, is a regression." These comments clearly support Eurocentric notions of the terms of cultural progress and link them to music. The significance of these comments is not in the ignorance they display but in the fact that the *New York Times* believed that these analyses carry enough social weight and legitimation to warrant publication without rebuttal.[50]

In response, some rap producers offer their lack of training as an explanation for the innovative nature of their approach. For example, claiming that rap producers are actually more creative than *real* musicians, Hank Shocklee defends rap producers' approach to music and explains the reasons for the antagonism between rap producers and formally trained musicians: "We don't like musicians. We don't respect musicians. The reason why is because they look at people who do rap as people who don't have any knowledge. As a matter of fact, it's quite the opposite. We have a better sense of music, a better concept of music, of where it's going, of what it can do."[51] Shocklee believes that his ignorance of formal musical training allows him to see beyond what has been understood as correct and proper sound construction, giving him a greater range of creative motion: "In dealing with rap, you have to be innocent and ignorant of music. Trained musicians are not ignorant to music, and they cannot be innocent to it . . . For example, certain keys have to go together because you have this training and it makes musical sense to you. We might use a black key and white key together playing together because it works for a particular part. A musician will go, 'No those are the wrong keys. The tones are clashing.' We don't look at it that way."[52] Shocklee's comments about formal training and its relationship to musical innovation as well as critical responses to Shocklee's approaches bear striking resemblance to the criticism of be-bop pianist Thelonius Monk's untrained approach to jazz piano playing. As jazz music historian Frank Tirro notes, in the 1950s, Monk's eclectic and unconventional compositions, which "had earlier been passed off as a lack of technical ability (were) now being viewed as a new way of creating musical sounds and organizing musical ideas." Jason Berry et al. have noted how black musicians find beats in everyday sounds, even using truck engines as rhythmic inspiration. As vocalist Aaron Neville recalls, "Me and [Allen] Toussaint would ride around with a tape recorder and one day we pulled up next to a big semi-truck. The motor was going 'rumble rum rumble' with a nice beat, you know, and Toussaint recorded that beat." Shocklee backs Neville and Toussaint up on this when he asserts that "music is nothing but organized noise. You can take anything—street sounds, us talking, whatever you want—and make it music by organizing it. That's still our philosophy, to show people that this thing you call music is a lot broader than you think it is."[53]

Shocklee claims that because their musical instincts are not "constrained" by formal rules and procedures, rap producers operate "more freely" with the available technology. Certainly, some of what Shocklee suggests about "innocence" to formal procedures is true. Fewer established parameters generally permit greater potential range of motion. But Shocklee's opposition between knowledge and innocence is a bit misleading. He is really referring to the differences between formal Western and black musical priorities as they are worked out, often contentiously, in the creative realm and in the marketplace. Shocklee's innocence is his lack of formal Western musical training. For Shocklee, "training" is formal Western training, and trained musicians use "knowledge" about a particular tradition to produce a particular arrangement of sounds that in turn produce particular effects. He, too, employs "knowledge" and musical strategies, not innocent (value-free) ones, but strategies commonly found in black musical traditions that often involve different cultural priorities. When he claims that to understand or deal with rap music you must be innocent, he suggests that a commitment to formal Western musical priorities must be abandoned, or at the very least interrogated and revised, especially as they are articulated in the rules of sound production and reproduction.

An absence of commitment to classical Western musical traditions is not sufficient to produce rap music. Shocklee refers to a presence, an alternative tradition that prioritizes openness, ruptures, breaks, and forces in motion. His inability to identify these characteristics as part of a discrete cultural history, coupled with the ease with which he references classical standards is an indication of the power of classically derived standards over creative efforts that represent alternative cultural logics, even in popular culture.

Hank Shocklee's defense of his musical creativity is connected to the perpetuation of a long-standing unwillingness to acknowledge black cultural traditions and practices in contemporary popular American forms. This may seem surprising given the fact that American popular music is a particularly significant territory for black cultural expressions. Yet, the study of popular music has been quite inattentive to the specificity of black practices in the popular realm. There is a significant intellectual divide between the study of black music and the study of American popular music. Not unlike racial segregation, black cultural practices and popular culture are treated as if they are mutually exclusive categories of analysis. For many cultural critics, once a black cultural practice takes a prominent place inside the commodity system, it is no longer considered a black practice—it is instead a "popular" practice whose black cultural priorities and distinctively black approaches are either taken for granted as a "point of origin," an isolated "technique," or rendered invisible. The last alternative has, so far, been a virtually impossible position to take in reference to rap music.[54] Yet, the category "dance" music has been a particularly slippery space in which black music has been linked to technological effects rather than black cultural priorities.

Along these lines, Andrew Goodwin's "Sample and Hold: Pop Music in the Age of Digital Reproduction" describes his project as one that will focus on the music itself, via comments on the "new technologies and their impact on rhythm and timbre." In an attempt to critique overly zealous reading of samplers as quintessential postmodern machines, Goodwin points out that high-tech samplers have been used most extensively in dance music, which he considers a communal practice. He argues that:

The most striking point in the analysis of both areas is the fact that music made by machines, or to sound like machines, has not taken pop's trajectory into electronic or art music, but has instead become the chief source of its *dance music*. . . . Synthesizers, drum machines and digital samplers are identified less with modern composers . . . than with dance genres like disco, hip hop, Hi-NRG, and House. In other words, while cultural studies critics such as Simon Frith debate the essentially critical and academic distinctions being made between technology on the one hand and "community" and nature on the other, pop musicians and audiences have grown increasingly accustomed to making an association between synthetic/automated music and the communal (dance floor) connection to nature (via the body). We have grown used to connecting machines and *funkiness*.[55]

Goodwin is correct to suggest that the deconstruction of recorded sound does not necessarily erase communal connections; such practices may recuperate history rather than deny it. And he is quite reasonably suspicious of a bifurcation of technology and community, which may suggest that the notion of community is a pretechnological condition. Yet, he refers to four major contemporary black dance forms—disco, hip hop, Hi-NRG, and house—as the bases for his argument regarding the way in which technology is made *funky* and the community-based nature of these forms without one reference to black cultural priorities, black musical traditions, or black people. He makes no mention of black practitioners and the possibility that these *dance* artists are using sampling technology to articulate black approaches to sound, rhythm, timbre, motion, and community. For Goodwin, technology is made *funky* but not as a result of black appropriation. His erasure of the overwhelmingly black approaches to music embodied in disco, hip hop, and house is at best a pernicious case of the anxiety of influence and at worst contributes to a body of cultural studies that has not yet confronted black popular presence other than as a stylistic effect ready for white popular consumption. His position, which reflects an incapacity to imagine the popular terrain as a site where contestations over black cultural forms take place, contributes to the discursive co-optation of black contributions in popular cultural criticism. Mead Hunter's comments on interculturalism in American music speak to the power dynamics that are inherent in these unequal forms of cultural exchange: "Considering that the adoption of American dance beats—for they are now effectively American, however African their lineage—must to some degree insinuate an American sensibility, the end-product cannot be wholly value free. Regional cultures act not as barriers, but as permeable membranes; even with the best of intentions, their penetration can be a subtle strain of colonialism."[56] Consequently, Goodwin's attempts to humanize technology—to affirm the community-based nature of dance music—is also an erasure of the very communities that are responsible for the dance musics he finds so compelling.

"Read it in Braille, It'll Still Be Funky":
Technological Orality and Oral Technology in Hip Hop

As I have suggested earlier, rap music is a technological form that relies on the reformulation of recorded sound in conjunction with rhymed lyrics to create its distinctive sound. Rappers bring black cultural priorities to bear on advanced technology.[57] Rappers also bring black oral practices into the technological mix. Rap's poetic force, its rearticulation of African-American oral practices, and its narrative strategies are central to rap. However, rap's oral and technological facets are more interactive than this disjuncture suggests. Rap music blurs the distinction between literate and oral modes of communication by altering and yet sustaining important aspects of African-American folk orality while embedding oral practices in the technology itself. Rap's orality is altered and highly informed by the technology that produces it; and in rap, oral logic informs its technological practices. Redefining the constitution of narrative originality, composition, and collective memory, rap artists challenge institutional apparatuses that define property, technological innovation, and authorship.

David Toop, one of rap's early and most thoughtful historiographers, argues that rap is rooted in twentieth-century African-American poetic traditions: "Raps forebears stretch back through disco, street funk, radio D.J.s, Bo Diddley, the bebop singers, Cab Calloway, Pigmeat Markham, the tap dancers and comics, The Last Poets, Gil Scott-Heron, Muhammad Ali, a cappella and doo wop groups, ring games, skip rope rhymes, prison and army songs toasts, signifying and the dozens. . . . No matter how far it *penetrates* into the twilight maze of Japanese video games and cool European electronics, its roots are still the deepest in all contemporary Afro-American music."[58] Toop, although he does have a solid grasp of the more prominent African-American oral influences in rap, draws a false dichotomy between rap's African-American roots and the high-tech equipment to which it is equally wedded. Rap then, is not simply a linear extension of other orally based African-American traditions with beat boxes and cool European electronics added on. Rap is a complex fusion of orality and postmodern technology. This mixture of orality and technology is essential to understanding the logic of rap music; a logic that, although not purely oral, maintains many characteristics of orally based expression and at the same time incorporates and destabilizes many characteristics of the literate and highly technological society in which its practitioners live. Harry Allen captures the relationship between orality and technology in rap when he suggests that, "hip hop humanizes technology and makes it tactile. In hip hop, you make the technology do stuff that it isn't supposed to do, get music out of something that's not supposed to give you music quite that way."[59]

Rap is in part an expression of what Walter Ong has referred to as "post-literate orality." Ong suggests that the electronic age is "an age of post-literate orality—the orality of telephones, radio, and television, which depends on writing and print for its existence." Although his book focuses primarily on the differences in mentality between oral and writing cultures, his conceptualization of postliterate orality is an innovative analytical tool for understanding contemporary developments in African-American culture. The concept of postliterate orality merges orally influenced traditions that are created and embedded in a postliterate, technologically sophisticated cultural context. Postliterate orality describes the way oral traditions are revised and presented in a technologically sophisticated context. It also has the capacity to explain the way literate-based technology is made to articulate sounds images and practices associated with orally based forms, so that rap simultaneously makes technology oral and technologizes orality.

In oral cultures, authorship is not essential to the performance of folk tales. According to Ong, "narrative originality lodges not in making up new stories, but in managing a particular interaction with this audience at this time—at every telling the story has to be introduced uniquely into a unique situation . . . formulas and themes are reshuffled rather than supplanted with new materials."[60] For example, the famous African-American oral tale of the Signifying Monkey has dozens of versions and no individual author, and "versioning" is an extremely common practice in Caribbean musics.[61]

Rappers have redefined this concept of communal authorship. Narrative originality *is* lodged in creating new stories, and these stories are associated with the rapper. However, rapper's rhymes are clearly influenced by, if not a direct outgrowth of, the African-American toast tradition. The dozen-playing bravado of toasts such as the Signifying Monkey is brilliantly captured in Kool Moe Dee's "How Ya Like Me Now."[62] Furthermore, in keeping with oral forms, unique introduction of materials takes on greater significance in the live performance.

On the whole, rappers carefully prepare and recite rhymes that become permanently associated with its author. References to the rapper and his or her DJ are extremely common. In Salt'N' Pepa's "Get Up Everybody (Get Up)," Salt says:

> Spindarella, my D.J., is a turntable trooper
> My partner Pepa, she's a power booster.

Word to life, I swear, she'll seduce ya
Don't take my word I'll introduce her.[63]

In Eric B & Rakim's "Follow the Leader," the chorus—"follow the leader Rakim a say"—is recited in staccato repetition to reinforce the identity of the performer.[64] Examples of such naming are endless. Rap lyrics are closely linked with the author; unlike traditional Western notions of composition in which the composer's text is in a separate sphere from that of the performer, rap lyrics are the voice of the composer and the performer. Rap fuses literate concepts of authorship with orally based constructions of thought, expression, and performance.

The content of a rap rhyme is sometimes so specific to its creator that to perform someone else's rhyme requires that references to its creator be rewritten. The significance of naming in rap is exemplified by a revision of L.L. Cool J.'s 1986 hit "I'm Bad."[65] In "Bad," L.L. brags that he is the best rapper in the history of rap and at a climax point instructs his fans to "forget Oreos eat Cool J. cookies." A famous go-go band from Washington, D.C., Trouble Funk, performed a live go-go version of "I'm Bad." To the delight of the audience, at the same climax point in the rhyme, the lead singer Chuck Brown announced: "forget Oreos eat Chuck Brown cookies!" while go-go's trademark brassy, rolling funky horns and drums supported his bold appropriation. The go-go audience responded to Brown's audacious appropriation of L.L. Cool J.'s rhyme as if it represented go-go's symbolic victory over rap music. The story told in "I'm Bad" is L.L. Cool J.'s story *and* a rap story. This authorial revision did not erase L.L. Cool J. as author; the absence of L.L. Cool J.'s name does not silence his presence, it displaces him. The power of Brown's insertion works best if the audience knows L.L. Cool J.'s "original" version. For another rapper to eat Cool J. cookies would be a major defeat; for L.L. to eat his own cookies renamed as Chuck Brown cookies is an outrageous moment of symbolic domination. Without L.L.'s presence and his identity as a rap artist, the theft of the rhyme has little significance. In this context L.L. Cool J.'s presence and the communal knowledge base it represents is a necessary element in go-go's symbolic victory over rap.

Although power is located in the oral presentation of rap, rap rhymes are not the "fixed, rhythmically balanced expressions" that Ong refers to in his description of oral cultures but rhymes constructed in linear, literate (written) patterns. They are rhymes, written down first, memorized, and recited orally. In oral cultures, there is no written context to aid in memorization. As Ong notes, "In an oral culture, to think through something in non-formulaic, non-patterned, non-mnemonic terms, even if it were possible, would be a waste of time, for such thought, once worked through, could never be recovered with any effectiveness, as it could be with the aid of writing."[66] By comparison, rap lyrics are oral performances that display written (literate) forms of thought and communication.

Informed by and dependent on literate forms of communication and reproduction for their complexity, rappers and their rhymes are a far cry from traditional oral poetic forms and performers. For example, in rap the rhymed word is often in the middle of a long sentence, and punctuated short phrases are worked against the meter of the bass line. The ability to easily reconstruct the rhyme and the music allows for greater flexibility in the construction and performance of rhymed lyrics. Simply to recite or to read the lyrics to a rap song is not to understand them; they are also inflected with the syncopated rhythms and sampled sounds of the music. The music, its rhythmic patterns, and the idiosyncratic articulation by the rapper are essential to the song's meanings.

The rap DJ and producer have a relationship to the concept of authorship and narrative originality that is more closely related to oral practices. In most rap music, the instruments are samplers that reproduce synthesized versions of traditional instruments, frighteningly real reproductions of other sounds (breaking glass, sirens, etc.), and the dynamic and explosive mixing and dubbing of new, previously recorded and seemingly fixed sound. Many of these samples are dubbed from other rhythm sections, other clearly and intentionally recognizable bass lines and horn sections, and reformulated in conjunction with beat box sounds and the rappers' style and accentuation.

Sampling technology as used by rap DJs and producers is strikingly similar to Ong's interpretation of narrative originality in oral cultures: "narrative originality lodges not in making up new stories . . . [instead] *formulas and themes are reshuffled* rather than supplanted with new materials."[67] Rap DJs and producers reshuffle known cultural formulas and themes. It is in this context that narrative originality is lodged. In the age of mechanical reproduction, these cultural formulas and themes are in the form of recorded sound, reshuffled, looped, and recontextualized.

Yet, sampling technology is also a means of composition, a means of (post) literate production. Using sounds and rhythms as building blocks, rap musicians store ideas in computers, build, erase, and revise musical themes and concepts. Similar to the way many live bands work through musical ideas, rap producers work with core concepts, improvising and building around them. Writing music in the age of electronic reproduction is a complex and dense process in which millions of sounds, rhythms, and melodies are made fantastically accessible. Eric Sadler describes how he *writes* music using the Bomb Squad's 20,000 record collection as his main source: "You decide you are going to write some songs. You just work. You just write, write, write. Sometimes Chuck (D) will come and say, 'Yo I got an idea here.' So what you try to do from there is to take the idea, put (the sample) in the drum machine, put a beat behind it and move on from there. Sometimes Keith (Shocklee) would get on the turntable and just start scratchin', like we were a band. I'd play the drum machine for the sample, and Keith would be throwing in records."[68] In a world of bytes and microprocessors, large and complex ideas can be rewritten, revised, "sampled" by computers and reorganized by composers. As a musical idea develops and changes, elements are added and deleted from the memory file. Still the interactive quality of live instrumentation and song writing remains, as individual contributions rub up against one another in the studio, creating a final (!) "composition."

Sampling in rap is a process of cultural literacy and intertextual reference. Sampled guitar and bass lines from soul and funk precursors are often recognizable or have familiar resonances. Some samples are taken from recent charted songs, making them eminently recognizable. Rap fans can recognize that Eric B. & Rakim took the bass line for their cut "Paid in Full" from Dennis Edwards "Don't Look Any Further" a popular R&B song that topped the charts only a year earlier. In addition to the musical layering and engineering strategies involved in these soul resurrections, these samples are highlighted, functioning as a challenge to know these sounds, to make connections between the lyrical and musical texts. It affirms black musical history and locates these "past" sounds in the "present."

More often than not, rap artists and their DJs openly revere their soul forebears. Stetsasonic defends this practice, claiming that it counteracts industry-fostered market conditions that dictate a particularly shallow shelf-life for black music. Dozens of soul artists' discographies have been reprinted as a result of rap's sampling strategies, and consequently, Daddy-O suggests, these soul artists have been placed in the foreground of black collective memory:

> You erase our music
> So no one could use it . . .
> Tell the truth—James Brown was old
> Til Eric B came out with 'I Got Soul.'
> Rap brings back old R&B
> If we would not
> People could have forgot.[69]

When Kool Moe Dee's explosive "How Ya Like Me Now" opens with "All aboard the night train!" sampled from a James Brown record, it not only verifies Brown as the author, it paradoxically undermines any fixed link his sound has to the label on which it was "originally" recorded. Brown's exclamation in the context of Moe Dee's piece is employed as a communal resource that functions in opposition to the recording industry's fixation with ownership. In the opening moment of "How Ya Like Me Now," James Brown is affirmed and valorized, Kool Moe Dee is situated within an African-American music tradition, and a self-constructed affirmative and resistive history is sounded.

Sampling is not the only method of narrative reformulation and resistance. Mixes of the old and the new, or "versioning," as it is referred to by Dick Hebdige in *Cut n Mix*, is at the heart of all African-American and Caribbean musics: "The original version takes on a new life and a new meaning in a fresh context."[70] Versioning, unlike sampling, entails the reworking of an entire composition. I concur with Hebdige's overall analysis but would like to dub in a different version of his quote. The *referenced* version takes on *alternative lives and alternative meanings* in a fresh context. Versioning, too, redefines traditional notions of authorship and originality as it incorporates it.

Sampling has had important resistive effects in the recording industry. To reuse portions of copyrighted material without permission undermines legal and capital market authority. Before rap music began grossing millions of dollars, the use of these musical passages went unnoticed by publishing administrators and copyright holders. Sampling clearance was a relatively minor legal issue. Limited visibility, relatively small profits and legal costs to pursue illegal uses of sampled materials made policing such theft undesirable for record executives. Furthermore, these samples encouraged the sale of new records. For a recording label to win a law suit in order to take a share of another label's profit raised the possibility that similar profits would have to be paid (in full) in another case. Because all major record companies distribute sampled material, law suits would be traded rather heavily. Today, rap is big business. With multimillion record sales by such rap artists as MC Hammer, Tone Loc, NWA, Public Enemy, and Vanilla Ice, the pursuit of the illegal use of sampled materials has become a complicated and high-profile legal issue in the entertainment industry.

At the center of the controversy is the scope and intent of the music copyright system and its limited applicability to sampling as practiced first by rap artists and now by a wide array of musicians and producers. Derived from nineteenth-century literary law, the current music copyright system is designed to protect musical scripts, to protect sheet music from theft or illegal use. Simon Frith elaborates:

The original musical commodity was a score, and even as the law changed to take account of audio recording—a new way of fixing sounds—the song, defined as a particular combination of *harmony, melody and lyric*, remained the object of legal protection . . . what is most significant about this is what is not copyrightable—timbre, rhythm the very qualities that became, with the rise of recording, central to pop pleasure. And that has served as one way in which black musicians have been exploited by the pop industry, via the law's definition of music in European rather than Afro-American terms.[71]

Although Frith does not actually raise the issue, one might wonder why the change from harmony to rhythm accompanied the advent of technology. It could have simply reinforced the centrality of melody and harmony. Obviously, reproduction technology (e.g., cassette tapes) allows for multiple contexts for usage, reception, and access to a variety of musics with different cultural priorities. Given the shift to rhythm and timbre as a source of popular pleasure in the age of reproduction and the undeniable centrality of black musical forms that heavily privilege rhythm and timbre, then it seems reasonable to suggest that recording technology has been the primary vehicle for providing access to black music and black cultural priorities, which have in turn had a critical impact on the terms of popular pleasure.

Computer sampling instruments create access to sounds formerly uncopyable and therefore unprotected.[72] Because very few sampling cases have been litigated (so far, virtually all contests have been settled out of court), questions regarding proper clearance, when it is necessary, what constitutes a recognizable portion, and what fee is reasonable for such usage remains unregulated.[73] In some cases publishers have begun to ask outrageous fees for relatively minor usages; in other cases, rappers have avoided clearing sample uses and have had to pay hefty fees after the album's successful release. In some instances, of course, no clearance is obtained, and the sample usage goes unnoticed by publishers, but, these cases are increasingly rare. To further complicate matters, the question of rights to future use are in part determined by the terms of original artists' contract at the time the "original" record was released. This means that if, for example, the record contract that covered the recording of Aretha Franklin's "Respect" did not have a provision that entitled her to a percentage of profits for future use of sound recordings or compositions, then she would not see much, if any, of the money being negotiated today for sample usages. Even more disturbing is the fact that many black artists do not have publishing rights to their songs, which means that sound recording use, the least legally protected area, is the most likely territory for older recording artists to make claims. In these cases, most proceeds from sampling claims would go to their record companies. It is also important to remember that, even when an artist has publishing rights, the record company generally retains over 94 percent of the record sales proceeds. It is the remaining 6 percent or less—and 6 percent is a generous estimate—that is paid to the artist. And it is out of this maximum of 6 percent that sampling usage fees are either taken or received.

Charges leveled against rappers for stealing from their musical forebears are valid; clearly, such musical forces as James Brown, Sly Stone, and Aretha Franklin should be compensated for the reformulation of their work. But these cries of thievery against rappers are suspect given that they have been used to obscure the most serious and profound thefts against black artists. When a sample is illegally used and the song generates substantial sales, it is the record company that loses control over its "product" and again the record company that reaps the greatest rewards when such samples are legally appropriated. The primary theft against the musical forebear took place in the record company offices long before many rappers finished grade school.[74] Although James Brown has spent substantial time and money in hot legal pursuit of his share of rap's profit from his music, George Clinton, the other godfather of rap samples, has taken an approach that seems acutely aware of this "initial" theft as it were. Clinton has recently released the first of a six-volume collection of sounds and previously unreleased out takes and songs entitled *Sample Some of Disc, Sample Some of D.A.T.* As reported in the *Village Voice*'s Rockbeat column, "while the original hits are still the property of the labels on which they were recorded, jam sessions and live recordings (even of classic tracks) owned by Clinton can be at your fingertips." *Sample Some of Disc* is designed to attract young artists and producers; it features a how-to-get sample clearance guide with a collaborative-minded fee system: No upfront fee is charged, producers or musicians are "charged only per record sold, so if your single flops, you won't be in the red."[75]

This issue of sampling thievery usually pertains to fairly recognizable samples, which in legal terms refers primarily to harmonic, melodic, and lyrical thefts. Drum samples, which are particularly difficult to claim, are the most widely used samples in rap music, not the "hooks" or "key phrases" that constitute the traditional material usage issues. So, even with the legal explosion that rap sampling has caused, the current state of sampling clearance does not begin to scratch the surface of rapper's use of prerecorded sounds: "While a Sly Stone organ sample may catch a layman's ear, the essence of the hip-hop song may be a snare drum from the Honeydrippers' 'Impeach the President,' added to Ziggy Modeliste's kick drum, or Larry Grahams' bass, rearranged into a rhythmic pattern from J.B.'s drummer John 'Jabo' Starks (if you've heard Eric B. and Rakim, you've heard Jabo.) Unless you're ordained, you may not recognize the source."[76] Maybe rap music represents the real "big payback." By defining music in such a way as to obscure black contributions and achievements, the music industry and the legal system have rendered current measurement of black rhythm, intonation, and timbre—for their profit—virtually inaccessible. The very laws that justified and aided in the theft from and denigration of an older generation of black artists have created a profitable, legal loophole and a relatively free-play zone for today's black artists. This creative cul-de-sac is rapidly evaporating. The record companies are increasingly likely to hold albums until all samples are cleared, until publishers and other record companies negotiate their profits. And many artists past and present are claiming their shares. Sadler and others have been emphatic that the crackdown has seriously affected rap music production, making bold sample uses, especially samples from the more powerful publishers and artists less likely. It does ensure that musicians (including sampled rappers) are being compensated for their work, and on the flip side it encourages more sophisticated cloaking devices—ways to use interesting material without detection.

Eric B. and Rakim's 1986 debut album represents a critical moment in the development of rap's sonic presence, the articulation of technology as a colleague in the creation and a forthright acknowledgment of music as commodity. *Paid in Full* is explicit both about the economic and cultural considerations at work in rap music. The album cover art features a collection of heavy gold rope chains, rings, and clips, $100 bills, and a personal check that appears to be signed by Ronald Reagan and whose dollar amount and payee are obscured by gold chains. Eric B. and Rakim are so good at what they do that even Reagan had to pay up. Musically speaking, few rap albums have been able to match the gritty, heavy, dark beats and overall character of *Paid in Full*, although a number of attempts have been made.[77] The title cut opens with a multi-drum rhythm section and a dialogue between Eric B. and Rakim that locates them within a particular recording and production camp. The first verse opens with the bass line from Dennis Edward's "Don't Look any Further"; in it, Rakim tells the story of life on the edge and constantly returns to money, the means of survival. The constant cutting and mixing of Eric B.'s music keeps the listener in a perpetual state of anticipation; the walking bass line and the flute riff give the illusion of a lyric and purposeful gait. Rakim's deep and ominous voice combined with sarcastic references to life on the edge of respectability keep the listener on edge:

Thinkin' of a master plan
This ain't nothin' but sweat inside my hand
So I dig into my pocket all my money's spent
So I dig deeper—still comin' up with lint
So I start my mission and leave my residence
Thinkin' how I'm gonna get some dead Presidents
I need money, I used to be a stick up kid
So I think of all the devious things I did
I used to roll up, "this is a hold up—ain't nuttin' funny
Stop smiling ain't still don't nothin' move but the money"
But now I learned to earn cause I'm righteous
I feel great, so maybe I might just
Search for a nine to five
And if I thrive, then maybe I'll stay alive.[78]

After Rakim's rhyme, they get ready to leave the studio. Rakim suggests that they, "pump up the music and count [their] money." Eric B. then tells Ely, the engineer: "Yo, but check this out, yo Ely! Turn the bass down, and just let the beat keep rockin.'" Eric B. and Rakim sign off with "Peace" right before a long and complex scratch and sample solo by Eric B. Surely Eric B. is not counting his money while Ely mixes this solo, but the illusion of effortlessness further proves his/their expertise and mastery over technology. A second conversation between Eric B. and Rakim brings the listener back to the confines of the studio, and, in what seems to be an afterthought, Eric B. asks, "what happened to peace?" Good question. The piece closes with "Peace" echoed in the mix.[79]

This rap's acknowledgment of the presence of the recording studio juxtaposed against Rakim's rhyme about life on the street without money, demystifies technology and its production and highlights the reality of rap as a means of upward mobility for young blacks for whom meaningful jobs for meaningful pay are scarce. In this rap, the studio and the rehearsed monitored production (or absence of improvisation) associated with it are deemphasized by Eric B. and Rakim. They seem to have just walked in off the street and started rolling the tapes. Simultaneously, the power of technology (the recording industry) is posited as the reason for their material success. Eric B. and Rakim suggest that they are *in control* of what technology produces—including its on-site manager, Ely, the engineer. Needless to say, actual artistic control over recording production is quite circumscribed for musicians. Instead, Eric B.

and Rakim's control over Ely is to be understood as symbolic domination over the process of technological reproduction. Their overt concern with profit and commodity production reveals the primary agenda of the recording industry as well as the real need to be compensated for one's performance. They implicitly contradict the myth of artistic freedom and anxiety over mass cultural marketing limits and yet seem to perform creatively. Eric B. and Rakim resist the masked and naturalized dominance of the institutional structure by overtly expressing its presence and logic.

Rap music is a technologically sophisticated and complex urban sound. No doubt, its forebears stretch far into the orally influenced traditions of African-American culture. But the oral aspects of rap are not to be understood as primary to the *logic* of rap nor separate from its technological aspects. Rap is fundamentally literate and deeply technological. To interpret rap as a direct or natural outgrowth of oral African-American forms is to romanticize and decontextualize rap as a cultural form. It requires erasing rap's significant sonic presence and its role in shaping technological, cultural, and legal issues as they relate to defining and creating music. Retaining black cultural priorities is an active and often resistive process that has involved manipulating established recording policies, mixing techniques, lyrical construction, and the definition of music itself.

The lyrical and musical texts in rap are a dynamic hybrid of oral traditions, postliterate orality, and advanced technology. Rap lyrics are a critical part of a rapper's identity, strongly suggesting the importance of authorship and individuality in rap music. Yet, sampling as it is used by rap artists indicates the importance of collective identities and group histories. There are hundreds of shared phrases and slang words in rap lyrics, yet a given rap text is the personal and emotive voice of the rapper.[80] The music is a complex cultural reformulation of a community's knowledge and memory of itself. Rap lyrics and the sampled sounds that accompany them are highly literate and technological, yet they articulate a distinct oral past.

Like many groundbreaking musical genres, rap has expanded popular aural territory. Bringing together sound elements from a wide range of sources and styles and relying heavily on rich Afrodiasporic music, rap musicians' technological in(ter)ventions are not ends in and of themselves, they are means to cultural ends, new contexts in which priorities are shaped and expressed. Rap producers are not so much deliberately working against the cultural logic of Western classical music as they are working within and among distinctly black practices, articulating stylistic and compositional priorities found in black cultures in the diaspora. As has been made clear, these practices do not take place in a cultural and political vacuum. Rap's sonic forces are often contested on the grounds that they are not creative, constitute theft, and are nonmusical. In other cases, these black approaches to the use and manipulation of new technologies are rendered invisible as they are joyfully appropriated. Sampling, as employed by rap producers, is a musical time machine, a machine that keeps time for the body in motion and a machine that recalls other times, a technological process whereby old sounds and resonances can be embedded and recontextualized in the present. Rap technicians employ digital technology as instruments, revising black musical styles and priorities through the manipulation of technology. In this process of techno-black cultural syncretism, technological instruments *and* black cultural priorities are revised and expanded. In a simultaneous exchange, rap music has made its mark on advanced technology, and technology has profoundly changed the sound of black music.

© Lisa Leone

CHAPTER FOUR

Prophets of Rage
Rap Music and the Politics of Black Cultural Expression

✦

With vice I hold the mike device
With force I keep it away of course
And I'm keepin' you from sleepin'
And on the stage I rage
And I'm rollin'
To the poor, I pour it on in metaphors
Not bluffin', it's nothin'
We ain't did before.
—Public Enemy[1]

Public Enemy's prophet of rage, Chuck D, keeps poor folks alert and prevents them from being lulled into submission by placating and misleading media stories and official "truths." He holds the microphone with a vice grip and protects it from perpetrators of false truths, speaking directly to the poor, using indirection and symbolic reference. When Chuck D says that pouring it on in metaphor is nothing new, he refers to the long history of black cultural subversion and social critique in music and performance. In this sense, rap is "nothing we ain't did before." Slave dances, blues lyrics, Mardi Gras parades, Jamaican patios, toasts, and signifying all carry the pleasure and ingenuity of disguised criticism of the powerful. Poor people learn from experience when and how explicitly they can express their discontent. Under social conditions in which sustained frontal attacks on powerful groups are strategically unwise or successfully contained, oppressed people use language, dance, and music to mock those in power, express rage, and produce fantasies of subversion. These cultural forms are especially rich and pleasurable places where oppositional transcripts, or the "unofficial truths" are developed, refined, and rehearsed. These cultural responses to oppression are not safety valves that protect and sustain the machines of oppression. Quite to the contrary, these dances, languages, and musics produce communal bases of knowledge about social conditions, communal interpretations of them and quite often serve as the cultural glue that fosters communal resistance.

In an expansive cross-cultural study, *Domination and the Arts of Resistance*, James Scott explores the dynamics of cultural and political domination and resistance by investigating how power relationships are solidified and challenged through social transcripts. Referring to these transcripts of power and resistance respectively as "public" and "hidden" transcripts, Scott argues that the dominant "public" transcript, a "shorthand way of describing the open interaction between subordinates and those who dominate," supports the established social order, whereas the "hidden" transcript, the "discourse that takes place 'offstage,' or in disguised form," critiques and resists various aspects of social domination.[2]

These dominant public transcripts are maintained through a wide range of social practices and are in a constant state of production. Powerful groups maintain and affirm their power by attempting to dictate the staging of public celebrations, by feigning unanimity among groups of powerholders to make such social relations seem inevitable, by strategically concealing subversive or challenging discourses, by preventing access to the public stage, by policing language and using stigma and euphemism to set the terms of public debate or perception. Resistive hidden transcripts that attempt to undermine this power block do so by insinuating a critique of the powerful in stories that revolve around symbolic and legitimated victories over powerholders. They create alternative codes that invert stigmas, direct our attention to offstage cultures of the class or group within which they originated, and validate the perceptions of the less powerful. These hidden transcripts, are "often expressed openly—albeit in disguised form." Scott suggests that "we might interpret the rumors, gossip, folktales, songs, gestures, jokes and theater of the powerless as vehicles by which, among other things, they insinuate a critique of power."[3] He goes on to say that by examining the "discrepancy between the hidden transcript and the public transcript we may begin to judge the impact of domination on public discourse." His analysis of power relationships as they are acted out through social transcripts points to the critical role language and other modes of communication play in the sustenance, destabilization, and struggle over power.[4]

Rap music is, in many ways, a hidden transcript. Among other things, it uses cloaked speech and disguised cultural codes to comment on and challenge aspects of current power inequalities. Not all rap transcripts directly critique all forms of domination; nonetheless, a large and significant element in rap's discursive territory is engaged in symbolic and ideological warfare with institutions and groups that symbolically, ideologically, and materially oppress African Americans. In this way, rap music is a contemporary stage for the theater of the powerless. On this stage, rappers act out inversions of status hierarchies, tell alternative stories of contact with police and the education process, and draw portraits of contact with dominant groups in which the hidden transcript inverts/subverts the public, dominant transcript. Often rendering a nagging critique of various manifestations of power via jokes, stories, gestures, and song, rap's social commentary enacts ideological insubordination.

In contemporary America, where most popular culture is electronically mass-mediated, hidden or resistant popular transcripts are readily absorbed into the public domain and subject to incorporation and invalidation. Cultural expressions of discontent are no longer protected by the insulated social sites that have historically encouraged the refinement of resistive transcripts. Mass-mediated cultural production, particularly when it contradicts and subverts dominant ideological positions, is under increased scrutiny and is especially vulnerable to incorporation.[5] Yet, at the same time, these mass-mediated and mass-distributed alternative codes and camouflaged meanings are also made vastly more accessible to oppressed and sympathetic groups around the world and contribute to developing cultural bridges among such groups. Moreover, attacks on institutional power rendered in these contexts have a special capacity to destabilize the appearance of unanimity among powerholders by openly challenging public transcripts and cultivating the contradictions between commodity interests ("Does it sell? Well, sell it, then.") and the desire for social control ("We can't let *them* say *that*."). Rap's resistive transcripts are articulated and acted out in both hidden and public domains, making them highly visible, yet difficult to contain and confine. So, for example, even though Public Enemy know pouring it on in metaphor is nothing new, what makes them "prophets of rage with a difference" is their ability to retain the mass-mediated spotlight on the popular cultural stage and at the same time function as a voice of social critique and criticism. The frontier between public and hidden transcripts is a zone of constant struggle between dominant and subordinate groups. Although electronic mass media and corporate consolidation have heavily weighted the battle in favor of the powerful, contestations and new strategies of resistance are vocal and contentious. The fact that the powerful often win does not mean that a war isn't going on.

Rappers are constantly taking dominant discursive fragments and throwing them into relief, destabilizing hegemonic discourses and attempting to legitimate counterhegemonic interpretations. Rap's contestations are part of a polyvocal black cultural discourse engaged in discursive "wars of position" within and against dominant discourses.[6] As foot soldiers in this "war of position," rappers employ a multifaceted strategy. These wars of position are not staged debate team dialogues; they are crucial battles in the retention, establishment, or legitimation of real social power. Institutional muscle is accompanied by social ideas that legitimate it. Keeping these social ideas current and transparent is a constant process that sometimes involves making concessions and adjustments. As Lipsitz points out, dominant groups "must make their triumphs appear legitimate and necessary in the eyes of the vanquished. That legitimation is hard work. It requires concession to aggrieved populations . . . it runs the risk of unraveling when lived experiences conflict with legitimizing ideologies. As Hall observes, it is almost as if the ideological dogcatchers have to be sent out every morning to round up the ideological strays, only to be confronted by a new group of loose mutts the next day."[7] Dominant groups must not only retain legitimacy via a war of maneuver to control capital and institutions, but also they must prevail in a war of position to control the discursive and ideological terrain that legitimates such institutional control.[8] In some cases, discursive inversions and the contexts within which they are disseminated directly threaten the institutional base, the sites in which Gramsci's wars of maneuver are waged.

In contemporary popular culture, rappers have been vocal and unruly stray dogs. Rap music, more than any other contemporary form of black cultural expression, articulates the chasm between black urban lived experience and dominant, "legitimate" (e.g., neoliberal) ideologies regarding equal opportunity and racial inequality. As new ideological fissures and points of contradiction develop, new mutts bark and growl, and new dogcatchers are dispatched. This metaphor is particularly appropriate for rappers, many of whom take up *dog* as part of their nametag (e.g., Snoop Doggy Dog, Tim Dog, and Ed O.G. and the Bulldogs). Paris, a San Francisco-based rapper whose nickname is P-dog, directs his neo-Black Panther position specifically at ideological fissures and points of contradiction:

> P-dog commin' up, I'm straight low
> Pro-black and it ain't no joke
> Commin' straight from the mob that broke shit last time,
> Now I'm back with a brand new sick rhyme.

> So, black, check time and tempo
> Revolution ain't never been simple[9]

Submerged in winding, dark, low, bass lines, "The Devil Made Me Do It" locates Paris's anger as a response to white colonialism and positions him as a "low" (read underground) voice backed up by a street mob whose commitment is explicitly pro-black and nationalist. A self-proclaimed supporter of the revived and revised Oakland-based Black Panther movement, Paris (whose logo is also a black panther) locates himself as a direct descendent of the black panther "mob that broke shit last time" but who offers a revised text for the nineties. Paris's opening line, "this is a warning" and subsequent assertion, "So don't ask next time I start this, the devil made me do it," along with his direct address to blacks "so, black, check time and tempo," suggest a double address both to his extended street mob and to those whom he feels are responsible for his rage. "Check time and tempo" is another double play. Paris, a member of the Nation of Islam (NOI) is referring to the familiar NOI cry, "Do you know what time it is? It's nation time!" and the "time and tempo" based nature of his electronic, digital musical production. Later, he makes more explicit the link he forges between his divinely inspired digitally coded music and the military style of NOI programs:

> P-dog with a gift from heaven, tempo 116.7
> Keeps you locked in time with the program
> When I get wild I'll pile on dope jams.[10]

Speaking to and about dominant powers and offering a commitment to military mob-style revolutionary force, P-dog seems destined to draw the attention of Hall's ideological dogcatchers.[11] Although revolution has never been simple, it seems clear to Paris that not only will it be televised, it will have a soundtrack, too.

Attempts to delegitimate powerful social discourses are often deeply contradictory, and rap music is no exception. To suggest that rap lyrics, style, music, and social weight are predominantly counterhegemonic (by that I mean that for the most part they critique current forms of social oppression) is not to deny the ways in which many aspects of rap music support and affirm aspects of current social power inequalities. Few would deny the resistive weight of male rappers' critique of the so-called "peacekeeping" and "just mission" of urban police forces and the resulting redefinition of what constitutes violence, as well as which groups have the power to exercise hidden or institutional violence. At the same time rappers also tend to reinforce the male sexual domination of black women and confirm and sustain the construction of black women as objects and status symbols. Although sexism in rap has been described as a means by which young black males buttress their socially devalued sense of patriarchal privilege, these attacks against black women are not critiques of social oppression and in too many instances they are frighteningly regressive. These attacks on black women ultimately reinforce the social domination of black women and have no place in politically progressive struggles. Similarly, rap's commentary on alienating and racist educational structures and curricula clearly critiques dominant ideologies regarding the reasons and solutions for the crisis in public education, yet some rap artists' homophobic and anti-Semitic lyrics are neither progressive nor resistive.

Such contradictions are not unique to rap, popular expressions, or organized political protest. Countless popular expressions and social and political movements have been rife with similar contradictions. The blues has long been considered a musical form critical of dominant racial ideologies and a resistive cultural space for African Americans under harsh racist conditions. Yet, blues lyrics usually contain patriarchal and sexist ideas and presumptions. British punk offered a biting working-class critique of British culture and society in the 1970s, yet simultaneously perpetuated sexist ideas and social formations. Feminist thought and organized protests have rightfully been recognized for their role in protecting, advancing, and redefining women's rights; yet many women of color and working-class women have criticized leading, white middle-class, feminist activists and thinkers for significant class and racial blind spots that have aided in the perpetuation of some inequalities as they attempted to abolish others. These contradictions are not reducible to the pitfalls of limited vision (although limited vision has often been a part of the problem) but, instead, characterize the partiality and specificity of cultural struggle. Nonetheless, these contradictions are not to be accepted fatefully; they are also to be contested and critiqued.

In the case of rap music, which takes place under intense public surveillance, similar contradictions regarding class, gender, and race are highlighted, decontextualized, and manipulated so as to destabilize rap's resistive elements. Rap's resistive, yet contradictory, positions are waged in the face of a powerful, media-supported construction of black urban America as the source of urban social ills that threaten social order. Rappers' speech acts are also heavily shaped by music industry demands, sanctions, and prerogatives. These discursive wars are waged in the face of sexist and patriarchal assumptions that support and promote verbal abuse of black women. Yet, at the same time, rap's social criticism

opposes and attempts to counteract the ways in which public educational institutions reinforce and legitimate misleading historical narratives and erase from the public record the resistance to domination that
women, people of color, and the working classes have persistently maintained.[12]

A close examination of politically explicit raps from three central
and well-established figures will give us some insight into how rap's
social criticism is crafted and how such criticism is related to everyday
life and social protest. The primary raps under consideration are KRS-
One's "Who Protects Us from You?," L.L. Cool J.'s "Illegal Search," and
Public Enemy's "Night of the Living Baseheads." KRS-One's "Who
Protects Us" and L.L. Cool J.'s "Illegal Search" are compared as two
related, but distinct, critiques of police harassment and brutality specifically against black males, and these texts are read in relationship to two
incidents, one that illustrates the use of these texts as a part of lived cultures and the other that situates the song as a counterdominant revision
of a well-publicized incident of police harassment and the conditions
surrounding it.

This is followed by a close reading of the video, lyrics, and music
in Public Enemy's "Night of the Living Baseheads," a multilayered critique of the government, the police, the media, and the black bourgeoisie. Visual and narrative elements in "Baseheads" symbolically refer
to corporate development and to related anticorporate social protests,
specifically to grassroots struggles against corporate real-estate acquisi-
tions in Harlem and the symbolic and political relevance of community
opposition. "Baseheads" is a productive example to examine closely because it analyzes several powerful groups at once and because it explicitly
references on-going social protest.

The police, the government, and dominant media apparatuses are the
primary points of institutional critique in rap, and these institutions are
primarily critiqued by male rappers. Female rappers rarely address police
brutality or media coverage of rap music and are instead more likely to
render social and political critiques against limitations on female independence, identity, community, and most critically, the sexist character
of black heterosexual relations.[13]

The cultural contestations articulated here are both black and masculine. Yet, race is a commonly shared category of oppression, even as
it is articulated from a male perspective. Consequently, many of the
issues addressed in the raps that I discuss speak both to black female
and black male experiences of discrimination and oppression. These
transcripts are part of a larger discursive struggle over legitimate inter-

pretations of black expression, urban America, and black contemporary youths. In some cases, these discursive battles have had significant social implications for and material effects on both male and female African Americans.

The second part of this exploration turns to the social and institutional constraints imposed on rap; or as I call it, the hidden politics of rap—that is, the politics of rap that are not generally given much attention in the public transcript. This section on the hidden politics will explore insurance policies, public space policing of rap fans, media coverage of violence at rap concerts, and rappers' collective responses to the media's interpretations.

Cultural Contestations: Discursive and Institutional Critiques in Rap Music

For many poor and working-class African Americans, police and brutality are synonymous. This is all the more the case after the April 1992 Rodney King videotaped beating at the hands of Los Angeles officers and the judicial responses to their crimes. As soldiers in the war against crime, police officers have a significant degree of power that is exercised, except in those highly egregious and publicized cases, autonomously. Outside the territory of "fighting street crime," the police have played a key role in averting black freedom struggles, brutalizing protesters, and intimidating activists.[14] Police brutality, racism, and harassment form the political core of male rappers' social criticism, and lyrics that effectively and cleverly address these issues carry a great deal of social weight in rap music.[15]

In the Reagan and Bush era's war on drugs, urban police forces have been soldiers of war, and poor and minority communities are the enemy battleground. The antidrug war metaphor intensifies an already racially fractured urban America and labels poor minority communities an alien and infested social component and a hot spot for America's drug problem. The nature and character of this drug effort has collapsed categories of youths, class, and race into one "profile" that portrays young black males as criminals. What war has no casualties? The public dominant transcript identifies police officers as "our" troops, and young black and Hispanic males as the enemy, the primary targets. In this scenario, mistakes made by officers are combat errors; the victims are casualties of war.[16]

KRS-One, the central figure and lyricist in a group of rappers and musicians organized under the name Boogie Down Productions, addresses the power, perspective, and history of harassment of the police in a philosophical rap, "Who Protects Us from You?" In "Who Protects Us," KRS-One, the lead voice, challenges the equation of institutional power and truth as it relates to police authority:

FIRE! Come down fast!
You were put here to protect us, but who protects us from you?
Everytime you say, "that's illegal," does it mean that it's true?
[*Chorus*:] Un hun.
Your authority's never questioned, no one questions you
If I hit you, I'll be killed, if you hit me, I can sue
[*Chorus*:] Order, Order!
Looking through my history book, I've watched you as you grew
Killing blacks, and calling it the law, and worshipping Jesus, too
[*Chorus*:] Bo Bo Bo!
There was a time when a black man couldn't be down with your crew
[*Chorus*:] Can I have a job please?
Now you want all the help you can get. Scared? Well ain't that true
[*Chorus*:] Goddamn right.
You were put here to protect us, but who protects us from you?
It seems that when you walk the ghetto
You walk with your own point of view
[*Chorus*:] Look at that gold chain.
You judge a man by the car he drives or if his hat matches his shoe
[*Chorus*:] You're looking kind of fresh.
But back in the days of Sherlock Holmes, a man was judged by a clue
Now he's judged by if he's Spanish, Black, Italian or Jew
So do not kick my door down and tie me up
While my wife cooks the stew.
[*Chorus*:] You're under arrest!
Cause you were put here to protect us,
But who protects us from you? [17]

Organized as an aggressive verbal address to the police, "Who Protects Us" speaks on behalf of a poor black community voicing cynicism, fear, and suspicion. KRS-One focuses on the slippage between law and morality, pressing us to reflect on the distinction between legal codes and moral codes, between law and truth. "Killing blacks and calling it the law" and "everytime you say, 'that's illegal,' does it mean it that's true?" attempt to destabilize the institutional and moral authority of the police. Rendering the police criminals, KRS-One points to the fragility and historical variability of notions of legality. "Who Protects Us" not only raises the question of who will police the police but also to the larger issue of relative power when it connects racial harassment to racial privilege by asking, "Who are the police protecting when they harass '*us*'?"

Although it is absolutely clear that "Who Protects Us" is about police harassment, the police are never mentioned by name. They are an alien, external force "put here" by other outside forces. Unnamed, but clearly identified, the force of the police is challenged while its institutional name (its power) is silenced, marginalized and a critique of authority is positioned dead center. KRS-One is calling out to the police: "hey you," objectifying them, rendering their behavior suspect. When he says, "You were put here to protect us, but who protects us from you," his voice is harsh, pointed, and in an echo chamber, magnifying and doubling his authority.

"Who Protects Us" is a conversational drama. At strategic points in the address, unidentified voices dramatize and comment on KRS-One's statements. These voices are call-and-response reactions to his sermon, local comments on KRS-One's theoretical reflections. When KRS-One asks if police charges of illegality are true, a voice resounds "Un hun," acknowledging that whatever the police say functions as truth. When he points out that the police force, understaffed and fearful are now eager to recruit minorities after retaining long-standing antiblack discriminatory policies, a voice calls out, "Goddamn right," suggesting perhaps that they have reason to fear for their lives, given their mistreatment of blacks. At the end, when they kick in his door and tie KRS-One up, the same voice shouts, "You're under arrest," a move that impersonates the police and calls for their arrest simultaneously. The police have been silent up to this point; when their victory cry is voiced, it is voiced against them. Anything you say can be used against you.

Accompanied by strikingly stark electronic beats, "Who Protects Us" opens with a powerful reggae cry, "Fire! come down fast," a symbolic call for fire's total destruction of current social structures. Fire is a common Rastafarian metaphor for massive social change, the destruction that precedes revelation, precedes new knowledge.[18] "Who Protects Us" is offering and calling for new knowledge, new ways of thought as public service. The title and chorus of "Who Protects Us" borrows a key phrase from the Gil Scott-Heron poem, "No-Knock" that also speaks of police brutality in a different time and place.[19] Scott-Heron's use of the phrase "who protects us from you," and the Rastafarian cry for destruction and reformation frame KRS-One's social critique, suggesting that this new knowledge will be diasporic in nature, reflective, historical, and collective.

"Who Protects Us" is from Boogie Down Productions' 1989 album

Ghetto Music: The Blueprint of Hip Hop, released in early 1989. New York urban contemporary radio stations occasionally played "You Must Learn," a black history rap. Throughout the spring of 1989, I heard "Who Protects Us from You" played more frequently than "You Must Learn" at a number of hip hop parties and caught the chorus and sparse beats blaring from dozens of Jeeps and other cars in New York City and New Haven, Connecticut. During the summer of 1989, I witnessed a moment in which the chorus "Who protects us from you?" was used in direct response to an incident of police harassment. In New Haven, on a street that is considered the dividing line between Yale University and a solidly black working-class community, I noticed a confrontation brewing between a young black teenager and a white New Haven police officer. On this narrow street, a teenager was aimlessly weaving his bicycle back and forth in the street and between the parked cars while he bantered with his male friend, who was talking with a young woman on a nearby porch. A slow-moving police car turned onto the street behind him, expecting him to move out of the way. It appeared that the vehicle was of no consequence to the teenage bike rider; whether he actually saw the vehicle or not, I am not sure. The officer did not beep his horn—he waited a brief moment and then stopped the car, emerging angrily. He went over to the porch and questioned the tallest boy, bellowing for identification, for information regarding where they lived and why they were on this street.

The boy on the bicycle lived in the house where the others were standing, and he continued to encircle the area where the police car was stopped and the area in front of his house. (I have no explanation for the officer's apparent disregard for the boy on the bicycle; perhaps it would have seemed too petty to address him directly.) The officer asked the young man what business he had there and demanded identification. The young man didn't have identification and asked the officer pointedly why he had to have it. He opened his pockets to show that he only had money, but no wallet. The officer glanced at me and my friend (the only two adults around) and as he continued speaking, he lowered his voice, apparently trying to ensure that we didn't hear him. We moved closer to them. The young man asked, loudly, if it was a crime to stand on this porch, yet, in his voice I could hear his anxiety, his embarrassment. The officer told him not to answer him with a smart mouth if he knew what was good for him. From the street, the boy on the bicycle said, "Who protects us from you?" The officer stopped for a moment and looked at us again, hoping we had gone away, I imagined. The boy repeated himself, this time a bit louder: "Who protects us from you?"

The words rang out like a communal protest; I could sense the tables being turned on the officer. His consensual authority slipping, he told the boy to watch his step, returned to his vehicle, and sped off.

The officer expected submission; instead he found contemptuous indifference, which in the context of tense power relationships is public transcript insubordination. The coded behavior of the subordination and domination was broken; as Scott points out, "if subordination requires a credible performance of humility and deference, so domination seems to require a credible performance of haughtiness and mastery."[20] "Who Protects Us from You," a phrase that at that time had considerable weight and communal resonance, was part of a hidden transcript that was used as a means to destabilize the police officer's performance of mastery.

I recount this incident not merely as an evidence of police harassment but, instead, as an illustration of the relationship between rap music as a musical text and as a communal African-American social discourse. At this moment, "Who Protects Us" was voiced as an open contestation of the public transcript, one that challenged police authority with hidden textual language and meanings. KRS-One's words conjured meanings and references that fortified a group act of resistance to police authority. KRS-One's words were used as a way to articulate communal knowledge of mistreatment at the hands of the police. These words are part of a contemporary discourse about social injustice; they have social weight and meaning. These words resonated for the bystanders as codes from a hidden text; the officer knew the meaning but not the reference, thereby temporarily destabilizing his verbal authority if not his physical, institutional authority.

"ILLEGAL SEARCH"

L.L. Cool J.'s "Illegal Search" is a similarly pointed antipolice rap that offers a version of "profile" arrests from the perspective of a profilee. "Illegal Search," which takes place on the New Jersey Turnpike, offers a detailed description of an incident in which L.L. Cool J. is stopped, searched, and arrested by a New Jersey State Trooper.[21] Police harassment, especially "profile harassment" (my term for what takes place prior to or in lieu of a profile arrest), has significant emotional and social costs. "Illegal Search" is a hidden text on what subordinate individuals would like to say directly to dominant authority figures but cannot because they fear reprisals. "Illegal Search" narrates the hidden injuries generated by practices of domination, offering this normally hidden subordinate commentary as the public and dominant text:

What the hell are you lookin' for?
Can't a young man make money anymore?
Wear my jewels and like freakin' on the floor
Or is it your job to make sure I'm poor?
Can't my car look better than yours. . . .

Get that flashlight out of my face
I'm not a dog so damn it put away the mace
I got cash and real attorneys on the case
You're just a joker perpetrating the ace
You got time, you want to give me a taste
I don't smoke cigarettes so why you lookin' for base?
You might plant a gun, and hope I run a race
Eatin' in the mess hall sayin' my grace
You tried to frame me, it won't work.
Illegal search.

On the Turnpike and everything is nice
In the background is flashing lights (sirens)
Get out the car in the middle of the night
It's freezing cold and you're doin' it for spite
Slam me on the hood, yo that ain't right
You pull out your gun if I'm puttin' up a fight
The car, the clothes, and my girl is hype
But you want to replace my silk for stripes
You're real mad, your uniform is tight
Fingerprint me, take my name and height
Hopin' it will, but I know it won't work.
Illegal Search.

And all them cops out there,
Who did the wrong thing to one of my brothers in Jersey
Keep on searchin'. Cause that was foul. Peace.[22]

Few young black males would dare speak out loud in the middle
of the night to an angry state trooper as L.L. does here. Bringing to
light the social context justifying the arrest, the discrimination that
takes place within the confines of an officially color-blind justice system, "Illegal Search" is a symbolic confrontation in which subtexts are
positioned above ground, center stage. It tells both the story of being
searched and the angry responses that are usually repressed; it fuses aspects of the official story with the indignities that are usually rendered
invisible in official texts. As is the case in profile arrests, L.L. need only be
a young black male in an expensive car to warrant his being questioned,
searched, and detained by the police on a cold night.

The rap's title is a legal term for such profile arrests gone awry; yet,
the lyrics really address the expectation that the rapper will be stopped
on the basis of his race and gender and the humiliation such treatment
causes. L.L. tells his girlfriend in the beginning of the song: "Put your
seat belt on. I got my paperwork, don't worry. It's cool." This introduc-

tion suggests that he expects to be stopped on the basis of his race and gender. The opening line also suggests that L.L.'s girlfriend may have asked him about his paperwork (e.g., registration) to protect herself from threatening confrontations with the police. Yet, even his excessive caution doesn't prevent him from being harassed; paperwork or not, he is likely to be detained and subjected to the hostility and presumption of guilt that often accompanies police profiling. The incident confirms the conditional nature of black masculine authority by pointing toward L.L.'s limited capacity to escort his girlfriend in public without fear of unwarranted state surveillance, a basic facet of masculine privilege. "Illegal Search" also hints at the relationship between conditional black masculine authority and the increased vulnerability of black women in public spaces.

At the song's end, L.L. addresses and challenges the New Jersey State Troopers and makes direct reference to the reality of illegal searches, specifically on the New Jersey Turnpike. *Mama Said Knock You Out*, the album that contains "Illegal Search," was released during the summer of 1990, four months after the press coverage of an incident that bears striking similarity to L.L. Cool J.'s story. Charles E. Jones and his wife Linda from Newark, New Jersey, were driving a rental car with California plates when they were stopped by New Jersey Troopers and subsequently charged with assaulting an officer and possession of cocaine. They have maintained their innocence and according to the *New York Times* were not informed of the reason they were stopped. This particular case was highlighted in the press because the defense attorney used statistical information from an undercover operation that strongly suggested that drug profiles that determine which vehicle will be stopped and searched, are in fact racial profiles. Profiling has resulted in heavy targeting of blacks driving late-model cars, especially those with out-of-state license plates. The study illustrated that although occupants in autos with out-of-state plates make up approximately 5 percent of the traffic, 80 percent of the contraband arrests referred to the Public Defenders office between February and December of 1988 involved black motorists driving out-of-state vehicles. According to Rutgers professor of statistics Joseph I. Naus, the difference between the typical traffic pattern and the rate of arrests of blacks in vehicles registered out of New Jersey "is dramatically above thresholds used to establish prima facie evidence of racial discrimination."[23]

Keep in mind that these statistics show arrests, not people who are stopped and illegally searched, but not charged. It is likely that illegal searches based on race would illustrate even more dramatic figures.

Given the racially motivated behavior of the State Troopers, it seems that not only are many white drug dealers slipping by unnoticed but also that many innocent black people are being stopped and harassed on the basis of race. Under these conditions, it is clear that race is a critical factor in police judgment regarding the potentiality of criminal behavior and that such assumptions can be expected to shape behavior attitude and treatment of African Americans.[24]

"Profile arrests," arrests of individuals that "look suspicious," require making categorical judgments that clearly discriminate on the basis of race. In *Looking for America on the New Jersey Turnpike*, a study of the Turnpike's history and culture, Gillespie and Rockland illustrate that racially discriminatory profile arrests are a common, if informal, policy of the New Jersey State Troopers: "A New Jersey sociologist tells of a criminology class . . . in which one of her students was a state police officer. He candidly admitted that black and hippies *are* often stopped on the turnpike on some pretext. 'But that's because the numbers are there,' he said. 'There's a good chance we're going to find drugs or a weapon or something.'"[25] Profile arrests were confirmed by Turnpike Authority chairman Joseph Sullivan and seem a close cousin to urban police profile arrests that draw almost a direct one-to-one correlation between young minority teenage males in sneakers and street gear and suspicious or criminal characters.[26] Profiling provides implicit sanction or justification for police officers to behave in profoundly racially discriminatory ways. Among other effects, this kind of explicit institutional racism perpetuates social stigma among young African Americans, as well as police brutality, antipolice responses, and a profound sense of alienation among black youths.

"Illegal Search" is a discursive revision of such incidents. Although he cannot prevent the incident from taking place, in his symbolic inversion L.L. challenges the assumptions that make such incidents possible, using his money and legitimate status as a means of taunting the officer. In the final verse, L.L. describes a court scene in which he wears a suit to court and the case gets thrown out, using profiling (along with his *real* legitimate status) against the justice system. His suit is important; L.L. seems to suggest that had he been wearing one when he was out on the Turnpike, he would have been stopped (blacks in suits are still "black" but not necessarily treated as harshly). In court, he uses the symbols of respectability to which he has access against the officers and as a means of self-protection, as they had used his hip hop, street symbols against him on the Turnpike. L.L.'s fantasy of revenge is situated inside the systematic and discriminatory practice of profiling and is therefore part of a collective hidden transcript. As Scott argues, "An individual who is affronted may develop a personal fantasy of revenge and confrontation, but when this insult is but a variant of affronts suffered systematically by a whole race, class or strata, then the fantasy can become a collective cultural product. Whatever form it assumes—offstage parody, dreams of violent revenge, millennial visions of a world turned upside down—the collective hidden transcript is essential to any dynamic view of power relations."[27] Yet, these collective texts have class dimensions as well. L.L.'s method of retaliation is more accessible to persons with considerable economic privilege. Without his money and legitimate status ("I've got cash and real attorneys on the case"), he would have been less capable of negotiating the judicial system. L.L.'s confidence in dealing with the Turnpike officer is not only a consequence of his orderly paperwork, it is also a consequence of his status as a "legitimate" (read privileged) middle-class male. In this sense, his answer to KRS-One's question "who protects us from you?" is a privileged response that affirms institutionally based law-abiding revenge. He protects himself with quiet indignation and official legal means. Economically disadvantaged citizens, especially those of color, are less likely to have access to fair treatment by the judicial system and consequently expect less from it.

KRS-One takes a decidedly working-class and group-oriented position by focusing on incidents of police harassment that take place in the home and on the street, sites of heightened working-class vulnerability to surveillance. KRS-One refers primarily to the group in his analysis ("who protects *us* from you?"). In KRS-One's story, the law and court system cannot be depended on as a site for redress. L.L. Cool J.'s story depends on such institutions as arenas for his restitution.

Each story tells a tale of the degree to which race is a critical and unifying site of discrimination and oppression, but at the same time each speaks to the central importance of class as a point of either greater or lesser capacity to combat racially discriminatory practices. Both stories also use patriarchal heterosexual coupling as a setting within which to highlight the conditional status of black masculine privilege. More central to each narrative, however, is the way in which the raps place at center stage the generally submerged subordinate *group* hidden text, placing it in direct confrontation to the official one. Articulating a desire for risk-free confrontation and revenge, "Who Protects Us" and "Illegal Search" represent a contemporary African-American collective critique of police harassment in urban America.

> Capitalism used to be like an eagle, but now it's more like a vulture . . . it can
> only suck the blood of the helpless. . . . You have to have someone else's
> blood to suck to be a capitalist. He's got to get it from somewhere other
> than himself, and that's where he gets it.   —Malcolm X[28]

Public Enemy's "Night of the Living Baseheads"[29] is a multilayered critique of several primary social narratives and institutions. "Baseheads" builds on the use of symbolic references to particular social events, multifaceted address, and the contradictory and discriminatory nature of policing as articulated in "Who Protects Us" and "Illegal Search." It is a narrative bricolage that offers critical commentary on the police, drug dealers, drug addicts, the black middle-class, the federal government, media discourse, and music censorship groups. A visual, symbolic, and conceptual tour de force, "Baseheads" is one of rap music's most extravagant displays of the tension between postmodern ruptures and the continuities of oppression. The video for "Baseheads" is an elaborate collage of stories, many of which move in and around the lyrical narratives, all of which address a variety of oppressive conditions and offer stinging media critiques and political statements. As "Baseheads" is one of the most ambitious and multilayered politically explicit rap videos, I present an in-depth analysis of it, followed by a reading of the video's political significance, social commentary, and implications.

The music video for "Baseheads" opens with Public Enemy (PE) in black-and-white footage, standing over a disheveled headstone marked "R.I.P. Basshead." This still image is spliced with a moving and flashing image of young black men and women writhing in bunches on the floor, eyes glazed and wide-open like zombies, the camera moving over them in short jagged motions. Over these two images the voice of Malcolm X booms: "Have you forgotten, that once we were brought here, we were robbed of our name, robbed of our language, we lost our religion, our culture, our god. And many of us by the way we act, we even lost our mind." Two quick jump cuts follow: first to an image of the famous PE target logo, a silhouette of a young black male in the center of a rifle sight and then, to the same logo alongside a station identification for PETV, both suspended above a television news anchor desk. The set lights come up on Sherelle Winters (a character played by a music video actress) and Flavor Flav (from Public Enemy) as PETV anchors. Flavor Flav irrepressibly blurts out his signature expression, "Yeah Boy-ee!!" while Winters smiles tightly, waiting for her turn to address the camera. Professionally, she announces that tonight's show will "address the devastating effects drugs are having on our society and what has been termed the basehead syndrome." The show will "also feature the controversial group Public Enemy and their new album, *It Takes a Nation of Millions to Hold Us Back*, which is causing a ruckus everywhere."

Using this studio news desk as an anchor, the video moves swiftly and irregularly through several images and settings. The musical tracks are spare; sharply punctuated by a syncopated two-note tenor horn sample that loops urgently and endlessly. The lyrical point of departure is Chuck D rapping in front of the abandoned and boarded-up entrance to the Audubon Ballroom in Harlem where Malcolm X was assassinated (the caption reads: "Audubon Ballroom 23 years later"). Chuck points down sharply, directly into a ground-level camera, and begins his rhyme:

> Here it is,
> BAAMM!
> And you say goddamn,
> This is the dope jam
> But let's define the term called dope
> And you think it means funky now, no [30]

Static interferes with the reception, and the video cuts back at the studio with Flavor Flav shouting, "Hey, yo Sherelle, kick the ballistics, G!" [31] She looks at him impatiently and then announces another news item for the audience: "An ultra-hyper faction known as the Brown Bags lodged a protest today against rap music."

The video cuts to live coverage of the Brown Bag protests with field reporter Chris Thomas (host of Rap City, a nationally syndicated rap show on cable television's Black Entertainment Television network) engaged in an interview with a protester who stands in front of a group of white males with brown bags over their faces, holding placards that read, "Elvis Lives" and "No More Rap," while protestors chant the latter slogan in the background. A representative for the Brown Bags announces to Thomas that, "All the rap noise and the violence associated with it is bringing our country to our knees, and we're not going to stand for it anymore. And, we, the Brown Bags have a plan to put an end to it all."

Cut again to Chuck D rapping from the entrance to the Audubon, then alongside drug addicts in the street, and then immediately—another static reception transition—to female rapper MC Lyte, as investigative reporter, standing in front of the New York Stock Exchange. She announces to the audience: "In the never-ending search for baseheads, we've come to a new hiding place." And then she adds with cynical emphasis: "Yeah that's right Wall Street." Static transition back to Chuck D at the Audubon:

Check out the justice and how they run it
Sellin' Smellin'
Sniffin' Riffin'
And brothers try to get swift an'
Sell to their own, rob a home
While some shrivel to the bone
Like comatose walking around
Please don't confuse this with the sound
I'm talking 'bout . . . BASS [32]

MC Lyte sneaks into a Wall Street office and surprises several white business men and women sitting around a conference table covered with lines of cocaine. They try to hide from the camera and collect their belongings, but the cameras swarm around them, there is no escape. While investment bankers crawl around the floor trying to hide their faces, Chuck's image and booming voice is sampled in syncopated stutter: "BASS BASS—BASS—BASS BASS!"

Another abrupt cut to the street where Chuck and Flavor Flav are moving among zombie-like baseheads, speaking on the devastation of drugs. These scenes are spliced with documentary-style night footage of shadowy figures hugging building doorways, avoiding the camera lights. Again, a jump cut to the newsroom: "Just in this red alert." (Legendary DJ Red Alert passes a news flash to Winters).[33] "Chuck D, leader of the controversial group Public Enemy has been taken hostage by the Brown Bags. We'll have more on this story as it develops." Next we see Chuck D rapping while tied to a chair struggling with his brown bag kidnappers.

Another abrupt jump cut to a young black male in jeans, sneakers, and a jacket who is being pulled down a mid-Manhattan street by two cops while he shouts, "Yo man, get off me, Get off me!! I'm not a drug dealer, I'm not a drug dealer!" A middle-aged, balding white salesman peers into the camera: "Did this ever happen to you before? They think you're a drug dealer? We know you're not." The salesman exclaims, "Well, now there's Beeper Tie! Yes, for a limited time only, for only $99.99 you can have your own beeper tie. To order, just call 1-800-555-1234. Woops, gotta go, beeper calling." The same teenager reenters the frame now wearing a suit, broad smile, and beeper tie around his neck. He flips it up to show the hidden beeper underneath the widest point of the necktie as two officers stroll past him without notice.

The video collage continues to move abruptly between several themes/narratives: Chris Thomas enters a mock home of a family destroyed by a drug-addicted father and describes the effects of drug addiction on the mother and children; Flavor Flav, seated at his anchor desk, calls for the release of Chuck D; baseheads dance like zombies; Chuck gestures to a homicide body marking with sneakers on a dark city street. Finally, a large still image of a skull with a white picket fence for teeth framed by "Crack House" on the top of the skull and "White House" below momentarily freezes the video's kinetic pace. Chuck's rap weaves through the images:

> Daddy-O one said to me
> He knew a brother who stayed all day in his jeep
> And at night he went to sleep
> And in the mornin' all he had was
> The sneakers on his feet
> The culprit used to jam and rock the mike, yo'
> He stripped the jeep to fill his pipe
> And wander around to find a different kind of
> . . . BASS

The SIWs (PE's Security of the First World) storm the hiding place to rescue Chuck; Professor Griff yells into a telephone receiver on the street: "Succotash is a means for kids to make cash, selling drugs to the brother man instead of the other man." Sampled shout: "Brothers and Sisters!" is followed by a more intense pastiche of images ending with the SIWs on a steaming dark city street with Chuck stalking toward the camera, punching his fist into the screen shouting "BASS!" As his voice echoes "BASS" four times, the rifle site logo freeze frames the opening graveyard scene. In time with his sampled "Bass!" each of the four target segments is filled in with a yellow screen.

"Night of the Living Baseheads" is, at the most obvious level, a black nationalist antidrug statement that revises the central concept in the cult horror film "Night of the Living Dead" using it as a metaphor for the way in which drugs can become a form of physical possession. The addicts are zombies possessed by drugs, the walking dead among us.[34] Bassheads, a reference to "baseheads" (a slang word for addicts who smoke freebase cocaine) is PE's play on the powerful, possessive capacity of the bass tones in black music, "don't confuse this with the sound. . . . I'm talkin' bout BASS!" Chuck replaces *base*heads with *bass*heads and wants his listeners to do the same. Chuck's urgent bellowing chorus "I'm talkin' bout BASS" calls for the music and the power of the drums, the rhythm of life to be the guiding light, the core black addiction. "Bass! How low can you go?" he warns in "Bring the Noise." This powerful phrase is sampled and thus resonates here in "Baseheads." How low can you go? How much of your life can you relinquish to the base? Alternatively: how much commitment can you make to African America? How far are you willing to go to free black people? How much of your soul will you relinquish to the bass? In "Baseheads" black music is the medium through which one's commitment to community and culture is realized. Using television as the loudspeaker, "Baseheads" revolves around these two competing seductions; "bass" and "base" form this work's most consistent conceptual tension.

Malcolm's imposing voice in the video's opening is about loss, the reality of absences and their effect on African-American self-worth and cultural reproduction. Produced in the year and a half prior to the 25th anniversary of the assassination of Malcolm X in the Audubon Ballroom, "Baseheads" uses the currently dilapidated and abandoned marquee and entrance as PE's philosophical point of departure. The Audubon Ballroom is a symbol of black protest and loss. Twenty-three years ago it was a site where "truth" was spoken. But, today the Audubon is closed and gutted—Chuck cannot speak from its podium. Instead, he locates himself as close to the Audubon as he can possibly get and speaks through today's primary communication medium—television—but invents his own channel.

PETV is a spoof on Black Entertainment Television, the primary, national outlet for black music videos and the network's bourgeois news programming. PETV provides news items of interest to black urban Americans and comic interpretations of hip hop–related issues. Sherelle Winters, in white blouse, bow tie, and navy blue blazer represents the epitome of the responsible, respectable black professional. On PETV, she is seated next to Flavor Flav, rap's most kinetic trickster. In "Baseheads" Flavor Flav is the source of the "real truth," urging her to "kick the ballistics" and offering his own version of the news when she fails to deliver. Flavor Flav is a news activist, his role is to tell you the news and what to do about it all in the same breath. He is a "truth" watchdog, urging Winters to speak on behalf of black people by attending to the issues that concern rap fans and the black poor. BET professes dedication to black programming but fails to address black outrage and working-class black social issues; Flavor Flav and Chuck D fill this void. Furthermore, partially because of financial constraints, MTV viewers are far more likely than BET viewers to get the latest news on rap music stars, their lives, travels, and runins with the police and media.[35]

On PETV these stories are brought center stage in a black context and in the language of the subordinate groups' hidden text. Such a juxtaposition suggests that BET is a central carrier of black bourgeois ideology and is not committed to the hidden transcripts, the messages such transcripts carry, or to contextualizing black social issues so that they focus on the class-related dynamics of black oppression. For example, the surprise-attack search for cocaine in offices on Wall Street to prove that the rich have serious drug problems, the need for black teenagers to hide one's beeper from the police, the symbolic confrontations between the right wing and rap artists are represented by Chuck's kidnap by the Brown Bags each suggest that class is an important facet of racial discrimination. Catching rich, protected Wall Street brokers snorting massive amounts of cocaine is sweet revenge for people especially vulnerable to police surveillance. Beeper Tie is a clever subversion of the class-based aspect in profile harassment. Police "profiling" on city streets is primarily a problem for young kids in working-class jobs or with no jobs at all; it is not a problem for suit-clad corporate managers whose beepers are symbols of responsibility and privilege. The Brown Bags are antirap activists whose name signifies a group without imagination or distinction, but who cover their faces like the Klu Klux Klan.[36] Like the censorship groups and their allies, the Brown Bags hunt down and attempt to silence (kidnap) rap artists to curtail their impact on American culture. Again, few middle-class black art forms are the target of such reactionary groups.

PE's target logo, a central symbol for the group, is heavily represented in "Baseheads." The rifle sight with a young black male at the center is the PETV logo in the video, but it is also the primary image on all merchandising and it appears prominently on their album covers and in PE press coverage. The target captures the widely held belief among African Americans that young black males are sighted for elimination by way of police brutality, poor education, drug access, and truncated economic opportunities.[37] It is a visualization of police profiling and surveillance against young black working-class males. This target covers the back of many PE tee-shirts, turning young fans explicitly into moving targets, externalizing the process of sighting and targeting that circumscribes black social space. Targeting also effectively silences the group under surveillance. Yet, in the context of PE's music and imagery, which is unapologetically pro-black, the target represents focus and commitment to black males. Public Enemy targets black males too, addressing them directly, placing them in focus and bringing their issues and concerns to the foreground. Women who wear this tee-shirt add another dimension of complexity to this sign. Because women are often moving targets for male sexual expression, the target takes on a sexual dimension not articulated in "Baseheads." Yet, without such explicit revisions, women wearing their tee-shirt may remain moving targets for men.

The fleeting skull image framed by "Crack House"/"White House" is a vivid image in "Baseheads" that draws an explicit link between the government and its responsibility for the drug trade. The Reagan/Bush Administration-sponsored war on drugs has contributed to national press focus on "cunning Colombians" and "enterprising urban teens," leaving questions regarding federal responsibility for such trade generally unasked and unanswered. The "Basehead's" death skull, which equates crack houses with the White House, is a racial metaphor that rests responsibility for the drug trade at the door of the federal government.

Public Enemy's selection of the abandoned Audubon Ballroom carries even greater weight than its role as a silent monument to Malcolm X and the social context out of which he emerged. At the same time as the video for "Baseheads" was released, Columbia University plans were underway to purchase the Ballroom and the northern three blocks, demolish the Audubon, and build Audubon Park, a 100,000-square-foot commercial biotech lab complex. Audubon Park would be a complex of multinational corporate laboratories dedicated to generating new life forms more resistant to disease and poisons. Columbia doctors and scientists would be working hand in hand with major pharmaceutical companies: Johnson and Johnson, DuPont, Monsanto, and Mitsubishi, "transferring information developed in 'nonprofit' academic pursuits over to the commercial labs for profit-making ventures." In answer to questions regarding plans for safe use and policing of microorganisms, fungi, bacteria, and radioactive materials used in these labs, Columbia University planner Bernard Haeckle responded, "we as owners will have a management plan." [38]

Seven years in planning, Audubon Park was submitted to City Planning in the fall of 1989 for review. Harlem residents and grassroots leaders protested the Park, calling instead for a monument to Malcolm X and for the restoration of the Ballroom for community-related services. [39] Harlem residents and activists see the project as a means of displacement, not economic investment in the community. Not only is New York estimated to pay $18 million out of the $22 million construction costs, the City would also give Columbia a 99-year lease and invest $10 million in equity through the Public Development Corporation. Claims that the biotech lab will provide a shot in the arm for Harlem residents by way of new jobs and retail opportunities have fallen on deaf ears, and not without cause:

The lion's share of employment flows far from the local block. When the $212 million project gleams with rows of microscopes, 90 per cent of the jobs will go to Ph.D.'s making $38,000 and up; two-thirds of them will be in the commercial labs. Furthermore, most of the employees in the commercial labs will be drawn from outside New York City. . . . In a city where the poor cannot afford to take care of their health, where hospitals have closed and those that remain open labor with patient gurneys often crammed in hallways, in a city where the voluntary hospitals—including Columbian Presbyterian—could not afford to give their employees a raise without a strike . . . the working poor, through the government, will subsidize a new frontier adventure for profit-making biology research, whose medicines they cannot afford.[40]

In a single step, Audubon Park would reinforce social commitment to life not yet formed and attempt to erase the symbolic meaning of the Ballroom as a critical moment in African-American protest and mobilization.

Public Enemy's use of the Audubon Ballroom in "Baseheads" as the narrative point of departure is part of a larger community dialogue and struggle over social space and political power. Using the Ballroom as his "base," Chuck D situated PE's vision as an extension of Malcolm X and focused attention on the Audubon Park controversy while the issue was being hotly contested. His explicitly antimedia, antigovernment stance suggests that he supports the community-based distrust of the Audubon Park project and its effects on the surrounding Harlem community. "Baseheads" video images and lyrical focus on the dangers of drug addiction, the loss of power and agency it produces and its devastating effect on black people, is in brutal contrast with the City's proposed Audubon Park biotechnical complex, whose purpose is to create non-human life forms that can resist disease and poisons.

Under the guidance and direction of Chuck D, the collaborative process that brought together the video, lyrics, and music for "Baseheads" has produced a media-savvy, socially grounded, and relevant collage that not only offers biting criticism and commentary on contemporary American class and race relations but also does it to swirling and mesmerizing beats and rhymes. It is no wonder that so many folks, cultural critics included, look to rappers rather than politicians for political direction and vision.

During the February 1990 "We Remember Malcolm Day," just two months before the "Baseheads" video debuted on BET, Chuck D, along with a number of rappers, activists, and political leaders addressed the significance of Malcolm not only as a historical figure but also as a spiritual force in contemporary black America. Some speakers pointed out that the Audubon was a special place for African-American history and memory. After Reverend Calvin Butts, Betty Shabazz, Haki Madhubuti (Don L. Lee), Percy Sutton, Lisa Williamson (aka Sister Souljah), and others addressed the crowd at the Abyssinian Baptist Church, a petition to stop the Audubon project was passed around. It suggested that the ballroom should be renovated for use as a social center, library, or other community-based organization. Not surprisingly, it was widely supported by the crowd.

This kind of interactive, dialogical quality in rap's social commentary is quite common. References to recent social issues of particular concern to black urban communities are frequent and timely. D-Nice's rap, "21 to Life" and Ed O.G. and the Bulldogs' "Speak upon It" devote lyrical passages to summarizing the Charles Stuart case in Boston, Massachusetts, in which a white male murdered his wife and blamed the crime on a vaguely described black male. The local press's willingness to believe his badly crafted story was strongly encouraged by the social hysteria regarding the black male street criminal. Female rap trio Bytches with Problems (BWP) used the footage of Los Angeles citizen Rodney King being brutally beaten by a large group of Los Angeles police officers in their video for "Comin' Back Strapped." "Arizona," on Public Enemy's *Apocalypse 91* reminds the listener that the state of Arizona would not recognize Martin Luther King's birthday as a national holiday and critiques the racist logic in the governor's refusal.

Rap music's desire to respond to social issues that pertain to black life in America is part of a long-standing tradition in black culture to refashion dominant transcripts that do not sufficiently address racial slights and insults. Rap's capacity to respond to local and contemporary social issues so quickly is enhanced by technological advances in home studio systems and tape reproduction that allow rappers to incorporate their comments on recent events into their recorded and distributed material almost immediately. And so, rap's timely dialogical quality is situated in the current configuration of the means of production and distribution as well as in the history of black social criticism. Recent moves toward increased corporate consolidation and efforts to sanction and censor rap will most probably seriously affect the speed with which rap artists respond to contemporary concerns and the character of their criticism.

To understand the nature of oppression and its relationship to cultural production, we must concern ourselves not only with economic or institutional discrimination but also with social indignities carried out in public transcripts and acted out by individual representatives of the state. The experiences of domination and the hidden transcripts produced in relation to these experiences of domination are culturally coded and culturally specific. That is to say, although oppressed groups share common traits, oppression is experienced inside specific communities. Consequently, these hidden transcripts emerge not as overt cross-referential moments of protest but as culturally specific forms and expressions. They depend at some level on the addressed group's having special access to meanings or messages and can assume the privileging of in-group experiences. Although they share traits with other forms of social protest, the language, style, form, and substance in rap music's articulation of social protest are moments of black social protest. Black hidden transcripts are at once discrete moments of cultural expression and examples of discursive resistance to structures of domination. It is the specificity of a cultural practice such as rap, as well as structures of domination surrounding it, that shape the hidden transcripts that emerge.

Hidden Politics: Discursive and Institutional Policing of Rap Music

Confining the discussion of politics in rap to lyrical analysis addresses only the most explicit dimension of the politics of contemporary black cultural expression. Rap's cultural politics lies in its lyrical expression, its articulation of communal knowledge, and in the context for its public reception. As is the case for cultural production in general, the politics of rap music involves the contestation over public space, the meanings, interpretations, and value of the lyrics and music, and the investment of cultural capital. In short, it is not just what you say, it is where you can say it, how others react to it, and whether you have the power to command access to public space. To dismiss rappers who do not choose "political" subjects as having no politically resistive role ignores the complex web of institutional policing to which all rappers are subjected, especially in large public space contexts. The struggle over context, meaning, and access to public space is critical to contemporary cultural politics. Power and resistance are exercised through signs, language, and institutions. Consequently, popular pleasure involves physical, ideological, and territorial struggles. Black popular pleasure involves a particularly thorny struggle.

My central concern here is the exercise of institutional and ideological power over rap music and the manner in which rap fans and artists relate and respond to ideological and institutional constraints. More specifically, I try to untangle the complex relationships between the political economy of rap and the sociologically based crime discourse that frames it. This involves a close examination of the resistance to rap in large venues, media interpretations of rap concerts, and incidents of "violence" that have occurred.[41] In addition, venue security reaction to a predominantly black rap audience is an important facet of this process

© Lisa Leone

of institutional policing. It sets the tone of the audience's relationship to public space and is a manifestation of the arena owners' ideological position on black youths.

THIS IS CALLED THE SHOW

> Voice 1: The Economy, Phuhh!
> Voice 2: Yeah, I know.
>   Voice 1: Politics, Phuffh!
>   Voice 2: Yeah, say that also.
>   Voice 1: The Police . . .
>   Voice 2: Guilty, guilty . . .
>   Voice 1: Everything!
>   Voice 2: uhuh. Wait a, wait wait wait . . .
>   Voice 1: Except for the youth.
>   Voice 2: Yeah, yeah, wait wait.
>
> Voice 1: It's about to come back!
> Voice 2: Yeah I know. . . . Here it comes, ALRIGHT OKAY!
> —"Youthful Expressions," A Tribe Called Quest[42]

The way rap and rap-related violence are discussed in the popular media is fundamentally linked to the larger social discourse on the spacial control of black people. Formal policies that explicitly circumscribe housing, school, and job options for black people have been outlawed; however, informal, yet trenchant forms of institutional discrimination still exist in full force. Underwriting these de facto forms of social containment is the understanding that black people are a threat to social order. Inside of this, black urban teenagers are the most profound symbolic referent for internal threats to social order. Not surprisingly, then, young African Americans are in fundamentally antagonistic relationships to the institutions that most prominently frame and constrain their lives. The public school system, the police, and the popular media perceive and construct young African Americans as a dangerous internal element in urban America; an element that, if allowed to roam freely, will threaten the social order; an element that must be policed. Since rap music is understood as the predominant symbolic voice of black urban males, it heightens this sense of threat and reinforces dominant white middle-class objections to urban black youths who do not aspire to (but are haunted by) white middle-class standards.

My experiences and observations while attending several large-venue rap concerts in major urban centers serve as disturbingly obvious cases of how black urban youth are stigmatized, vilified, and approached with hostility and suspicion by authority figures. I offer a description of my confrontation and related observations not simply to prove that such racially and class-motivated hostility exists but, instead, to use it as a case from which to tease out how the public space policing of black youth and rap music feeds into and interacts with other media, municipal, and corporate policies that determine who can publically gather and how.

*   *   *

Thousands of young black people milled around waiting to get into the large arena. The big rap summer tour was in town, and it was a prime night to see and be seen. The "pre-show show" was in full effect. Folks were dressed in the latest fly-gear: bicycle shorts, high-top sneakers, chunk jewelry, baggie pants, and polka-dotted tops. Hair style was a fashion show in itself: high-top fade designs, dreads, corkscrews, and braids with gold and purple sparkles. Crews of young women were checking out the brothers; posses of brothers were scoping out the sisters, each comparing styles among themselves. Some wide-eyed pre-teenyboppers were soaking in the teenage energy, thrilled to be out with the older kids.

As the lines for entering the arena began to form, dozens of mostly white private security guards hired by the arena management (many of whom are off-duty cops making extra money), dressed in red polyester V-neck sweaters and grey work pants began corralling the crowd through security checkpoints. The free-floating spirit began to sour, and in its place began to crystallize a sense of hostility mixed with humiliation. Men and women were lined up separately in preparation for the weapon search. Each of the concertgoers would go through a body pat down, pocketbook, knapsack, and soul search. Co-ed groups dispersed, people moved toward their respective search lines. The search process was conducted in such a way that each person being searched was separated from the rest of the line. Those searched could not function as a group, and subtle interactions between the guard and person being searched could not be easily observed. As the concertgoers approached the guards, I noticed a distinct change in posture and attitude. From a distance, it seemed that the men were being treated with more hostility than the women in line. In the men's area, there was an almost palpable sense of hostility on behalf of the guards as well as the male patrons. Laughing and joking among men and women, which had been loud and buoyant up until this point, turned into virtual silence.

As I approached the female security guards, my own anxiety increased. What if they found something I was not allowed to bring inside? What was prohibited, anyway? I stopped and thought: All I have in my small purse is my wallet, eyeglasses, keys, and a notepad—nothing "dangerous." The security woman patted me down, scanned my body with an electronic scanner while she anxiously kept an eye on the other black women in line to make sure that no one slipped past her. She opened my purse and fumbled through it pulling out a nail file. She stared at me provocatively, as if to say "why did you bring this in here?" I didn't answer her right away and hoped that she would drop it back into my purse and let me go through. She continued to stare at me, sizing me up to see if I was "there to cause trouble." By now, my attitude had turned foul; my childlike enthusiasm to see my favorite rappers had all but fizzled out. I didn't know the file was in my purse, but the guard's accusatory posture rendered such excuses moot. I finally replied tensely, "It's a nail file, what's the problem?" She handed it back to me, satisfied, I suppose, that I was not intending to use it as a weapon, and I went in to the arena. As I passed her, I thought to myself, "This arena is a public place, and I am entitled to come here and bring a nail file if I want to." But these words rang empty in my head; the language of entitlement couldn't erase my sense of alienation. I felt harassed and unwanted. This arena wasn't mine, it was hostile, alien territory. The unspoken message hung in the air: "You're not wanted here, let's get this over with and send you all back to where you came from."

I recount this incident for two reasons. First, a hostile tenor, if not actual verbal abuse, is a regular part of rap fan contact with arena security and police. This is not an isolated or rare example, incidents similar to it continue to take place at many rap concerts.[43] Rap concertgoers were barely tolerated and regarded with heightened suspicion. Second, arena security forces, a critical facet in the political economy of rap and its related sociologically based crime discourse, contribute to the high level of anxiety and antagonism that confront young African Americans. Their military posture is a surface manifestation of a complex network of ideological and economic processes that "justify" the policing of rap music, black youths, and black people in general. Although my immediate sense of indignation in response to public humiliation may be related to a sense of entitlement that comes from my status as a cultural critic, thus separating me from many of the concertgoers, my status as a young African-American woman is a critical factor in the way I was *treated* in this instance, as well as many others.[44]

Rap artists articulate a range of reactions to the scope of institutional policing faced by many young African Americans. However, the lyrics that address the police directly—what Ice Cube has called "revenge fantasies"—have caused the most extreme and unconstitutional reaction from law-enforcement officials in metropolitan concert arena venues. The precedent-setting example took place in 1989 and involved Compton-based rap group NWA (Niggas with Attitude) that at that time featured Ice Cube as a lead rapper. Their album *Straight Outta Compton* contained a cinematic, well-crafted, gritty, and vulgar rap entitled "__the Police," which in the rap itself filled in the f.u.c.k. at every appropriate opportunity. This song and its apparent social resonance among rap fans and black youths in general provoked an unprecedented official FBI letter from Milt Ahlerich, an FBI assistant director, which expressed the FBI's concern over increasing violence (indirectly linking music to this increase) and stating that, as law-enforcement officials "dedicate their lives to the protection of our citizens . . . recordings such as the one from NWA are both discouraging and degrading to the brave, dedicated officers." He justifies this targeting of NWA by suggesting that the song allegedly advocates violence against police officers. As far as Ahlerich knows, the FBI has never adopted an official position on a record, book, or artwork in the history of the agency.[45] NWA's "__the Police" is what finally smoked them out. This official statement would be extraordinary enough, given its tenous constitutionality, but what follows is even worse. According to Dave Marsh and Phyllis Pollack, nobody at the agency purchased the record, nor could Ahlerich explain how he had received these lyrics other than from "responsible fellow officers." Furthermore, Ahlerich's letter fueled an informal fax network among police agencies that urged cops to help cancel NWA's concerts. Marsh and Pollack summarize the effects of this campaign:

Since late spring (of 1989), their shows have been jeopardized or aborted in Detroit (where the group was briefly detained by cops), Washington, D.C., Chattanooga, Milwaukee, and Tyler, Texas. NWA played Cincinnati only after Bengal lineback and City Councilman Reggie Williams and several of his teammates spoke up for them. During the summer's tour, NWA prudently chose not to perform "＿＿ the Police" (its best song), and just singing a few lines of it at Detroit's Joe Loius arena caused the Motor City police to rush the stage. While the cops scuffled with the security staff, NWA escaped to their hotel. Dozens of policemen were waiting for them there, and they detained the group for 15 minutes. "We just wanted to show the kids," an officer told the Hollywood Reporter, "that you can't say 'fuck the police' in Detroit."[46]

Unless, of course, you're a cop. Clearly, police forces have almost unchallengable entree in these arenas. If the police break through security to rush the stage, whom do security call to contain the police? Or as KRS-One might say, "Who Protects Us from You?" These large arenas are not only surveilled, but also they are, with the transmission of a police fax, subject to immediate occupation. What "justifies" this occupation? A symbolic challenge to the police in a song that, as Marsh and Pollack observe, "tells of a young man who loses his temper over brutal police sweeps based on appearance, not actions, like the ones frequently performed by the LAPD. In the end the young man threatens to smoke the next flatfoot who fucks with him." It is clearly not in the interests of business owners to challenge the police on these matters, they cannot afford to jeopardize their access to future police services, so that the artists, in this case, find themselves fleeing the stage after attempting to perform a song that is supposed to be constitutionally protected. NWA's lyrics have even more resonance after the FBI's response:

> Fuck the police, comin' straight from the underground
> A young nigga got it bad 'cause I'm brown
> And not the other color, so police think
> They have the authority to kill a minority.[47]

It is this ideological position on black youth that frames the media and institutional attacks on rap and separates resistance to rap from attacks sustained by rock 'n' roll artists. Rap music is by no means the only form of expression under attack. Popular white forms of expression, especially heavy metal, have recently been the target of increased sanctions and assaults by politically and economically powerful organizations, such as the Parent's Music Resource Center, The American Family Association, and Focus on the Family. These organizations are not fringe groups, they are supported by major corporations, national-level politicians, school associations, and local police and municipal officials.[48]

However, there are critical differences between the attacks made against black youth expression and white youth expression. The terms of the assault on rap music, for example, are part of a long-standing sociologically based discourse that considers black influences a cultural threat to American society.[49] Consequently, rappers, their fans, and black youths in general are constructed as coconspirators in the spread of black cultural influence. For the antirock organizations, heavy metal is a "threat to the fiber of American society," but the fans (e.g., "our children") are *victims* of its influence. Unlike heavy metal's victims, rap fans are the youngest representatives of a black presence whose cultural difference is perceived as an internal threat to America's cultural development. *They* victimize *us*. These differences in the ideological nature of the sanctions against rap and heavy metal are of critical importance, because they illuminate the ways in which racial discourses deeply inform public transcripts and social control efforts. This racial discourse is so profound that when Ice-T's speed metal band (*not rap group*) Body Count was forced to remove "Cop Killer" from their debut album because of attacks from politicians, these attacks consistently referred to it as a rap song (even though it in no way can be mistaken for rap) to build a negative head of steam in the public. As Ice-T describes it, "there is absolutely no way to listen to the song Cop Killer and call it a rap record. It's so far from rap. But, politically, they know by saying the word *rap* they can get a lot of people who think, 'Rap-black-rap-black-ghetto,' and don't like it. You say the word *rock*, people say, 'Oh, but I like Jefferson Airplane, I like Fleetwood Mac—that's rock.' They don't want to use the word rock & roll to describe this song."[50]

According to a December 16, 1989, *Billboard* magazine article on rap tours, "venue availability is down 33% because buildings are limiting rap shows." One apparent genesis of this "growing concern" is the September 10, 1988, Nassau Coliseum rap show, where the stabbing death of 19-year-old Julio Fuentes prompted national attention on rap concert-related "violence": "In the wake of that incident, TransAmerica cancelled blanket insurance coverage for shows produced by G Street Express in Washington, D.C., the show's promoter. Although G Street has since obtained coverage, the fallout of that cancellation has cast a pall over rap shows, resulting in many venues imposing stringent conditions or refusing to host the shows at all."[51]

I do not contest that the experience was frightening and dangerous for those involved. What I am concerned with here is the underlying racial and class motivation for the responses to the episode. This incident was not the first to result in an arena death, nor was it the largest or most threatening. During the same weekend of the Fuentes stabbing, 1,500 people were hurt during Michael Jackson's performance in Liverpool, England. At Jackson's concert a crowd of youths without tickets tried to pull down a fence to get a view of the show. Yet, in an Associated Press article on the Jackson incident entitled "1500 Hurt at Jackson Concert," I found no mention of Jackson-related insurance company cancellations, no pall was cast over his music or the genre, and no particular group was held accountable for the incident.[52] What sparked the venue owners' panic in the Coliseum event was a preexisting anxiety regarding rap's core audience—black working-class youths—the growing popularity of rap music, and the media's interpretation of the incident, which fed directly into those preexisting anxieties. The Coliseum incident and the social control discourse that framed it provided a justification for a wide range of efforts to contain and control black teen presence while shielding, behind concerns over public safety, Coliseum policies aimed at black-dominated events.

The pall cast over rap shows was primarily facilitated by the New York media coverage of the incident. A *New York Post* headline, "Rampaging Teen Gang Slays 'Rap' Fan" fed easily into white fears that black teens need only a spark to start an uncontrollable urban forest fire.[53] Fear of black anger, lawlessness, and amorality was affirmed by the media's interpretation and description of this incident. Venue owners all over the country were waiting to see what happened that night in Nassau County, and press interpretations were a critical aid in constructing a memory of the event. According to Haring, Norm Smith, assistant general manager for the San Diego Sports Arena, "attributes the venue's caution to the influence of discussions building management has had with other arenas regarding problems at rap shows." These "discussions" between venue managers and owners are framed by incident reports (which are documented by venue security staff and local police) as well as by next-day media coverage. These self-referential reports are woven together into a hegemonic interpretation of "what took place." According to the *New York Times* coverage of the incident, the stabbing was a by-product of a "robbery spree" conducted by a dozen or so young men. Fuentes was stabbed while attempting to retrieve his girlfriend's stolen jewelry. Staff writer Michel Marriott noted that out of the 10,000 concertgoers, this dirty dozen were solely responsible for the incident. Although the race of the perpetrators was not mentioned in the text, a photo of a handcuffed black male (sporting a Beverly Hills Polo Club sweatshirt!) and mention of their Bedford Stuyvesant residences stereotypically positioned them as members of the inner-city black poor.[54] The portrait of black male aggression was framed by an enlarged inset quote that read: "a detective said the thieves 'were in a frenzy, like sharks feeding.'"[55] The vast majority of poor youths who commit street crimes do so to get money and consumer goods. In a society in which the quality and quantity of amassed consumer goods are equated with status and prowess, it should not be surprising that some of these teenagers who have accurately assessed their unlikely chances for economic mobility steal from other people.[56] Described as black predators who seek blood for sustenance, these twelve black boys were viciously dehumanized. Marriott not only mischaracterized their motives but also set a tone of uncontrolled widespread violence for the entire concert. There were no quotes from other patrons or anyone other than Police Commissioner Rozzi and detective Nolan. The event was framed exclusively by the perspective of the police. However, in my own conversations with people who attended the event, I learned that many concertgoers had no idea the incident took place until they read about it in the newspapers the next day.

In Haring's article on venue resistance, Hilary Hartung, director of marketing for the Nassau Coliseum, reports that there have been no rap shows since the September 1988 stabbing incident and that she "suspects it's by mutual choice": "The venue looks at every concert individually. We check with all arenas before a concert comes here to check incident reports for damage or unruly crowds. It could be [a] heavy metal concert or [a] rap concert."[57] In the Nassau Coliseum case, the police reports and the media coverage work in tandem, producing a unified narrative that binds racist depictions of blacks as animals to the ostensibly objective, statistically based police documentation, rendering any other interpretation of the "rampage" irrelevant. They provide perfect justification for venue owners to significantly curtail or ban rap performances from performing in their arenas.

The social construction of "violence," that is, when and how particular acts are defined as violent, is part of a larger process of labeling social phenomena.[58] Rap-related violence is one facet of the contemporary "urban crisis" that consists of a "rampant drug culture" and "wilding gangs" of black and Hispanic youths. When the *Daily News* headline reads, "L.I. Rap-Slayers Sought" or a *Newsweek* story is dubbed "The Rap Attitude," these labels are important, because they assign a particular meaning to an event and locate that event in a larger context.[59] Labels are critical to the process of interpretation, because they provide a context and frame for social behavior. As Stuart Hall et al. point out in *Policing the Crisis*, once a label is assigned, "the use of the label is likely to mobilize this whole referential context, with all its associated meaning and connotations."[60] The question then, is not "is there really violence at rap concerts," but how are these crimes contextualized, labeled? In what already existing categories was this pivotal Nassau Coliseum incident framed? Whose interests do these interpretive strategies serve? What are the repercussions?

Venue owners have the final word on booking decisions, but they are not the only group of institutional gatekeepers. The other major power-broker, the insurance industry, can refuse to insure an act approved by venue management. In order for any tour to gain access to a venue, the band or group hires a booking agent who negotiates the act's fee. The booking agent hires a concert promoter who "purchases" the band and then presents the band to both the insurance company and the venue managers. If an insurance company will not insure the act, because they decide it represents an unprofitable risk, then the venue owner will not book the act. Furthermore, the insurance company and the venue owner reserve the right to charge whatever insurance or permit fees they deem reasonable on a case-by-case basis. So, for example, Three Rivers Stadium in Pittsburgh, Pennsylvania, tripled its normal $20,000 permit fee for the Grateful Dead. The insurance companies who still insure rap concerts have raised their minimum coverage from about $500,000 to between $4 and 5 million worth of coverage per show.[61] Several major arenas make it almost impossible to book a rap show, and others have refused outright to book rap acts at all.

These responses to rap music bear a striking resemblance to the New York City cabaret laws instituted in the 1920s in response to jazz music. A wide range of licensing and zoning laws, many of which remained in effect until the late 1980s, restricted the places where jazz could be played and how it could be played. These laws were attached to moral anxieties regarding black cultural effects and were in part intended to protect white patrons from jazz's "immoral influences." They defined and contained the kind of jazz that could be played by restricting the use of certain instruments (especially drums and horns) and established elaborate licensing policies that favored more established and main-stream jazz club owners and prevented a number of prominent musicians with minor criminal records from obtaining cabaret cards.[62]

During an interview with "Richard" from a major talent agency that books many prominent rap acts, I asked him if booking agents had responded to venue bans on rap music by leveling charges of racial discrimination against venue owners. His answer clearly illustrates the significance of the institutional power at stake:

These facilities are privately owned, they can do anything they want. You say to them: "You won't let us in because you're discriminating against black kids." They say to you, "Fuck you, who cares. Do whatever you got to do, but you're not coming in here. You, I don't need you, I don't want you. Don't come, don't bother me. I will book hockey, ice shows, basketball, country music and graduations. I will do all kinds of things 360 days out of the year. But I don't need you. I don't need fighting, shootings and stabbings." Why do they care? They have their image to maintain.[63]

Richard's imaginary conversation with a venue owner is a pointed description of the scope of power these owners have over access to large public urban spaces and the racially exclusionary silent policy that governs booking policies. It is also an explicit articulation of the aura created by the ideological soldiers: the red and grey arena security force described earlier. Given this scenario, the death of Julio Fuentes was not cause for regret over an unnecessary loss of life, it was the source of an image problem for venue owners, a sign of invasion by an unwanted element.

Because rap has an especially strong urban metropolitan following, freezing it out of these major metropolitan arenas has a dramatic impact on rappers' ability to reach their fan base in live performance. Public Enemy, Queen Latifah, and other rap groups use live performance settings to address current social issues, media miscoverage, and other problems that especially concern black America. For example, during a December 1988 concert in Providence, R.I., Chuck D from Public Enemy explained that the Boston arena refused to book the show and read from a *Boston Herald* article that depicted rap fans as a problematic element and that gave its approval of the banning of the show. To make up for this rejection, Chuck D called out to the "Roxbury crowd in the house," to make them feel at home in Providence. Each time Chuck mentioned Roxbury, sections of the arena erupted in especially exuberant shouts and screams.[64] Because black youths are constructed as a permanent threat to social order, large public gatherings will always be viewed as dangerous events. The larger arenas possess greater potential for mass access and unsanctioned behavior. And black youths, who are highly conscious of their alienated and marginalized lives, will continue to be hostile toward those institutions and environments that reaffirm this aspect of their reality.

The presence of a predominantly black audience in a 15,000 capacity arena, communicating with major black cultural icons whose music, lyrics, and attitude illuminate and affirm black fears and grievances, provokes a fear of the consolidation of black rage. Venue owner and insurance company anxiety over broken chairs, insurance claims, or fatalities are not important in and of themselves; they are important because they symbolize a loss of control that might involve challenges to the current social configuration. They suggest the possibility that black rage can be directed at the people and institutions that support the containment and oppression of black people. As West Coast rapper Ice Cube points out in *The Nigga Ya Love to Hate*, "just think if niggas decided to retaliate?"[65]

Venue resistance to rap music is driven by both economic calculations and the hegemonic media interpretation of rap fans, music, and violence. The relationship between real acts of violence, police incident reports, economic calculations, and media accounts is complex and interactive and has most often worked to reproduce readings of rap concert violence as examples of black cultural disorder and sickness. This matrix masks the source of institutional power by directing attention away from blatant acts of discrimination and racially motivated control efforts by the police and discriminatory insurance and booking policies. Media accounts of these rap-related incidents solidify these hegemonic interpretations of black criminality. Paul Gilroy's study of race and class in Britain, *There Ain't No Black in the Union Jack*, devotes considerable attention to deconstructing dominant images of black criminality. Gilroy's study reveals several ideological similarities between dominant media and police interpretations of race and crime in the United States and Britain. His interpretation of the construction of black criminality in Britain is appropriate here:

Distinctions between the actual crimes which blacks commit and the symbolism with which the representation of these crimes has become endowed is highly significant. . . . The manner in which anxiety about black crime has provided hubs for the wheels of popular racism is an extraordinary process which is connected with the day to day struggle of police to maintain order and control at street level, and at a different point, to the political conflicts which mark Britain's move towards more authoritarian modes of government intervention and social regulation.[66]

Deconstructing the media's ideological perspective on black crime does not suggest that real acts of violence by and against black youths do not take place. However, real acts are not accessible to us without critical mediation by hegemonic discourses. Consequently, this "real" violence is always/already positioned as a part of images of black violence and within the larger discourse on the urban black threat. Although violence at rap concerts can be understood as a visible instance of crimes by and against blacks, because it takes place in a white safety zone, it is interpreted as a loss of control on home territory. The fact that rap-related concert violence takes place outside the invisible fence that surrounds black poor communities raises the threat factor. Rappers have rearticulated a long-standing awareness among African Americans that crimes against blacks (especially black-on-black crimes), do not carry equal moral weight or political imperative.

The two exceptions to the rule remain within the logic of social control discourse: black-on-black crimes that occur *outside* designated black areas (blacks can kill each other as long as they do it in "their" neighborhoods) and the undeniably racist attacks against blacks (as in the Howard Beach incident) that result in social outcry. (These unwarranted attacks might result in race wars that could seriously disrupt the current social configuration.) Each of these exceptions is circumscribed by the logic of social control and carries with it hefty institutional scrutiny.[67] The rap community is aware that the label "violence at rap concerts" is being used to contain black mobility and rap music, not to diminish violence against blacks. Ice Cube captures a familiar reading of state-sanctioned violence against young black males:

> Every cop killer ignored
> They just send another nigger to the morgue
> A point scored
> They could give a fuck about us
> They'd rather find us with guns and white powder
>
> . . .
>
> Now kill ten of me to get the job correct.
> To serve, protect and break a nigga's neck[68]

Cognizant of the fact that violence is a selectively employed term, KRS-One points out the historical links between music, social protest, and social control:

> When some get together and think of rap,
> They tend to think of violence
> But when they are challenged on some rock group
> The result is always silence.
> Even before the rock 'n' roll era, violence played a big part in music
> It's all according to your meaning of violence
> And how or in which way you use it.
> By all means necessary, it is time to end the hypocrisy,
> What I call violence I can't do,
> But your kind of violence is stopping me.[69]

Since the Nassau Coliseum incident, "violence" at rap concerts has continued to take place, and the media's assumption of links between rap and disorder has grown more facile. On more than a dozen occasions I have been called by various media outlets around the country to comment on the violence that is expected to or has taken place at a given rap concert. The violence angle is the reason for the article, even in cases where incidents have not taken place. When I have challenged the writers or radio hosts about their presumptions, they have almost always returned to their own coverage as evidence of the reality of violence and usually ignored my comments. In one striking case I was told that without the violence angle they would kill the story. In effect, they were saying that there was no way around it. The media's repetition of rap-related violence and the urban problematic that it conjures are not limited to the crime blotters, they also inform live performance critiques. In both contexts, the assumption is that what makes rap newsworthy is its spatial and cultural disruption, not its musical innovation and expressive capacity.[70] Consequently, dominant media critiques of rap's sounds and styles are necessarily conditioned by the omnipresent fears of black influence, fears of a black aesthetic planet.

In a particularly hostile *Los Angeles Times* review of the Public Enemy 1990 summer tour at the San Diego Sports Arena, John D'Agostino articulates a complex microcosm of social anxieties concerning black youths, black aesthetics, and rap music. D'Agostino's extended next-day rock review column entitled: "Rap Concert Fails to Sizzle in San Diego" features a prominent sidebar that reads: "Although it included a brawl, the Sports Arena concert seemed to lack steam and could not keep the under-sized capacity audience energized." In the opening sentence, he confesses that "rap is not a critics' music; it is a disciples' music," a confession that hints at his cultural illiteracy and should be enough to render his subsequent critique irrelevant. What music *is* for critics? To which critics is he referring? Evidently, critical reviews of rap music in *The Source* and the *Village Voice* are written by disciples. D'Agostino's opening paragraph presents the concert audience as mindless and dangerous religious followers, mesmerized by rap's rhythms:

For almost five hours, devotees of the Afros, Queen Latifah, Kid 'N Play, Digital Underground, Big Daddy Kane and headliners Public Enemy were jerked into spasmodic movement by what seemed little more than intermittent segments of a single rhythmic continuum. It was hypnotic in the way of sensory deprivation, a mind- and body-numbing marathon of monotony whose deafening, prerecorded drum and bass tracks and roving klieg lights frequently turned the audience of 6,500 into a single-minded moveable beast. Funk meets Nuremberg Rally.[71]

Apparently, the music is completely unintelligible to him, and his inability to interpret the sounds frightens him. His reading, which makes explicit his fear and ignorance, condemns rap precisely on the grounds that make it compelling. For example, because he cannot explain why a series of bass or drum lines moves the crowd, the audience seems "jerked into spasmodic movement," clearly suggesting an "automatic" or "involuntary" response to the music. The coded familiarity of the rhythms and hooks that rap samples from other black music, especially funk and soul music, carries with it the power of black collective memory. These sounds are cultural markers, and responses to them are not involuntary at all but in fact densely and actively intertextual; they immediately conjure collective black experience, past and present.[72] He senses the rhythmic continuum but interprets it as "monotonous and mind- and body-numbing." The very pulse that fortified the audience in San Diego, left him feeling "sensory deprived." The rhythms that empowered and stimulated the crowd, numbed his body and mind.

His description of the music as "numbing" and yet capable of moving the crowd as a "single-minded, moveable beast" captures his confusion and anxiety regarding the power and meaning of the drums. What appeared "monotonous" frightened him precisely because that same pulse energized and empowered the audience. Unable to negotiate the relationship between his fear of the audience and the wall of sound that supported black pleasure while it pushed him to the margins, D'Agostino interprets black pleasure as dangerous and automatic. As his representation of the concert aura regressed, mindless religious rap disciples no longer provided a sufficient metaphor. The hegemonic ideology to which D'Agostino's article subscribes was displaced by the sense of community facilitated by rap music as well as the black aesthetics the music privileged.[73] He ends his introduction by linking funk music to an actual Nazi rally to produce the ultimate depiction of black youths as an aggressive, dangerous, racist element whose behavior is sick, inexplicable, and orchestrated by rappers (that is, rally organizers). Rap, he ultimately suggests, is a disciples' soundtrack for the celebration of black fascist domination. The concert that "failed to sizzle" was in fact too hot to handle.

Once his construction of black fascism is in place, D'Agostino devotes the bulk of his review to the performances, describing them as "juvenile," "puerile," and, in the case of Public Enemy, one that "relies on controversy to maintain interest." Half-way through the review, he describes the "brawl" that followed Digital Underground's performance:

After the house lights were brought up following DU's exit, a fight broke out in front of the stage. Security guards, members of various rappers' entourages, and fans joined in the fray that grew to mob size and then pushed into a corner of the floor at one side of the stage. People rushed the area from all parts of the arena, but the scrappers were so tightly balled together that few serious punches could be thrown, and, in a few minutes, a tussle that threatened to become a small scale riot instead lost steam.[74]

From my mezzanine-level stage side seat, which had a clear view of the stage, this "brawl" looked like nothing more than a small-scale scuffle. Fans did not rush from all areas to participate in the fight, which was easily contained, as he himself points out, in a few minutes. In fact, few people responded to the fight except by watching silently until the fracas fizzled out. He neglects to consider that the 20-plus minute waiting periods *between each act* and the overarching sense of disrespect with which young black fans are treated might have contributed to the frustration. Out of 6,500 people, a group of no more than 20, who were quickly surrounded by security guards, falls significantly short of a "mob" and "threatened to become a small scale riot" only in D'Agostino's colonial imagination.

D'Agostino's review closes by suggesting that rap is fizzling out, that juvenile antics and staged controversy no longer hold the audience's attention and therefore signify the death of rap music. What happened to the "single-minded moveable beast" that reared its ugly head in the introduction? How did black fascism dissolve into harmless puerility in less than five hours? D'Agostino had to make that move; his distaste for rap music, coupled with his fear of black youths, left him little alternative but to slay the single-minded beast by disconnecting its power source. His review sustains a fear of black energy and passion and at the same time allays these fears by suggesting that rap is dying. The imminent death of rap music is a dominant myth that deliberately misconstructs black rage as juvenile rebellion and at the same time retains the necessary specter of black violence, justifying the social repression of rap music and black youths.

Mass media representations and institutional policing have necessarily leavened rap's expressive potential. "Rap-related violence" media coverage has had a significant impact on rappers' musical and lyrical content and presentation. The most explicit response to rap-related violence and media coverage has been music industry-based Stop the Violence movement (STV). Organized in direct response to the pivotal Nassau Coliseum incident in September 1988, "it was," in the words of STV's primary organizer, writer and music critic Nelson George, "time for rappers to define the problem and defend themselves." STV was an attempt to redefine the interpretation and meaning of rap-related violence and discourage black-on-black crime: "The goals of the STV [were] for the rappers to raise public awareness of black on black crime and point out its real causes and social costs; to raise funds for a charitable organization already dealing with the problems of illiteracy and crime in the inner city; [and] to show that rap music is a viable tool for stimulating reading and writing skills among inner-city kids."[75] In January of 1990, STV released a 12-inch single entitled "Self-Destruction" featuring several prominent rappers "dropping science" on the cost of black-on-black crime for African Americans, on crime and drugs as dead-end professions, and on the media's stereotypical depiction of rap fans as criminals. The lyrics for "Self-Destruction" focused on the need to crush the stereotype of the violent rap fan. They separated rap fans from the "one or two ignorant brothers" who commit crime and they called for unity in the community. At one point, rapper Heavy D pointed out that blacks are often considered animals and although he doesn't agree with these depictions he thinks rap fans are proving them right by exhibiting violent, self-destructive behavior.[76] In addition to producing the all-star single music video and organizing several public marches, STV published a book in photo essay style on the STV movement. *Stop the Violence: Overcoming Self-Destruction* offered a history of STV, pages of black crime statistics, and teen testimonials about black-on-black violence. STV targeted young, urban African Americans with the hope to "educate and reform" them, to help them to "overcome" self-destruction. The book and the overall project were cosponsored by the National Urban League, which also served as the beneficiary for all donations raised as a result of STV's efforts.

Unfortunately, STV's reform-oriented response did not redefine the problem; it accepted the sociologically based terms laid out in the media's coverage. STV responded within the parameters already in place regarding black youth behavior. Uncritically employing the labels "black-on-black crime" and "self-destruction," STV's self-help agenda fit comfortably into the social pathology discourse that explained rap-related violence in the first place. STV's minimal attempts to position these acts of violence and crimes as symptoms of economic inequality were not sufficient to compensate for the logic of cultural pathology that dominated their statements. Pages of statistics documenting the number of blacks killed by other blacks reinforced the dominant construction of black pathology, while the economic, social, and institutional violence to which blacks are subjected remained unexplored.

The media's systematic avoidance of the destructive elements in urban renewal, deindustrialization, corporate crime, and the woefully flawed public education system were left undiscussed, effectively severing the mass media and government from their critical role in perpetuating the conditions that foster violent street crime. As Michael Parenti's study on the politics of the mass media, *Inventing Reality*, makes clear, minimal coverage of these larger social crimes, coupled with maximum coverage of street crimes, are directly related and illuminate the significance of class and race in defining the public transcript:

Press coverage focuses public attention on crime in the streets with scarcely a mention of "crime in the suites," downplaying such corporate crimes as briberies, embezzlements, kickbacks, monopolistic restraints of trade, illegal uses of public funds by private interests, occupational safety violations . . . and environmental poisonings which can cost the public dearly in money and lives . . . How the press defines and reports on crime, then is largely determined by the class and racial background of the victim and victimizer . . . blacks, Latinos and other minorities are more likely to be publicized as criminals than the corporate leaders whose crimes may even be more serious and of wider scope and repercussion than the street criminal's.[77]

Economically oppressed black communities face scarce and substandard housing and health services, minimal municipal services (911, as Public Enemy says, *is* a joke), constant police harassment and brutality, and economic, racial, and sexual discrimination; these conditions are fundamentally linked to "black-on-black crime" and constructions of social violence. The label *black-on-black* crime, Congressman John Conyers points out, "gives the erroneous impression of a strange, aberrant, or exotic activity, when it is taken out of the context of the social and economic roots of crime."[78] Furthermore, as Bernard Headley argues, the violence experienced by black and working-class people as a result of poor medical services, police use of deadly force, and industrial negligence far exceeds the threat of black-on-black crime." Black-on-black crime is a concept that necessarily severs crime from the conditions that create it: "Crime is not the result of blackness (which is what the notion of 'black on black' crime implies), but rather of a complex of social and economic conditions—a negative 'situational matrix'—brought on by the capitalist mode of production, in which both the black victim and the black victimizer are inextricably locked in a deadly game of survival."[79]

These missed connections were critical flaws in the STV movement. The STV agenda should have retained a dialectical tension between black self-destructive behavior *and* the immense institutional forces that foster such behaviors. Cries in the lyrics of "Self-Destruction" to avoid walking the (destructive) path that has been laid, to "keep ourselves in check," and to "love your brother, treat him as an equal," overemphasized the autonomy of black agency in the face of massive structural counterforces. There is an inherent tension between a desire to preserve personal agency and free will (e.g., fight the power, *self*-destruction) and a necessary acknowledgment of structural forces that constrain agency (e.g., institutional racism, white supremacy, class oppression). The illu-

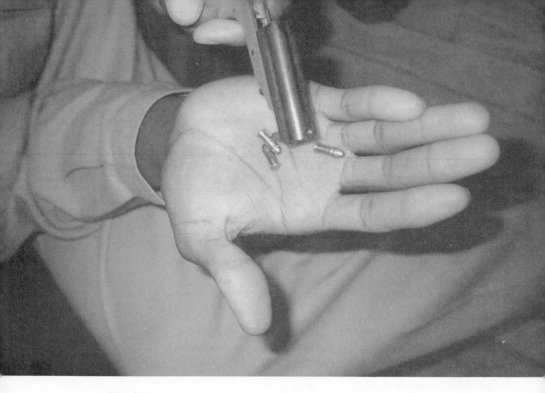

© suekwon

sion that exercising black agency can be undertaken outside of the racist and discriminatory context within which such action takes place ignores the tension between individual agency and structural oppression. Once severed from social context, agency is easily translated into theories of cultural pathology that blame the victim for his or her behavior and, therefore, circumstances. This discursive tension is a critical element in contemporary black cultural politics; the forces that constrain black agency must be acknowledged while the spirit and reality of black free will must be preserved. Agency and oppression must be joined at the hip, otherwise an incapacity to "overcome" self-destructive behavior is no longer connected to structures of oppression and is easily equated with cultural pathology. Unfortunately, STV did not successfully negotiate this tension. Instead, they garnered significant financial resources and mobilized a critical mass of rap music representatives to speak on behalf of social control in the name of black free will.

The greatest irony of the STV movement is that it borrowed its name and spirit from a 1988 KRS-One rap that sustained the tensions and contextualizations that remained unrealized in the STV movement. KRS-One's "Stop the Violence" draws direct links between the media, the educational system, the government, and the frustrations that contribute to street crime, especially as it relates to hip hop. His portrait of the relationships between class, race, institutional power, and crime is subtle and complex and contrasts sharply with the lyrics from the STV project:

> Time and time again, as I pick up the pen,
> As my thoughts emerge, these are those words
> I glance at the paper to know what's going on,
> Someone's doing wrong, the story goes on
> Mari Lou had a baby, some one else decapitated
> The drama of the world shouldn't keep us so frustrated
> I look, but it doesn't coincide with my books
> Social studies will not speak upon political crooks
> It's just the presidents and all the money they spent
> All the things they invent and how the house is so immaculate
> They create missiles, my family's eating gristle
> Then they get upset when the press blows the whistle
>
> . . .
>
> What's the solution to stop all this confusion?
> Re-write the constitution, change the drug which you're using?
> Re-write the constitution, or the emancipation proclamation
> We're fighting inflation, yet the president is still on vacation
>
> . . .
>
> This might sound a little strange to you
> But here's the reason I came to you
> We got to put our heads together and stop the violence
> 'Cause real bad boys move in silence
> When you're in a club you come to chill out
> Not watch someone's blood just spill out
> That's what these other people want to see
> Another race fight endlessly [80]

KRS-One's narrative weaves social conditions and violence together, illustrating the links between them. He calls on hip hop fans to stop killing one another, to avoid turning their rage against society on one another, but he refuses to identify their behavior as the source of the problem. He captures the essence of the illusions created in the "dangerous street criminal" narrative in one critical line: "We've got to put our heads together and stop the violence 'Cause real bad boys move in silence." For KRS-One, young black teenage males killing each other and their neighbors are acts of violence, but they are not any more violent than the federal government's abandonment of black and Hispanic Vietnam veterans and billion-dollar expenditures for weapons while "his family eats gristle"; no more violent than the educational system's historical narratives that "will not speak upon political crooks," giving the green light to tomorrow's generation of powerful criminals.

The first stanza in KRS-One's "Stop the Violence" is organized as a series of news fragments punctuated by his interpretations. At first, the fragments seem self-contained, but his comments begin to tie them together, weaving a narrative that illustrates contradictions in dominant transcripts and suggesting the existence of a common enemy. In the second main stanza, KRS-One addresses the hip hop community directly, suggesting that the first stanza was necessary background for his real agenda: violent crimes among poor black teenagers. Unfortunately, KRS-One does not have a "solution to stop this confusion"; his suggestion to rewrite the Constitution reads like rhetorical sarcasm, not a solution. What he does quite effectively, however, is to illustrate the self-destructive nature of crime among black teenagers without identifying black teenagers as the problem. KRS-One's "Stop the Violence" contextualizes these crimes as an outgrowth of the immense institutional forces that foster such behaviors. In this version, individual agency and structural oppression are in tension. Finally, unlike many social scientists, he bypasses the culture of poverty trap as an explanation for contemporary inequality and the conditions it fosters.[81]

The institutional policing of rap music is a complex and interactive process that has had a significant impact on rap's content, image, and reception. The Nassau Coliseum incident, which necessarily includes the social construction of the incident, the already existing discourse on black urban crime and fears of rap's political and social power, served as a catalyst for the explicit and sanctioned containment of rap's influence and public presence. This pivotal incident allowed an already suspicious public to "blame rap for encouraging urban violence," placed the rap community on the defensive, and effectively refocused attention away from the systemic reasons for street crime.

Rap music is fundamentally linked to larger social constructions of black culture as an internal threat to dominant American culture and social order. Rap's capacity as a form of testimony, as an articulation of a young black urban critical voice of social protest has profound potential as a basis for a language of liberation.[82] Contestation over the meaning and significance of rap music and its ability to occupy public space and retain expressive freedom constitute a central aspect of contemporary black cultural politics.

During the centuries-long period of Western slavery, there were elaborate rules and laws designed to control slave populations. Constraining the mobility of slaves, especially at night and in groups, was of special concern; slave masters reasoned that revolts could be organized by blacks who moved too freely and without surveillance.[83] Slave masters were rightfully confident that blacks had good reason to escape, revolt, and retaliate. Contemporary laws and practices curtailing and constraining black mobility in urban America function in much the same way and for similar reasons. Large groups of African Americans, especially teenagers, represent a threat to the social order of oppression. Albeit more sophisticated and more difficult to trace, contemporary policing of African Americans resonates with the legacy of slavery.

Rap's poetic voice is deeply political in content and spirit, but rap's hidden struggle, the struggle over access to public space, community resources, and the interpretation of black expression constitutes rap's hidden politics; hegemonic discourses have rendered these institutional aspects of black cultural politics invisible. Political interpretations of rap's explosive and resistive lyrics are critical to understanding contemporary black cultural politics, but they reflect only a part of the battle. Rap's hidden politics must also be revealed and contested; otherwise, whether we believe the hype or not won't make a difference.

CHAPTER FIVE

Bad Sistas

Black Women Rappers
and Sexual Politics in Rap Music

✦

Some think that we can't flow (can't flow)
Stereotypes they got to go (got to go)
I'm gonna mess around and flip the scene into reverse
With what?
With a little touch of ladies first.
                    —Queen Latifah [1]

She that has an ear, let her hear
The words I'm about to speak are black but clear
I bring light for us to fight the right fight
So that in darkness you might have sight, alright?
All won't come along but Harmony is still singing that song
Cause I'm strong
This is when—when and where I enter
The impact I have is the focus the center.
                    —Harmony [2]

Women have to work twice as hard to get half the credit. Unfortunately, that's just how
it is for women in this society. Rap is no different. It's fucked up.
                    —Kid (from Kid-N-Play) [3]

Black women rappers interpret and articulate the fears, pleasures, and
promises of young black women whose voices have been relegated to the
margins of public discourse. They are integral and resistant voices in rap
music and in popular music in general who sustain an ongoing dialogue
with their audiences and with male rappers about sexual promiscuity,
emotional commitment, infidelity, the drug trade, racial politics, and
black cultural history. By paying close attention to female rappers, we
can gain some insight into how young African-American women provide for themselves a relatively safe free-play zone where they creatively
address questions of sexual power, the reality of truncated economic
opportunity, and the pain of racism and sexism. Like their male counterparts, they are predominantly resistant voices that at times voice ideas

that are in sync with elements of dominant discourses. Where they differ from male rappers, however, is in their thematic focus. Although male rappers' social criticism often contests police harassment and other means by which black men are "policed," black women rapper's central contestation is in the arena of sexual politics.

Female rappers have been uniformly touted as sexually progressive, antisexist voices in rap music. Given the prominence and strength of these black women's voices in the popular terrain, it is not surprising that they have been heralded as rap's politically correct underdogs.[4] Their media status as antisexist rappers is necessarily accompanied by an understanding of male rappers as uniformly sexist. This opposition between male and female rappers serves to produce imaginary clarity in the realm of rap's sexual politics, rather than confront its contradictory nature.

The complexity of male and female sexual narratives rarely, if ever, find their way into discussions of sexism or feminism in rap. In the case of critical writing on male rappers, nonsexist and pro-women commentary about women and gender are virtually nonexistent. Instead, discussions of sexual references in male rappers' work are limited to considerations of the nature of rap's sexism. Similarly, critical commentary on female rappers rarely confronts the ways in which some of their work affirms patriarchal family norms and courtship rituals.

Repositioning women rappers as part of a dialogic process with male rappers (and others), rather than in complete opposition to them, I want to consider the ways black women rappers work within and against dominant sexual and racial narratives in American culture. For example, some female rappers affirm aspects of sexual power relationships as they raise incisive questions that seriously challenge the current distribution of power between men and women. Works by black women rappers that place black women's bodies in the spotlight have a similarly contradictory effect; they affirm black female beauty and yet often preserve the logic of female sexual objectification.

Three central themes predominate in the works of black female rappers: heterosexual courtship, the importance of the female voice, and mastery in women's rap and black female public displays of physical and sexual freedom. Here, these themes are contextualized in two ways; first, in dialogue with male rappers' sexual discourses, and then in dialogue with larger social discourses, including feminism. Clearly, female rappers are at least indirectly responding to male rappers' sexist constructions of black women. However, female rappers' sexual discourse is not simply part of a dialogue with male rappers, but also it responds to a variety of related issues, including dominant notions of femininity, feminism, and black female sexuality. At the very least, black women rappers are in dialogue with one another, black men, black women, and dominant American culture as they struggle to define themselves against a confining and treacherous social environment.

The concept of dialogue, exchange, and multidirectional communication is a useful way to understand the contradictory aspects and partiality of means of communication in popular music and cultural expression. In his application of Russian philosopher and literary critic Mikhail Bakhtin's concept of dialogism to popular music, George Lipsitz argues that: "Popular music is nothing if not dialogic, the product of an ongoing historical conversation in which no one has the first or last word. The traces of the past that pervade the popular music of the present amount to more than mere chance: they are not simply juxtapositions of incompatible realities. They reflect a dialogic process, one embedded in collective history and nurtured by the ingenuity of artists interested in fashioning icons of opposition."[5] Lipsitz's interpretation of popular music as a social and historical dialogue is an extremely important break from traditional, formalist interpretations of music. By grounding cultural production historically and avoiding the application of a fixed inventory of core structures, Lipsitz in his use of dialogic criticism is concerned with how popular music "arbitrates tensions between opposition and co-optation at any given historical moment." Linking popular musical discourses to the social world, Lipsitz's use of dialogic criticism in popular music shares a number of similarities with James Scott's interpretation of the hidden and public transcripts in rituals, gossips, folktales, and other popular practices. Both approaches examine power relationships as they are acted out, resisted, and affirmed in popular practices, and each understands that popular practices enter into and revise dialogues already in progress.[6]

Lipsitz's use of dialogic criticism is especially productive in the context of black women rappers. Negotiating multiple social boundaries and identities, black women rappers are in dialogue with one another, with male rappers, with other popular musicians (through sampling and other revisionary practices), with black women fans, and with hip hop fans in general. Dialogism resists the one-dimensional opposition between male and female rappers as respectively sexist and feminist. It also accommodates the tension between sympathetic racial bonds among black men and women as well as black women's frustration regarding sexual oppression at the hands of black men. As Cornel West aptly describes it, "the pressure on Afro-Americans as a people has forced the black man closer to the black woman: they are in the same boat. But they are also at each other's throat. The relation is internally hierarchical and often mediated by violence: black men over black women."[7] In addition, dialogism allows us to ground apparent inconsistencies and contradictions in rap's sexual politics within the complexity and contradictions of everyday life and protest, and it also allows us to make sense of the contradictory modes of resistance in women rappers' work.

Unfortunately, most discussions of rap's sexual politics and black women rappers do not account for these real-life complexities. Instead, discussions of women rappers can be divided into two related positions: (1) women rappers are feminist voices who combat sexism in rap; and/or (2) the sexist exclusion or mischaracterization of women's participation in rap music devalues women's significance and must be countered by evidence of women's contributions. In the former position, female rap lyrics, such as those by Latifah cited in the epigraph, are frequently offered as indirect critiques of infamous such works as those of the 2 Live Crew, Geto Boys, NWA, and others. In this battle between the sexes, male rappers are constructed as sexist and female rappers are constructed as feminist or womanist.[8] For example, Michelle Wallace's *New York Times* article, "When Black Feminism Faces the Music and the Music is Rap," concludes with a call for dialogue between male and female rappers regarding sex and sexism; yet the bulk of the piece, in fact, describes male rapper's references to sex as displaying "little regard for the humanity of the black woman" and positions female rappers in opposition to these male rappers.[9]

There are at least two problems with the monolith of male sexism and women rapper's opposition to it. First, and most obviously, it places female rappers in a totalizing oppositional relationship to male rappers. This is not to say that women rappers do not directly criticize sexist male rap lyrics, but their relationship to male rappers cannot be characterized as one of complete opposition. For example, during the height of the 2 Live Crew controversy over obscenity in popular music, a number of prominent female rappers were asked to comment on the 2 Live Crew and the sexist content of their lyrics. I only observed Salt from Salt 'N' Pepa speaking out against 2 Live Crew, and she did so in terms that resembled familiar black nationalist calls for "respecting" black women, rather than calling for an end to sexism. MC Lyte, Queen Latifah, Sister Souljah, and Yo-Yo refused to criticize their male colleagues—not necessarily because they did not find the lyrics offensive, but because they were acutely aware of the dominant discursive context within which their responses would be reproduced. Cognizant that they were being constructed in the mainstream press as a progressive response to regressive male rappers, these female rappers felt that they were being used as a political baton to beat male rappers over the head, rather than being affirmed as women who could open up public dialogue to interrogate sexism and its effects on young black women. Furthermore, they remain acutely aware of the uneven and sometimes racist way in which sexist offenses are prosecuted, stigmatized, and reported. And so, in several public contexts, women rappers defended male rappers' freedom of speech and focused their answers on the question of censorship rather than on sexism in rap lyrics.[10] This is not to say that their evasive tactics are not problematic in so far as they may implicitly sanction verbal attacks on women in rap. My point here is that women rappers cannot be situated in total opposition to male rappers; they support and critique male rappers' sexual discourse in a number of contradictory ways.[11]

Second, this way of thinking cannot account for the complexity and contradictory nature of the sexual dialogues in rap; not only those taking place between male and female rappers but within male sexual themes and within female sexual themes in rap: male rappers' sexual discourse is not consistently sexist, and female sexual discourse is not consistently feminist. Not only do women rappers defend male rappers' sexist speech in a larger society that seems to attack black men disproportionately, but their lyrics sometimes affirm patriarchal notions about family life and the traditional roles of husbands, fathers, and lovers. Similarly, there are many lyrics in male rappers' work that not only chastise men for abusing women but also call for male responsibility in childrearing and support the centrality of black women in black cultural life. For example, several male rappers' works take an explicit stand against sexual violence toward women. De La Soul's "Millie Pulled a Pistol on Santa" is a brilliant and poignant story about a young girl whose father's sexual abuse of her and her inability to convince adults of his crime drives her to kill him. A Tribe Called Quest's "Description of a Fool" defines a fool as, among other things, a man who hits a woman; and Tribe's "Date Rape" takes a decidedly pro-woman position about the coercive power men have in date rape situations. Some examples are not so easily positioned as progressive or regressive. In a single lyrical stanza in Tim Dog's "Fuck Compton," Tim Dog criticizes and chastises NWA producer Dr. Dre for his cowardly real-life physical abuse of female rapper and video host Dee Barnes; yet, a few phrases later he solidifies his power over Dr. Dre by bragging about how he "fucked" Dr. Dre's girlfriend behind his back. Gangster rapper Ice Cube calls for killing police officers and then turns his rage on black women, calling for slaying "bitches" in the same phrase.

Cube's lyrics suggest that state authority figures and black women are similarly responsible for black male disempowerment and oppression. Similar contradictions appear in women rappers' work. Yo-Yo's "Don't Play with My Yo-Yo" features Ice Cube repeating the song's title as part of the chorus, a move that allows Yo-Yo to be possessed by Ice Cube, albeit as a way to protect her from enemies and unwanted male advances. Salt 'N' Pepa's "Independent" attacks a man whose weakness is a product of his incapacity to provide material possessions and his limited economic means, a move that sustains the link between masculinity and economic privilege. In a number of raps by women, men who are being insulted are referred to as "fruity" or "punks," hinting at their possible homosexuality as a way to emasculate them. This sort of homophobia affirms oppressive standards of heterosexual masculinity and problematizes a simplistic reading of female rappers' sexual narratives.[12]

The second approach to black women rappers and rap's sexual politics, the sexist exclusion or mischaracterization of black women's participation in rap music, has two faces. Either analyses of rap are aggressively masculine and render women rappers invisible, or black female contributions are rightfully and extensively presented to counter previous deletions. A subtle but important example of the former is Houston Baker's "Hybridity, the Rap Race and Pedagogy for the 1990s," in which Baker explains rap's emergence as, in part, a "resentment of disco culture and a reassertion of black manhood." To define rap's emergence as a reassertion of black manhood not only affirms the equation of male heterosexuality with manhood, but also it renders sustained and substantial female pleasure and participation in hip hop invisible or impossible. The centrality of heterosexual male pleasure and identity in his construction is not the problem; it is, instead, his formulation of male pleasure in rap coupled with the total absence of women at the conceptual level that render his analysis incorrect and problematic.[13]

Nelson George's 1989 ten-year anniversary tribute to rap is a much more explicit case of what I call the "what women?" syndrome. In honor of rap's birthday in the recording industry, George, a black music historian and pro–hip hop music critic, published a sentimental rap retrospective in which he mourned rap's movement from a street subculture into the cold, sterile world of commercial record production.[14] George pointed out that, until recently, music industry powers have maintained a studied indifference to rap music. And now that rap's "commercial viability has been proven," many major recording companies are signing any halfway decent act they can find.

What worries George is that corporate influence on black music has led, in the past, to the dissolution of vibrant black cultural forms and that rap may become the latest victim. The problem is complex, real, and requires analysis. However, Nelson George and media critics generally, embed their descriptions of "authentic rap" and fears of recent corporate influence on it, in gender-coded discourse that mischaracterizes rap and silences women rappers and consumers. In his tenth-anniversary piece, George traces major shifts in rap, naming titles, artists, and producers. He weaves over twenty rap groups into his piece and names not a single female rapper. His retrospective is chockfull of prideful urban black youths (read men) whose contributions to rap reflect "the thoughts of city kids more deeply than the likes of Michael Jackson, Oprah Winfrey et al." His concluding remarks make apparent his underlying perception of rap: "To proclaim the death of rap is to be sure, premature. But the farther the control of rap gets from its street corner constituency and the more corporations grasp it—record conglomerates, Burger King, Minute Maid, Yo! MTV Raps, etc.—the more vulnerable it becomes to cultural emasculation." For George, corporate meddling not only dilutes cultural forms, but also it reduces strapping, testosterone-packed men into women! Could we imagine anything worse? Nelson George's concluding remarks are extreme but not unusual; his is but one example of media critics' consistent coding of rap music as male in the face of a significant and sustained female presence. Furthermore, George's mindboggling, yet emblematic, definition of rap as a "ultra-urban, unromantic, hyperrealistic, neo-nationalist, antiassimilationist, aggressive Afrocentric impulse," not only simplifies the complexity of masculinity, but also his definition is designed to conjure only a heterosexual masculine subject without drawing critical attention toward *how* black male heterosexuality is socially-constructed. For George, and for media critics in general, it is far easier to regender women rappers than it is to revise their own masculinist analysis of rap music. My immediate reaction to this article took the form of a letter to the editor of the *Village Voice*, which was published with the name tag "Lady Complainer," a petty and sexist attempt to devalue my criticism while retaining the appearance of being committed to open critique and dialogue. (We will return to this strategy of designating women's public speech as "complaint" a bit later.)

Many of the articles that have attempted to address the deletion of women in rap have been written by women and offer feminist analyses of the contributions of women to hip hop.[15] As several of these writers point out, the marginalization, deletion, and mischaracterization of women's role in black cultural production is routine practice. Nancy

Guevara charges that the "exclusion and/or trivialization of women's role in hip hop" is no mere oversight. In response to these exclusions, Guevara's "Women Writin', Rappin' and Breakin'" documents black and Latino female participation in hip hop from the earliest stages in the mid-1970s and it articulates the ways in which young women were discouraged from participating in hip hop youth culture.[16]

Two essays began to draw on the dialogic aspects of popular music via an exploration of the nature and character of black women's popular musical production in relationship to black culture and to larger cultural discourses. In her article, "Black Women and Music: A Historical Legacy of Struggle," Angela Davis puts forth three related arguments of particular importance. First, she challenges the marginal representation of black women in the documentation of African-American cultural developments and suggests that these representations do not adequately reflect women's participation. Second, she notes that music, song, and dance are especially rich places to look for the collective consciousness of black Americans. And third, she calls for a close reexamination of black woman's musical legacy as a way to understand black women's consciousness. She writes: "Music has long permeated the daily life of most African-Americans; it has played a central role in the normal socialization process; and during moments characterized by intense movements for social change, it has helped to shape the necessary political consciousness. Any attempt, therefore, to understand in depth the evolution of women's consciousness within the Black community requires a serious examination of the music which has influenced them—particularly that which they themselves have created."[17] Davis's argument is important, because it links black music to black politics; more important, it links black music to black women's racial, sexual, and political identities. Davis's approach identifies black music as a critical factor in the fashioning of a black collective consciousness—to which Lipsitz might add, a critical factor that "contributes to an on-going historical conversation in which no one has the first or last word."

Addressing similar issues regarding the absence or misrepresentation of black women's musical production, Hazel Carby charges that white-dominated feminist discourse has marginalized nonwhite women and questions of black sexuality. In responding to the reliance on black women's fiction as primary texts for analyzing black female discourse, Carby argues forcefully that representations of black women's sexuality in African-American literature differs significantly from representations of sexuality in black women's blues. Stating that, "different cultural forms negotiate and resolve different sets of social contradictions,"

Carby suggests that many literary and cultural studies scholars have perhaps allowed black women writers to speak on behalf of a large segment of black women whose daily lives and material conditions may not be adequately reflected in black women's fiction. For example, the consumption patterns and social contexts for reception of popular music differ significantly from those of fiction.[18] The dialogic capacity of popular music, particularly that of rap music, seems especially suited for engaging many of the social contradictions and ambiguities that pertain specifically to contemporary urban working-class black life.

Carby and Davis are calling for a multifaceted analysis of black women's identity and sexuality with special attention paid to their musical production. Placing black popular music and black women's musical production at center stage, Carby and Davis lay a foundation for analyses of black women rappers that can confront the complex and contradictory nature of popular expression and black female social identities.

*   *   *

Rap is co-ed now.   —Roxanne Shante

Although there are significantly fewer female than male rappers, they have a prominent role in rap and a substantial following. It is difficult to ignore the massive increase in record deals for women rappers following Salt 'N' Pepa's double platinum (2 million) 1986 debut album *Hot, Cool and Vicious*. Such volume album sales, even for a rap album by a male artist, were virtually unprecedented in 1986. Since then, several female rappers, many of whom have been rapping for years (some since the mid-1970s) have finally been recorded and promoted.[19] Says female rapper Ms. Melodie: "It wasn't that the male started rap, the male was just the first to be put on wax. Females were always into rap, and females always had their little crews and were always known for rockin' house parties and streets or whatever, school yards, the corner, the park, whatever it was."[20] In the early stages, women's participation in rap was hindered by gender-related considerations. M.C. Lady "D" notes that because she didn't put a female crew together for regular performances, she "didn't have to worry about getting (her) equipment ripped off, coming up with the cash to get it in the first place, or hauling it around on the subways to gigs, problems that kept a lot of other women out of rap in the early days."[21] For a number of reasons, including increased record industry support and more demand for rappers generally and female rappers specifically, women have greater access to production and transportation resources.

MC Lyte's 1988 release "Paper Thin" sold over 125,000 copies in the first six months with virtually no radio play. Lady B, who became the first recorded woman rapper in 1978, has since become Philadelphia's top rated DJ on WUSL and is founder and editor-in-chief of *Word Up!*, a tabloid devoted to hip hop.[22] Salt 'N' Pepa's first single "Expressions," from *Black's Magic*, went gold in the first week and stayed in the number one position on Billboard's Rap Chart for over two months. Most of these songs address black women's rejection of black male domination, an assertion of new terms for heterosexual courtship, and the centrality of black women's voices.

Courting Disaster

Raps written by women that specifically concern male-female relationships almost always confront the tension between trust and savvy; between vulnerability and control. Some raps celebrate their sisters for "getting over" on men, rather than touting self-reliance and honesty. For example, in Icey Jaye's "It's a Girl Thang," she explains how she and her friends find ways to spend as much of their dates' money as possible and mocks the men who fall for their tricks. Similarly, in the video for Salt 'N' Pepa's "Independent" Salt accepts several expensive gifts from a string of dates who hope to win her affection with diamond necklaces and rings. In raps such as these, women are taking advantage of the logic of heterosexual courtship in which men coax women into submission with trinkets and promises for financial security. Nikki D's "Up the Ante for the Panty" and B.W.P.'s "We Want Money" are more graphic examples of a similar philosophy. However, for the most part, when they choose to rap about male-female relations, women rappers challenge the depictions of women in many male raps as gold diggers and address the fears many women share regarding male dishonesty and infidelity.

MC Lyte and Salt 'N' Pepa have reputations for biting raps that criticize men who manipulate and abuse women. Their lyrics tell the story of men taking advantage of women, cheating on them, taking their money, and then leaving them for other unsuspecting female victims. These raps are not mournful ballads about the trials and tribulations of being a heterosexual woman. Similar to women's blues, they are caustic, witty, and aggressive warnings directed at men and at other women who might be seduced by them in the future. By offering a woman's interpretation of the terms of heterosexual courtship, these women's raps cast a new light on male-female sexual power relations and depict women as resistant, aggressive participants. Yet, even the raps that explore and revise women's role in the courtship process often retain the larger patriarchal parameters of heterosexual courtship.

Salt 'N' Pepa's 1986 single "Tramp" is strong advice, almost boot camp, for single black women. "Tramp" is not, as Salt 'N' Pepa warn, a "simple rhyme," but a parable about courtship rituals between men and women:

> Homegirls attention you must pay to what I say
> Don't take this as a simple rhyme
> Cause this type of thing happens all the time
> Now what would you do if a stranger said "Hi"
> Would you dis him or would you reply?
> If you'd answer, there is a chance
> That you'd become a victim of circumstance
> Am I right fellas? tell the truth
> Or else I'll have to show and prove
> You are what you are I am what I am
> It just so happens that most men are TRAMPS.[23]

In the absence of any response to "Am I right fellas?" (any number of sampled male replies easily could have been woven in here), Salt 'N' Pepa "show and prove" the trampings of several men who "undress you with their eyeballs," "think you're a dummy, on the first date, had the nerve to tell me he loves me" and of men who always have sex on the mind. Salt 'N' Pepa's parable defines promiscuous *males* as tramps, and thereby inverts the common belief that male sexual promiscuity is a status symbol. This reversal undermines the degrading "woman as tramp" image by stigmatizing male promiscuity. Salt 'N' Pepa suggest that women who respond to sexual advances made by these men are victims of circumstance. In this case, it is predatory, disingenuous men who are the tramps.

The music video for "Tramps" is a comic rendering of a series of social club scenes that highlight tramps on the make, mouth freshener in hand, testing their lines on the nearest woman. Dressed in the then-latest hip hop street gear, Salt 'N' Pepa perform the song on television, on a monitor perched above the bar. Because they appear on the television screen, they seem to be surveying and critiquing the club action, but the club members cannot see them. There are people dancing and talking together (including likeable men who are coded as "non-tramps"), who seem unaware of the television monitor. Salt 'N' Pepa are also shown in the club, dressed in very stylish, sexy outfits. Salt 'N' Pepa act as decoys, talking and flirting with the tramps to flesh out the dramatization of tramps on the prowl. They make several knowing gestures at the camera to reassure the viewer that they are unswayed by the tramps' efforts.

The tramps and their victims interact only with body language. The club scenes have no dialogue; we hear only Salt 'N' Pepa lyrics over the musical tracks for "Tramp," which serve respectively as the video's narrative and the club's dance music. Viewing much of the club action from Salt 'N' Pepa's authoritative position—through the television monitor—we can safely observe the playful but cautionary dramatization of heterosexual courtship. One tramp who is rapping to a woman, postures and struts, appearing to ask something like the stock pick-up line: "what is your zodiac sign, baby?" When she shows disgust and leaves her seat, he repeats the same body motions and gestures on the next woman who happens to sit down. Near the end of the video, a frustrated "wife" enters the club and drags one of the tramps home, smacking him in the head with her pocketbook. Salt 'N' Pepa are standing next to the wife's tramp in the club, shaking their heads as if to say "what a shame." Simultaneously, they are pointing and laughing at the husband from the television monitor. At the end of the video, a still frame of each man is stamped "tramp," and Salt 'N' Pepa revel in having identified and exposed them. They then leave the club together, without men, seemingly enjoying their skill at exposing the real intentions of these tramps.

Salt 'N' Pepa are "schooling" women about the sexual politics of the club scene, by engaging in and critiquing the drama of heterosexual courtship. The privileged viewer is a woman who is directly addressed in the lyrics and presumably can empathize fully with the visual depiction and interpretation of the scenes. The video's resolution can be interpreted as a warning to both men and women. Women: Don't fall for these men either by talking to them in the clubs or believing the lies they'll tell you when they come home. Men: You will get caught eventually, and you'll be embarrassed. Another message suggested by the video for "Tramp" is that women can go to these clubs, successfully play along with "the game" as long as the power of female sexuality and the terms of male desire are understood and negotiated.

However, "Tramp" does not interrogate "the game" itself. "Tramp" implicitly accepts the larger dynamics and power relationships between men and women. Although the tramps are embarrassed and momentarily contained at the end of the video, in no way can it be suggested that these tramps will stop hustling women and cheating on their wives. More important, what of women's desire? Not only is it presumed that men will continue their dishonest behavior, but women's desire for an idealized monogamous heterosexual relationship is implicitly confirmed as an unrealized (but not unrealizable?) goal. In their quest for an hon-

© suekwon

est man, should not the sobering fact that "most men are tramps" be considered a point of departure for rejecting the current courtship ritual altogether?

Salt 'N' Pepa leave the club together, seemingly pleased by their freedom and by their ability to manipulate men into pursuing them "to no end." But the wife drags her husband home—she is not shocked but rather frustrated by what appears to be frequent dishonest behavior. What conclusion is to be drawn from this lesson? Do not trust tramps, separate the wheat from the tramps, and continue in your quest for an honest, monogamous man. "Tramp" is courtship advice for women who choose to participate in the current configuration of heterosexual courtship, it does not offer an alternative paradigm for such courtship, and in some ways it works inside of the very courtship rules that it highlights and criticizes. At best, "Tramp" is an implicit critique of the club scene as a setting for meeting potential mates as well as of the institution of marriage that permits significant power imbalances clearly weighted in favor of men.

MC Lyte has a far less comedic response to Sam, a boyfriend whom she catches trying to pick up women. MC Lyte's underground hit "Paper Thin" is one of the most scathingly powerful raps about male dishonesty and infidelity and the tensions between trust and vulnerability in heterosexual relations. Lyte has been burned by Sam, but she has turned her experience into a black woman's anthem that sustains an uncomfortable balance between brutal cynicism and honest vulnerability:

When you say you love me it doesn't matter
It goes into my head as just chit chatter
You may think it's egotistical or just very free
But what you say, I take none of it seriously. . . .

I'm not the kind of girl to try to play a man out
They take the money and then they break the hell out.
No that's not my strategy, not the game I play
I admit I play a game, but it's not done that way.
Truly when I get involved I give it my heart
I mean my mind, my soul, my body, I mean every part.
But if it doesn't work out—yo, it just doesn't.
It wasn't meant to be, you know it just wasn't.
So, I treat all of you like I treat all of them.
What you say to me is just paper thin.[24]

Lyte's public acknowledgment that Sam's expressions of love were paper thin is not a source of embarrassment for her but a means of empowerment. She plays a brutal game of the dozens on Sam while wearing her past commitment to him as a badge of honor and sign of character. Lyte presents commitment, vulnerability, and sensitivity as assets, not indicators of female weakness. In "Paper Thin," emotional and sexual commitment are not romantic, Victorian concepts tied to honorable but dependent women; they are a part of her strategy, part of the game she plays in heterosexual courtship.

"Paper Thins'" high-energy video contains many elements present in hip hop. The video opens with Lyte, dressed in a sweatsuit, chunk jewelry, and sneakers, abandoning her new Jetta hastily because she wants to take the subway to clear her head. A few members of her male posse, shocked at her desire to leave her Jetta on the street for the subway, follow along behind her, down the steps to the subway tracks. (Her sudden decision to leave her new car for the subway and her male posse's surprised reaction seems to establish that Lyte rarely rides the subway anymore.) Lyte enters a subway car with an introspective and distracted expression. Once in the subway car, her DJ K-Rock, doubling as the conductor, announces that the train will be held in the station because of crossed signals. While they wait, Milk Boy (her female but very masculine-looking body guard) spots Sam at the other end of the car, rapping heavily to two stylish women and draws Lyte's attention to him. Lyte, momentarily surprised, begins her rhyme as she stalks toward Sam. Sam's attempts to escape fail; he is left to face MC Lyte's wrath. Eventually, she throws him off the train to the chorus of Ray Charles's R&B

classic, "Hit the Road Jack," and locks Sam out of the subway station and out of the action. The subway car is filled with young black teenagers, typical working New Yorkers and street people many of whom join Lyte in signifying on Sam while they groove on K-Rock's music. MC Lyte's powerful voice and no-nonsense image dominate Sam. The taut, driving music, which is punctuated by sampled guitar and drum sections and an Earth Wind and Fire horn section, complement Lyte's hard, expressive rapping style.

It is important that "Paper Thin" is set in public and on the subway, the quintessential mode of urban transportation. Lyte is drawn to the subway and seems comfortable there. She is also comfortable with the subway riders in her video; they are her community. During musical breaks between raps, we see passengers grooving to her music and responding to the drama. By setting her confrontation with Sam in the subway, in front of their peers, Lyte moves a private problem between lovers into the public arena and effectively dominates both spaces.

When her DJ, the musical and mechanical conductor, announces that crossed signals are holding the train in the station, it frames the video in a moment of communication crisis. The notion of crossed signals represents the inability of Sam and Lyte to communicate with one another, an inability that is primarily the function of the fact that they communicate on different frequencies. Sam thinks he can read Lyte's mind to see what she is thinking and then feed her all the right lines. But what he says carries no weight, no meaning. His discourse is light, it's paper thin. Lyte, who understands courtship as a game, confesses to being a player, yet expresses how she feels directly and in simple language. What she says has integrity, weight, and substance.

After throwing Sam from the train, she nods her head toward a young man standing against the subway door, and he follows her off the train. She will not allow her experiences with Sam to paralyze her but instead continues to participate on revised terms. As she and her new male friend walk down the street, she raps the final stanza for "Paper Thin" that sets down the new courtship ground rules:

> So, now I take precautions when choosing my mate
> I do not touch until the third or fourth date
> Then maybe we'll kiss on the fifth or sixth time that we meet
> Cause a date without a kiss is so incomplete
> And then maybe, I'll let you play with my feet
> You can suck the big toe and play with the middle
> It's so simple unlike a riddle . . .

Lyte has taken control of the process. She has selected her latest companion; he has not pursued her. This is an important move, because it allows her to set the tone of the interaction and subsequently articulates the new ground rules that will protect her from repeating the mistakes she made in her relationship with Sam. Yet, a central revision to her courtship terms involve withholding sexual affection, a familiar strategy in courtship rituals for women that implicitly affirms the process of male pursuit as it forestalls it. Nonetheless, Lyte seems prepared for whatever takes place. Her analysis of courtship seems to acknowledge that there are dishonest men and that she is not interested in negotiating on their terms. Lyte affirms her courtship rules as she identifies and critiques the terms of men such as Sam. In "Paper Thin" she has announced that her desire will govern her behavior and *his* ("you can suck my big toe and then play with the middle") and remains committed to her principles at the same time.

As "products of an ongoing historical conversation," "Paper Thin" and "Tramp" are explicitly dialogic texts that draw on the language and terms imbedded in long-standing struggles over the parameters of heterosexual courtship. These raps are also dialogic in their use of black collective memory via black music. Salt 'N' Pepa's "Tramp" draws its horns and parts of its rhythm section from the 1967 soul song of the same name performed by Otis Redding and Carla Thomas. Otis's and Carla's "Tramp" is a dialogue in which Carla expresses her frustration over Otis's failure in their relationship while he makes excuses and attempts to avoid her accusations.[25] Salt 'N' Pepa's musical quotation of Otis's and Carla's "Tramp" set a multilayered dialogue in motion. The musical style of Salt 'N' Pepa's "Tramp" carries the blues bar confessional mode of many rhythm and blues songs updated with rap's beats and breaks. Salt 'N' Pepa are testifying to Carla's problems via the music, at the same time providing their contemporary audience with a collective reference to black musical predecessors and the history of black female heterosexual struggles.

Lyte's direct address to Sam ("when you say you love it doesn't matter") is her half of a heated conversation in which Sam is silenced by her, but nonetheless present. Lyte's announcement that she "admits playing a game but it's not done that way" makes it clear that she understands the power relationships that dictate their interaction. Lyte encourages herself and by extension black women to be fearless and self-possessed ("sucker you missed, I know who I am") in the face of significant emotional losses. Her game, her strategy, have a critical sexual difference that lays the groundwork for a black female-centered communal voice that revises and expands the terms of female power in heterosexual courtship.

The dialogic and resistive aspects in "Tramps" and "Paper Thin" are also present the body of other women rappers' work. Many female rappers address the frustration heterosexual women experience in their desire for intimacy with and commitment from men. The chorus in Neneh Cherry's "Buffalo Stance" tells men not to mess with her, and that money men can't buy her love because it's affection that she's lookin' for; "Say That Then" from West Coast female rappers Oaktown 3-5-7, give no slack to "Finger popping, hip hoppin' wanna be bed rockin'" men; Monie Love's "It's a Shame" is a pep talk for a woman breaking up with a man who apparently needs to be kicked to the curb; Ice Cream Tee's "All Wrong" chastises women who allow men to abuse them; Monie Love's "Just Don't Give a Damn" is a confident and harsh rejection of an emotionally and physically abusive man; and MC Lyte's "I Cram to Understand U," "Please Understand," and "I'm Not Havin' It" are companion pieces to "Paper Thin."

This strategy, in which women square off with men, can be subverted and its power diminished. As Laura Berlant suggests, this mode of confrontational communication can be contained or renamed as the "female complaint." In other words, direct and legitimate criticism is reduced to "bitching" or complaining as way of containing dissent. Berlant warns that the "female complaint . . . as a mode of expression is an admission and recognition both of privilege and powerlessness . . . circumscribed by a knowledge of woman's inevitable delegitimation within the patriarchal public sphere." Berlant argues that resistance to sexual oppression must take place "in the patriarchal public sphere, the place where significant or momentous exchanges of power are perceived to take place," but that the female complaint is devalued, marginalized, and ineffective in this sphere. Berlant offers an interpretation of "Roxanne's Revenge," an early and popular rap record by black female rapper Roxanne Shante, as an example of the pitfalls of the "female complaint." Attempts were made to contain and humiliate Roxanne on a compilation record that included several other related answer records. Berlant says that "Roxanne's Revenge" is vulnerable to "hystericization by a readily available phallic discourse (which) is immanent in the very genre of her expression."[26]

Berlant is making an important point about the vulnerability of women's voices to devaluation. No doubt women's angry responses have long been made to appear hysterical and irrational or whiny and childlike. I am not sure, though, that we can equate attempts to render women's voices as "complaint" with the voices themselves. To do so may place too much value on the attempts to contain women. "Roxanne's Revenge" gave voice to a young girl's response to real-life street confrontations with men. She entered into black male-dominated public space and drew a great deal of attention away from the UTFO song to which she responded. More importantly, "Roxanne's Revenge" has retained weight and significance in hip hop since 1985 when it was released. This has not been the case for UTFO, the UTFO song, or any of the fabricated responses on the compilation record. Much of the status of the original UTFO song "Roxanne Roxanne" is a result of the power of Roxanne Shante's answer record. What Berlant illustrates is the ways in which Roxanne's "female complaint" needed to be labeled as such and then contained precisely because it was threatening. It did not go unnoticed, because it was a compelling voice in the public domain that captured the attention of male and female hip hop fans. The compilation record is clearly an attempt at containing her voice, but it was, in my estimation an unsuccessful attempt. Furthermore, such attempts at circumscription will continue to take place when partial, yet effective, attacks are made, whether in the form of the female complaint or not. Nonetheless, Berlant's larger argument, which calls for substantial female public sphere presence and contestation is crucial. These public sphere contests must involve more than responses to sexist male speech; they must also entail the development of sustained, strong female voices that stake claim to public space generally.

Preeminent Emcees: Who's the Boss?

Rapping skills involve verbal mastery, mastery of delivery, creativity, personal style, and virtuosity. Rappers seize the public stage, demanding the audience's attention and winning their admiration. Their rhymes are embedded in an aggressive self-possessed identity that exudes confidence and power. Given this, rhymes that boast, signify, and toast are an important part of women rappers' repertoire. Antoinette's "Who's the Boss," Ice Cream Tee's "Let's Work," Yo-Yo's "Stompin' to tha 90's," Salt 'N' Pepa's "Everybody Get Up," and Queen Latifah's "Latifah's Had It up to Here" and "Come into My House" establish black women rappers as hip hop MCs who can move the crowd, a skill that ultimately determines one's status as a successful rapper. Even introspective raps are delivered with edgy self-possession. Women rappers who seize the public stage and win the crowd's admiration under these highly competitive conditions, represent a substantial intervention in contemporary women's performance and popular cultural identities.

"Ladies First," Queen Latifah's second release from her debut album *All Hail the Queen* is a landmark example of centralizing a strong black female public voice. Taken together, the video and lyrics for "Ladies

First" are a statement for black female unity, independence, and power, as well as an anticolonial statement concerning Africa's southern region and recognition of the importance of black female political activists, which offers hope for the development of a pro-female pro-black diasporic political consciousness. "Ladies First" is a rapid-fire and powerful rap duet between Queen Latifah and her "European sister" Monie Love. A recital on the significance and diversity of black women, "Ladies First" exploded on the rap scene. Latifah's assertive, measured voice, and opening rhyme sets the tone:

> The ladies will kick it, the rhyme it is wicked
> Those who don't know how to be pros get evicted
> A woman can bear you, break you, take you
> Now it's time to rhyme, can you relate to
> A sister dope enough to make you holler and scream?[27]

In her rapid-fire, almost double-time verse, Monie Love responds:

> Eh, Yo! Let me take it from here Queen.
> Excuse me but I think I am about due
> To get into precisely what I am about to do
> I'm conversatin' to the folks who have no whatsoever clue
> So, listen very carefully as I break it down to you
> Merrily merrily, hyper happy overjoyed,
> Pleased with all the beats and rhymes my sisters have employed
> Slick and smooth—throwing down the sound totally, a yes.
> Let me state the position: Ladies First, Yes?

Latifah responds, "YES!"

Without referring to or attacking black men, "Ladies First" is a powerful rewriting of the contributions of black women in the history of black struggles. Opening with slides of black female political activists Sojourner Truth, Angela Davis, and Winnie Mandela, the video's predominant theme features Latifah as Third World military strategist. She stalks an illuminated map of Southern Africa the size of a conference table and with a long pointer shoves large, clay, chesslike figures of briefcase-carrying white men off from white-dominated countries, replacing them with large, black-power–style fists. In between these scenes, Latifah and Monie Love rap in front of and between more photos of politically prominent black women, and footage of black struggles, protests, and acts of military violence against protestors. Latifah positions herself as part of a rich legacy of black women's activism, racial commitment, and cultural pride.

The centrality of black women's political protest in "Ladies First" is a break from protest-footage rap videos, which have become quite popular over the last few years and have all but excluded footage of

© suekwon

black women leaders or foot soldiers. Footage of dozens of rural African women running with sticks raised above their heads toward armed oppressors, holding their ground alongside men in equal numbers and dying in struggle are rare media images. As Latifah explains: "I wanted to show the strength of black women in history. Strong black women. Those were good examples. I wanted to show what we've done. We've done a lot, it's just that people don't know it. Sisters have been in the midst of these things for a long time, but we just don't get to see it that much."[28] After placing a black power fist on each country in Southern Africa, Latifah surveys the map, nodding contentedly. The video ends with a still frame of the region's new political order.

Latifah's self-possession and independence are important facets of the new cultural nationalism in rap. The powerful, level-headed, and black feminist character of her lyrics calls into question the historically cozy relationship between nationalism and patriarchy. Latifah strategically samples the legendary Malcolm X phrase: "There are going to be some changes made here" throughout "Ladies First." When Malcolm's voice is introduced, the camera pans the faces of some of the more prominent female rappers and DJs, including Ms. Melodie, Ice Cream Tee, and

Shelley Thunder. The next sample of Malcolm's memorable line is used to narrate South African protest footage. Latifah calls on Malcolm as a part of a collective African-American historical memory and recontextualizes him not only as a voice in support of contemporary struggles in South Africa but also as a voice in support of the imminent changes regarding the degraded status of black women and specifically black women rappers. "Ladies First" is a cumulative product that, as Lipsitz might say, "enters a dialogue already in progress." Latifah's use of the dialogic processes of naming, claiming, and recontextualizing are not random; nor are they "juxtapositions of incompatible realities." "Ladies First" affirms and revises African-American traditions past and present at the same time that it forges new territory for black women.

Express Yourself: Black Women's Bodies in the Public Sphere

Black women rappers' public displays of physical and sexual freedom often challenge male notions of female sexuality and pleasure. Salt 'N' Pepa's rap duet, "Shake Your Thang" with E.U., a prominent go-go band, is a verbal and visual display of black women's sexual resistance. The rap lyrics and video are about Salt 'N' Pepa's sexual dancing and others' responses to them. The first stanza sets them in a club "shakin' [their] thang to a funky beat with a go-go swing" and noting the shock on the faces of other patrons. With attitude to spare, Salt 'N' Pepa chant: "It's my thang and I'll swing it the way that I feel, with a little seduction and some sex appeal." The chorus, sung by the male lead in E.U., chants "Shake your thang, do what you want to do, I can't tell you how to catch a groove. It's your thang, do what you wanna do, I won't tell you how to catch a groove."[29]

The video is framed by Salt 'N' Pepa's interrogation after they have been arrested for lewd dancing. Real New York police cars pull up in front of the studio where their music video is being shot, and mock policemen (played by Kid-N-Play and Herbie Luv Bug, their producer) cart Salt 'N' Pepa away in handcuffs. When their mug shots are being taken, Salt 'N' Pepa blow a kiss to the camera person as each holds up her arrest placard. Once in the interrogation room, Kid-N-Play and Herbie ask Salt 'N' Pepa authoritatively, "what we gonna do about this dirty dancing?" Pepa reaches across the table, grabs Herbie by the tie and growls, "We gonna do what we wanna do."

The mildly slapstick interrogation scenes bind a number of other subplots. Scenes in which Salt 'N' Pepa are part of groups of women dancing and playing are interspersed with separate scenes of male dancers, co-ed dance segments with Kid-N-Play, E.U.'s lead singer acting as a spokesman for a "free-Salt 'N' Pepa" movement and picketers in front of the police station calling for their release. When he is not gathering signatures for his petition, E.U. chants the chorus from a press-conference-style podium. The camera angles for the dance segments give the effect of a series of park or street parties. Salt 'N' Pepa shake their butts for the cameras and for each other while rapping, "My jeans fit nice, they show off my butt" and "I Like hip hop mixed with a go-go baby, it's my thang and I'll shake it crazy. Don't tell me how to party, it's my dance, yep, and it's my body."[30]

A primary source of the video's power is Salt 'N' Pepa's irreverence toward the morally based sexual constrictions placed on them as women. They mock moral claims about the proper modes of women's expression and enjoy every minute of it. Their defiance of the moral, sexual restrictions on women is to be distinguished from challenges to the seemingly gender-neutral laws against public nudity. Salt 'N' Pepa are eventually released because their dancing isn't against the law (as Salt 'N' Pepa say, "we could get loose, but we can't get naked"). But their "dirty dancing" also teases the male viewer who would misinterpret their sexual freedom as an open sexual invitation. Salt 'N' Pepa make it clear that their expression is no such thing: "A guy touch my body? I just put him in check." Salt 'N' Pepa force a wedge between overt female sexual expression and the presumption that such expressions are intended to attract men. "Shaking your thang" can create a stir, but that should not prevent women from doing it when and how they choose.

At the video's close, we return to the interrogation scene a final time. Herbie receives a call, after which he announces that they have to release Salt 'N' Pepa. The charges will not stick. Prancing out of the police station, Salt 'N' Pepa laughingly say, "I told you so." The police raid and arrests make explicit the real, informal yet institutionally based policing of female sexual expression. The video speaks to black women, calls for open, public displays of female expression, assumes a community-based support for their freedom, and focuses directly on the sexual desirability and beauty of black women's bodies.[31]

Salt 'N' Pepa's physical freedom, exemplified by their focusing on their butts, is no random expression; the black behind has an especially charged place in the history of both black sexual expression and white classification of it as a sign of sexual perversity and inferiority. It conjures a complex history of white scrutiny of black female bodies, from the repulsion and fascination with and naked exhibition of Sara Bartmann as "The Hottentot Venus" in the early 1800s to the perverse and exoticized pleasure many Europeans received from Josephine Baker's aggressively behind-centered dances. It is also a contemporary nod to the substantial black folk history of performers and dances and songs that involve celebration of big behinds for men and women (e.g., the Bump, the Dookey Butt, and E.U. and Spike Lee's black chart topper, "Da Butt"). As bell hooks points out, "contemporary popular music is one of the primary cultural locations for discussions of black sexuality. In song lyrics, the butt is talked about in ways that attempt to challenge racist assumptions that suggest it is an ugly sign of inferiority, even as it remains a sexualized sign.[32] Because female bodies are especially scrutinized in this way, such explicit focus on the protruding behind in black popular culture counters mainstream white definitions of what constitutes a sexually attractive female body. It also serves as a rejection of the aesthetic hierarchy in American culture that marginalizes black women. American culture, in defining its female sex symbols, places a high premium on long thin legs, narrow hips, and relatively small behinds. The vast majority of white female television and film actresses, musicians, and the highest paid black models fit this description. The aesthetic hierarchy of the female body in mainstream American culture, with particular reference to the behind and hips, positions many black women somewhere near the bottom. When viewed in this context, Salt 'N' Pepa's rap and video become an inversion of the aesthetic hierarchy that renders black women's bodies inadequate and sexually unattractive.[33]

Obviously, the common practice of objectifying all women's bodies complicates the interpretation of Salt 'N' Pepa shaking their collective thangs. For some, their sexual freedom could be considered dangerously close to self-inflicted exploitation. Such interpretations of the racial and sexual significance of black female sexual expression may explain the surprisingly cautious responses I have received from some white feminists regarding the importance of women rappers, particularly in their use of sexually overt gestures and lyrics. However, as Hortense Spillers and other prominent black feminists have argued, a history of silence has surrounded African-American women's sexuality. Spillers argues that this silence has at least two faces; either black women are creatures of male sexual possession, or they are reified into the status of nonbeing.[34] Room for self-defined sexual identity exists in neither alternative. In much of the video work by female rappers, black women's bodies are centered, possessed by women, and are explicitly sexual.

These black female rap videos share a visual and lyrical universe with male rappers' work in which black women are almost always creatures of male sexual possession. Increasingly, black women's asses are being depicted as the primary target for male predatory sexual behavior. Some videos represent an exaggerated mode of real-life visual and verbal tracking and stalking of women's behinds. Most notably, "Pop That Coochie" by 2 Live Crew and "Rump Shaker" by Wrecks-in-Effex, both extremely popular and highly requested videos, are from start to finish, camera pans of black women's scantily clad, gyrating, and, in some frames, visually distorted asses.[35] Another very popular example of this, Sir-Mix-a-Lot's "Baby Got Back," is complicated by the fact that the lyrics narrate both an explicit desire for black women's protruding behinds and at the same time mock the fashion industry for celebrating anorexic-looking white women. Sir-Mix-a-Lot basically announces that they can keep those skinny women from the covers of *Cosmopolitan* and other magazines, because he and most men want a woman with a big round behind, a woman with "back." His voicing of a familiar black male vernacular sentiment that affirms black women's bodies in a cultural environment in which they are aesthetically rejected may bring a sigh of relief to many women, but unfortunately it contributes to an already entrenched understanding of women's bodies as objects of consumption.

At the same time, we cannot escape the reality of black women's complicity in these displays. In a wide variety of videos, photos, and other aspects of creative production and marketing, women who are called "hotties" or more derogatorily "video ho's" or "skeezers" are willing participants in their own exploitation. As Carmen Ashhurst-Watson, president of Rush Communications points out, "we never have any difficulty finding women to appear in the videos."[36] So abundant are these women that one producer told me that he has "hottie files" with the vital statistics of innumerable young women, so that one can be located at the drop of a hat. The motivation for this cooperation is on one level incomprehensible and on another quite familiar. Participation in this video meat market is closely related to the rock/sports/film star groupie phenomenon, in which fans, especially female, get momentary star aura by associating closely or having sex with rich and famous figures. It speaks to a profound desire for attention and praise, and it is understood or misunderstood as a vehicle for one's budding career in show business or a potential form of upward mobility out of economically fragile circumstances.

This culture of sexual exchange is not limited to video production, rap parties, and the post–rap-show hotel lobbies are filled with young women hoping to "get lucky." For some, this sort of upfront exchange in which women do the pursuing can be interpreted as a mode of female empowerment. These women are choosing their sexual partners (more aggressively than most women do in regular situations) and collecting sexual experiences not unlike men do. For women rappers who must engage this environment regularly, this argument may not be so compelling. They are struggling for parity, fighting to be taken seriously in a music industry that has a horrible reputation for tolerating and participating in the abuse, sexual harassment, and sexist containment of women artists and employees. Women rappers who have commented on these dynamics at conferences and in rap lyrics are not calling for the patriarchal protection of women (the familiar flipside of the meat market); instead, they seem to be acknowledging that under these conditions, where male rappers and record executives have virtually all the social and institutional power, women cannot engage in this sort of display and sexual exchange in an empowering way. No matter how you slice it, these "hotties" are understood as expendable, and male desire is the driving force behind sexual encounters.

The resistant facets of black women's participation in rap and their attempts to redefine their own sexual imagery is better understood when we take the historical silence and sexual objectification of black women into consideration. The subject matter and perspectives presented in many women's rap lyrics challenge dominant notions of sexuality, heterosexual courtship, and aesthetic constructions of the body. Their visual presence in music videos and live performances displays exuberant communities of women occupying public space, sexual freedom, independence, and occasionally explicit domination over men. Through their lyrics and video images, such black women rappers as TLC, Queen Latifah, MC Lyte, Yo-Yo, and Salt 'N' Pepa form a dialogue with working-class black women and men, offering young black women a small but potent culturally reflexive public space.

By and large, black women rappers are carving out a female-dominated space in which black women's sexuality is openly expressed. Black women rappers sport distinctively black hairstyles and hip hop clothing and jewelry that ground them in a contemporary working-class black youth aesthetic. They affirm black female working-class cultural signs and experiences that are rarely depicted in American popular culture. Black women rappers resist patterns of sexual objectification at the hands of black men and of cultural invisibility at the hands of dominant American culture.

As I have said, sexual dialogues in rap involve intense power struggles over the meaning, terms, and conditions of male/female relationships. I have also pointed out women rappers' strategies to resist and revise current patriarchal norms. A great deal of these power struggles are waged over sex, sexuality, and control of black female bodies. Women rappers' work clearly takes up these battles by using their sexuality and knowledge to expose men ("Tramps," "Paper Thin") to center female spectators at the expense of male viewers ("Shake Your Thang") and to link women's power to their sexual capacities ("Ladies First"). To the contrary, male sexist narratives often involve devaluing and dominating black female sexuality and sexual behavior. The profound fear and hostility expressed toward women in the works of male rappers is a complex and multicausal phenomenon. Some of this hostility toward women is related to the dominant cultural formula that equates male economic stability and one's capacity to be a family breadwinner with masculinity, thus making black men's increasingly permanent position at the bottom of or completely outside the job market a sign of emasculation, dependence, or femininity. If financial and social clout cannot provide you with masculine virility, then the private social sphere is the next best alternative. At the same time, marriage in American culture is generally less and less an institution that serves as the primary vehicle for sexual interaction, financial security, and a sign of adult independence. Black women, especially under these larger economic and social conditions, are less likely to remain in unfulfilling and abusive relationships for economic reasons. As Robin Kelley has suggested in reference to gangsta rappers, "these transformations have had tremendous impact on the way in which masculinity is constructed by (them) . . . especially in their narratives about sexual relationships. 'Bringing home the bacon' is no longer a measure of manhood; instead, heterosexual conquest free of commitment is prized much more than marriage, which in some cases is even viewed as emasculating."[37]

Another factor contributes to the tenor and abundance of sexism in rap music: the specter of black female sexual power, which partially contextualizes the themes specific to black women rappers' work. In a *Village Voice* interview with ex-NWA member Ice Cube, notorious not only for harsh sexist raps but for brilliant, chilling stories of ghetto life, Greg Tate interrogated Ice Cube about the hostility toward women expressed in rap:

TATE: Do you think rap is hostile toward women?
ICE CUBE: The whole damn world is hostile toward women.
TATE: What do you mean by that?
ICE CUBE: I mean the power of sex is more powerful than the motherfuckers in Saudi Arabia. A girl that you want to get with can make you do damn near anything. If she knows how to do her shit right, she can make you buy cigarettes you never wanted to buy in life. . . . Look at all my boys out here on this

video shoot, all these motherfuckers sitting out here trying to look fly, hot as a motherfucker, ready to go home. But there's too many women here for them to just get up and leave. They out here since eight o'clock in the morning and ain't getting paid. They came for the girls.[38]

Ice Cube's answer may appear to be a non-sequitur, but his remarks address what I believe is a significant subtext in rap's symbolic male domination over women. Ice Cube suggests that many men are hostile toward women, because the fulfillment of male heterosexual desire is significantly checked by women's capacity for sexual rejection or manipulation of men. Ice Cube acknowledges the reckless boundaries of his desire and its consequences as well as the power women can exercise in this sexual struggle. In his rap entitled "The Bomb," Ice Cube warns men to keep an eye on the women with big derrieres, because, it is inferred, the greater your desire, the more likely you are to be blinded by it and, consequently, the more vulnerable you will be to female domination. Obviously, Ice Cube is not addressing the fact that the logic of patriarchy is in many ways contributing to making that desire aggressive, predatory, and consuming. Ice Cube and many black male rappers expose the vulnerability of heterosexual male desire in their exaggerated stories of total domination over women. These evil fantasies speak to the pervasiveness of sexism, yes, but they also speak to the realities of the struggle for power in heterosexual courtship in a sexist society in which women have power that can be and is wielded.

During my interview with MC Lyte, we discussed the indirect power women have in determining the decisions men make. At one point she described a conversation she had with her brother Giz that echoes Ice Cube's point:

Giz told me that the reason men work, everything that man does is for a woman. If he works, it's to get a house, it's a prop house to get women to see it . . . everything a man does is to attract women. . . . So, Giz goes and buys an $800 VCR with a digital picture. I asked him, "what the hell is this, Giz?" he said, "It's a prop for the women." So, he thinks that women are gonna be fascinated by it.

I asked her if she thought women were impressed by this and whether she would be impressed by it. She said:

It wouldn't impress me because I have my own. Some people like to live off other people. I like to have my own. I get no thrill from anybody giving me money. Some girls, you know they say, "ooh, my boyfriend gave me these earrings . . ." I'm like, "what did you get for yourself?"[39]

During the summer of 1990, a popular R&B/Rap crossover group, Bell Biv Divoe (BBD) raced up the charts with "Poison," a song about women whose chorus warns men not to "trust a big butt and a smile." The song cautions men about giving into their sexual weakness and then being taken advantage of by a sexy woman whose motives might be equally insincere. The degree of anxiety expressed is striking; "Poison" explains both their intense desire for and profound distrust of women. The capacity of a woman to use her sexuality to manipulate *his* desire for *her* purposes is an important facet of the sexual politics of male raps about women. BBD are cautioning men, as if to say, "you may not know what a big butt and a smile really means, it might not mean pleasure—it might mean danger—poison." BBD's warning tacitly acknowledges the sustained struggles over female sexuality that their sexist narrative attempts to reconstruct as easily contained skirmishes.

Women rappers effectively engage with male hip hop fans and rappers by acknowledging this aspect of heterosexual politics. By expressing their sexuality openly and in confrontational language, and "shaking their collective thangs"—yet distinguishing themselves from "poisonous, insincere women"—black women rappers signify on heterosexual male desire. Similarly, when TLC say that they like it when men kiss "both sets of lips," they are challenging patriarchal assumptions that interpret open displays of female-controlled sexuality as a threat to male privilege and power.

I am not suggesting that women have so much untapped power that once accessed it will lead the way to the dismantling of patriarchy. Ice Cube, Giz, and BBD's expressions must be understood in the context of their status as men and the inherent social power such a gender assignment affords. But the struggle over control of black female sexuality in heterosexual courtship relations particularly must also be understood as an ongoing and never fully achieved goal. We must not take these social narratives, however vicious, as fixed realities; to do so would be to erase black female agency and give even greater power to sexist narratives that have been invented precisely for that purpose. Without the capacity of women to revise, to control the exchange, to refuse, efforts to dominate women sexually and physically would be unnecessary.

Anxiety over sexual manipulation is also present in women's raps that often display fears of loss of control and betrayal at the hands of men. What is especially interesting about these women's raps is the way in which they shift the terms of the debate. Male rappers justify their promiscuous and selfish behavior by focusing on sexually promiscuous women who "want their money" (sometimes called "skeezers") and rarely offering a depiction of a sincere woman. Black women rappers do not deny their sexual experiences by pretending to be virginal counterparts to these "skeezers." Female rappers distinguish themselves as seasoned women with sexual confidence and financial independence who are tired of dishonest men who themselves seek sex from women (much like the women who seek money from men); a move that draws attention away from the behavior of these objectified so-called skeezers and toward the men who depend on them for establishing their much-needed sexual prowess.

Among a recent group of especially aggressive women rappers who have been dubbed "gangsta women," or "gangsta bitches," the presumption of betrayal and abuse at the hands of men has taken an aggressive and violent fantasy form similar to that of men's gangsta raps. In "Recipe of a Hoe" Boss, a female gangsta duo from Detroit who "take great pride in knocking niggas off," has pulled the trump card on gangsta posturing about sexual prowess. Boss not only derides truly promiscuous men for being used up and having too many miles on them to be worth anything but also reminds them that most of them are posturing wanna-be-pimps who can't get any women to go to bed with them at all. She ends the rhyme by saying that men are basically weak because of their slavishness to the "pussy." Lyrically, she seems to be trying to suggest that hoes are hoes regardless of gender, but in what may have been a tactical error, the chorus chant (which is about letting a hoe be a hoe) is sung by a group of men. This has the unfortunate effect of giving power and voice to the male and sexist labeling of women's sexual behavior as deviant, a move that in my estimation undermines her lyrical revisions of male sexual behavior.

These revenge fantasies against black men are as socially relevant as black men's revenge fantasies against the police. As dream hampton writes, "young Black women die at the hands of Black men who may or may not have claimed to love them, more often than they die at the hands of white men, police or otherwise." The track that follows "Recipe," entitled "a blind date with boss," is a vignette in which Boss has an upfront exchange with a man who has approached her about having sex at a party. After confirming that he wants "to fuck her," she then steps into the bathroom. He thinks she is going to return dressed in something more "comfortable," so he asks his homeboy for a condom all the while describing how hard he's gonna "fuck" her. When she re-enters the room, she cocks a pistol screaming among a string of epithets "give me your fuckin' money," they have a loud confused exchange not unlike that of a police raid and then she shoots them four times. All falls silent; a moment later she calls him a bastard.[40]

Surely, some of these musical narratives are far more confrontational than everyday exchanges between all young men and women. Nonetheless, they do speak to a profound distrust and anxiety over the vulnerability associated with sexual intimacy that does inform everyday life. During my interview with Salt, I pressed her about how she could envision a committed heterosexual relationship without some degree of emotional dependence on a man, she replied:

I just want to depend on myself. I feel like a relationship shouldn't be emotional dependence. I, myself, am more comfortable when I do not depend on hugs and kisses from somebody that I possibly won't get. If I don't get them then I'll be disappointed. So if I get them, I'll appreciate them.[41]

Salt's lyrics reflect much of how she feels personally: she does not want men for their money, she's independent, makes her own money, and doesn't expect men to tell her how to spend it; she reminds them how little she needs them and how much they need her.[42] In refusing to have any "expectations," she illustrates a deep mistrust of men and the possibility for a relationship in which expectations can be maintained. Drawing on personal experiences and her understanding of black women's desire for autonomy and intimacy, Salt's lyrics and comments articulate the complexity of heterosexual female autonomy and sexual desire in contemporary American culture. The battle lines have been drawn, and women seem less and less interested in doing most of the characteristically female emotional work that it would take to pry men's and women's hands from each other's throats. Perhaps Disposable Heroes of Hiphoprisy's rare moment of male sexual honesty in hip hop speaks to the possibility of a collective understanding of how important sexual political development is to black political and cultural struggle. In Hiphoprisy's "Music and Politics," rapper Michael Franti acknowledges how crucial personal sexual awareness and transformation are to cultural and political revolution:

If ever I would stop thinking about music and politics . . .
I would tell you that sometimes I use sex to avoid communication
It's the best escape when we're down on our luck
But I can express more emotions than laughter, anger and let's fuck . . .
I would tell you that the personal revolution is far more difficult
and is the first step in any revolution.[43]

When and Where I Enter: White Feminism and Black Women Rappers

In the epigraph cited at the beginning of the chapter, Harmony conjures the title of Paula Gidding's book *When and Where I Enter: The Impact of Black Women on Race and Sex in America* as a way of centralizing her voice in the history of black women's struggles.[44] Given the identities these women rappers have fashioned for themselves, one might expect them to feel comfortable understanding themselves as feminists. However, as I mentioned earlier, critical and journalistic writing on black women rappers implicitly and explicitly constructs them as feminist voices in rap. However, during my conversations with Salt, MC Lyte, and Queen Latifah it became clear that these women were uncomfortable with being labeled feminist and perceived feminism as a signifier for a movement that related specifically to white women. They also thought feminism involved adopting an antimale position, and although they clearly express frustrations with men, they did not want to be considered or want their work to be interpreted as anti-black male.

In MC Lyte's case, she remarked that she was often labeled a feminist even though she did not think of herself as one. Yet, after she asked for my working definition of feminist, she wholeheartedly agreed with my description, which was as follows:

I would say that a feminist believed that there was sexism in society, wanted to change and worked toward change. Either wrote, spoke, or behaved in a way that was pro-woman, in that she supported situations (organizations) that were trying to better the lives of women. A feminist feels that women are more disadvantaged than men in many situations and would want to stop that kind of inequality.

MC Lyte responded, "Under your definition, I would say I am." We talked further about what she imagined a feminist to be, and it became clear that once feminism was understood as a mode of analysis rather than as a label for a group of women associated with a particular social movement, MC Lyte was much more comfortable discussing the importance of black women's independence: "Yes, I am very independent, and I feel that women should be independent, but so should men. Both of us need each other and we're just coming to a realization that we do."[45] In her answer, Lyte constructs women's independence and male and female codependence as compatible forces. She also separates independence from the need for companionship. So, her resistance to feminism is not resistance to women's independence, it is a response to the history of white feminist movements, particularly in their self-serving blind spots regarding the significance of race and a response to the history of the backlash against such movements.

Part of the backlash against feminists is the result of antifeminist attacks from right-wing organizations and mainstream media depictions of pro-women activists as bitter man-hating women.[46] These facile and repetitive depictions have been especially compelling for communities of women who have little direct or local connection to feminist movements. Such attacks have contributed to making feminism a "dirty word" for women of a variety of ethnic, racial, and economic classes. If high-profile feminist organizations had a consistent and prominent grassroots commitment to young poor women of color at the local level, then these women would be far more suspicious of these backlash depictions of feminists. Yet, not all of their skepticism is the product of this social gap; the specificity of black women rappers' rejection of feminism is also directly linked to their status as *black* women, which places them in a contradictory position vis-à-vis black men in a racist society.

Queen Latifah was sympathetic to the issues associated with feminism but preferred to be considered pro-woman. She was unable to articulate why she was uncomfortable with the term feminist and preferred instead to talk about her admiration for Faye Wattleton, the black former president of Planned Parenthood and the need to support the pro-choice movement. "Faye Wattleton, I like her, I look up to her. I'm pro-choice, but I love god. But I think (abortion) is a woman's decision. In a world like we live in today you can't use (god) as an excuse all the time. They want to make abortion illegal, but they don't want to educate you in school."[47] Salt was the least resistant to the term feminism, yet, she made explicit her limits: "I guess you could say that [I'm a feminist] in a way. Not in a strong sense where I'd want to go to war or anything like that. [laughter] . . . But I preach a lot about women depending on men for everything, for their mental stability, for their financial status, for their happiness. Women have brains, and I hate to see them walking in the shadow of a man."[48]

For these women rappers, and many other black women, feminism is the label for members of a white women's social movement that has no concrete link to black women or the black community. Feminism signifies allegiance to historically specific movements whose histories have long been the source of frustration for women of color. Similar criticisms of women's social movements have been made vociferously by many black feminists.[49] As they have argued, race and gender are inextricably linked for black women. This is the case for both black and white women. However, in the case of black women, the realities of racism link black women to black men in a way that challenges cross-racial sisterhood. Sisterhood among and between black and white women will not be achieved at the expense of black women's racial identity.

Gender-based alliances across race, especially in a racist society, is a problematic move for black women. This may in part explain black women rappers' hesitancy in being labeled feminists. This tension also contributes to the silence with which black women rappers responded to the 2 Live Crew controversy in the mainstream press. In "safe" environments, such as black conferences and black media outlets, women rappers and other women who are involved with hip hop expressed a great deal of frustration over the way they were being treated by the press and the way they are being represented in some rap lyrics. Yet, they are also aware that sexism against black women is being used to attack black men, rather than reconstruct power relationships between black men and women; consequently, they remain wary of "feminism" and seem anxious to separate their criticisms of black male sexism from white feminist complaints. A special program called "If You're Dissin' the Sisters You're Not Fightin' the Power" on WBAI, a black diasporic and Third World–focused radio station in New York, featured an interview with Brigette Moore, a representative of the now-defunct Hip Hop Women's Progressive Movement (HWPM). In it, Moore made clear both her fears of being labeled and her frustration over black women's oppression:

One thing we stressed in our initial press release was that we do not consider ourselves feminists because of the stigma and the negative attitude and vibe that you get from the word *feminist* and we didn't want to alienate any women. We didn't want them to think that we were these angry volatile women. . . . Yes, we are angry, we're tired of being stepped on. There are problems that we don't want to deal with anymore. . . . One important book I read was Angela Davis's *Women, Culture and Politics*. She says that you cannot forget that we (black women) have a strong feminist movement, but that it is not part of the racist (feminist) movement that we grew up with and is all we knew about.[50]

Moore struggles to balance a frustrated acknowledgment of abuses of black women with a practical strategy that channels black women's anger without being subjected to the stigma of being labeled feminists. In part because of this minefield, women's organizations in hip hop find it difficult to sustain momentum. Not only do black women in hip hop have to worry about looking as if they are too sympathetic to white feminists, they also have to make sure that they don't look like they are jumping on the anti-black male band wagon and at the same time craft a black women's agenda. Not surprisingly, such groups as Yo Yo's Intelligent Black Women's Coalition (IBWC) that had an initial high profile seem to have sustained a limited national voice.

In the wake of the brutal public beating of Dee Barnes, female rapper and host of rap video show *Pump It Up*, at the hands of Dr. Dre from NWA, I brought together a group of black women writers, rappers, and black feminists to sit down and talk about possible responses to Dre's acknowledged act of violence against a young woman in the hip hop community. All of us who formed the group Sisters Speak were shocked by the incident, its logic, and most of all by Dr. Dre's response. Angered by an interview on *Pump It Up* that featured estranged ex-NWA member Ice Cube that was interspersed with mocking references to them, Dr. Dre later assaulted her in a crowded Los Angeles dance club, threw her up against the wall repeatedly, and tried to throw her down the stairs. With his own bodyguards (who appeared to be armed) keeping the crowd at bay, Dr. Dre kicked her in the ribs. She slipped free and ran to the women's bathroom, where he followed her in and "grabbed her from behind by the hair and proceeded to punch her in the back of the head" before running out of the club with his crew. In a videotaped interview aired on MTV, NWA members Ren and Eazy agreed that "the bitch deserved it." Dre's explanation demonstrates a frighteningly misdirected response to powerlessness, and naturalization of violence against women: "People talk all this shit, but you know, somebody fucks with me, I'm gonna fuck them. I just did it, you know. Ain't nothing you can do now by talking about it. Besides, it ain't no big thing—I just threw her through a door."[51] He held Dee "responsible" for a Fox television producer's decision to edit the materials in a way that mocked NWA, because it was clear that, although beating up a young black woman might give him a bad reputation, beating up a white man in the entertainment business might spell disaster for his career. His bad reputation has been buttressed by Barnes's multimillion-dollar civil and criminal suits, both of which are still pending. Not surprisingly, Dee isn't his only victim. Dre also has a reputation for beating up former girlfriends and other young men around him.

Sister Speak was both a support group for Dee Barnes and an attempt to bring together a cross-generational group of black women who understood themselves as either inside the hip hop community or sympathetic to it, to air our concerns about the way black women are treated and imagined in hip hop, and to discuss possible strategies for action. One favored, but unrealized, response was to put pressure on prominent male rappers such as Chuck D to speak out explicitly against this attack, especially as it was claimed that he and others condemned Dre's acts in private conversations. However, we never made enough contacts to pull this off, and no publicized statements on behalf of Dee were made by any prominent male figures. In hip hop, where loud and sustained responses reign, the silence following abuses of black women is deafening. It was difficult to keep Sisters Speak together. We, too, suffered from trying to straddle the fence that seems to separate black and female agendas and struggled to develop a media strategy that would deflect attempts to cast us as anti–hip hop and anti-male. This, coupled

For The Brothers That Ain't Here by Ninety-Nine

TIMMY TIBBLE CAN BARELY LIFT

　　　　　　　　　　　　LEGS OUT OF CRIB

POSSESSED BY　　　**ICE CUBE**

　　　　　　　　　　FROM THE FREEZER TRAY

HYPNOTIC VOICES LEAD
HYPNOTIC FLOCKS
TO THE LIQUOR STORE
WITH ALL EYES FIXED ON
THE　　　　　　　　CROOKED LETTER
　　　　CROOKED LETTER
　　　　　　　　I.

BARELY WEIGHING 2LBS
NOW DRINKING FORTY
OUNCES

AS HE POUNCES PISSY SIMILAC WITH CREAMY HEAD
TO A HIGH CHAIR
FINGERS FUMBLE WITH CAP NEEDING A FIX WITH FLAIR
LIMITING STATEWIDE CAPITAL OUT OF RANGE
PULLED FROM THE DEPTHS OF LINT FILLED LEVI'S

BUSINESS OF THE DAY RAPPERS SCHOOLIN TODDLERS
ON SUBSTANCE ABUSE
OF TOXIC JUICE JUST TO SPRUCE UP **DEMOGRAPHIC SALES:**

NIGGER TESTED: RAP INDUSTRY APPROVED

PITCH SOUNDED SMOOTH ON VINYL GROOVES
TO A NEEDLE
THE BOOM
　　　THE BOOM
　　　　　THE BOOM　　THE BIP!

TAKIN SWIGS FROM THE TIP AND SOME ARE READY TO RIP
INTO RIPE CUNTS OF NEWBORN STUNTS
BORN FROM THE BOTTLE AND BROUGHT UP ON THE

BLUNT...YO! So LIGHT ANOTHER L

NO LONGER THE AGE OF CLYDESDALE SOUPY SALES
SELLIN PALES OF PISSY ALE

GRIOTS ONCE SHOUTED TALES FROM BOT OMLESS BOATS
BY THE ORIGINAL COLT 45 NEW GHETTO CRIMINAL

　　　　SEE ME AND BILLY D FREED THE WEED FROM THE PLASTIC
　　　　DIDN'T QUIBBLE OVER WHO EXTERMINATED LAST ROACH
　　　　AS DRUG TRAMPLES BLINDLY DOWN MY THROAT

NINTEY-3 REVOLUTION
COMMERCIAL PROSTITUTION
NEEDS TO BE BANNED

　　　　　　　　　　　AS PSEUDO ROLE MODELS CHANT

　　　　　　A DICK AND MY GAT A FORTY
　　　　　　I CAN TAP A BITCH BY MY SIDE
　　　　　　AND A BLUNT FOR THE RIDE

　　　　　　　　　　　　　　CAUSE IM COOL LIKE THAT
　　　　　　　　　　　　　　SOLD OUT LIKE THAT
　　　　　　　　　　　　　　PLAYED LIKE THAT
　　　　　　　　　　　　　　LOST.

with the fact that we had our own demanding career responsibilities and no institutional support, further encouraged our demise.

In "Demarginalizing the Intersection of Race and Sex," Kimberle Crenshaw echoes Moore's sentiments and the experiences of Sisters Speak in a more theoretical voice when she argues that the single-axis framework that dominates feminist theory (as well as antidiscrimination law and politics) constructs race and gender as mutually exclusive categories of experience and analysis that leave black women between a rock and a hard place. The paralyzing effects of these seemingly separate categories of race and gender have their basis in both the history of black liberation and feminist movements. In reference to feminist theory, Crenshaw points out that:

> the value of (white) feminist theory to Black women is diminished because it evolves from a white racial context that is seldom acknowledged. Not only are women of color in fact overlooked, but their exclusion is reinforced when *white* women speak for us as *women*. The authoritative universal voice—usually white male subjectivity masquerading as non-racial, non-gendered objectivity—is merely transferred to those who, but for gender, share many of the same cultural, economic and social characteristics. . . . Feminists thus ignore how their own race functions to mitigate some aspects of sexism and moreover, how it often privileges them over and contributes to the domination of other women.[52]

Thus, for black women, feminism often reads white feminism and consequently represents a movement that has contributed to sustaining their oppression while claiming to speak on their behalf. It is in part this tension that complicates a reading of black women rappers as feminist voices that can be situated in opposition to male rappers'. For these women rappers, feminism is a movement that does not speak to men; on the other hand, they are engaged in constant communication with black male audience members and rappers and simultaneously support and offer advice to their young black female audiences. Consequently, white feminist theorists must not be satisfied with simply "letting the other speak" but should begin a systematic reevaluation of how feminism is conceptualized and how ethnicity, class, and race seriously fracture gender as a single-axis category. Until this kind of analysis takes place a great deal more often than it does, many black women will be unable to rely on feminist analysis, and what white feminists say to MC Lyte will remain paper thin.

The scope of critical, feminist work on black women's cultural production should be broadened to include popular production, especially popular music. Popular cultural production often attends to the day-to-day conflicts and pressures faced by young black women. Black women rappers attract large male followings and consistently perform their explicitly pro-women material in co-ed settings. They are able to sustain dialogue with and consequently encourage dialogue between young black men and women. Their material supports black women and challenges some sexist male behavior. As MC Lyte explains, "When I do a show, the women are like, 'Go ahead Lyte, tell em!' and the guys are like, 'Oh, shit. She's right.' And they sit there laughing because I pulled their card."[53] It would be naive to expect that such instances will lead directly to a widespread black feminist male-female alliances; on the other hand, it would be cynical and misdirected to presume that the dialogues facilitated by these female rappers will not contribute to its groundwork.

The presence of black female rappers and the urban, working-class black hairstyles, clothes, expressions, and subject matter of their rhymes provide young black women with a small culturally reflective public space. Black women rappers affirm black female popular pleasure and public presence by privileging black female subjectivity and black female experiences in the public sphere. Public performance also provides a means by which young black women can occupy public space in ways that affirm the centrality of their voices. As Salt observes, "The women look up to us, they take us dead seriously. It's not a fan type of thing, it's more like a movement. When we shout 'The year 1989 is for the ladies' they go crazy. It's the highlight of the show. It makes you realize that you have a voice as far as women go."[54]

Black women rappers have effectively changed the interpretive framework for the work of male rappers and have contested public sphere discourses, particularly those pertaining to race and gender. As women who challenge sexism expressed by male rappers, yet sustain dialogue with them, who reject the racially coded aesthetic hierarchies in American popular culture by privileging black female bodies, and who support black women's voices and history, black female rappers constitute an important and resistive voice in rap and contemporary black women's cultural production in general.

Epilogue

✦

In 1994, fifteen years after its commercial debut and seventeen years or so after its emergence in the South Bronx, rap remains at the forefront of cultural and political skirmishes and retains its close ties to the poorest and least represented members of the black community. After the Los Angeles riots erupted in response to the acquittal of the Los Angeles police officers who savagely beat Rodney King, Ice Cube was immediately called to comment but declined, because he was frantically trying to contact relatives whom he had not heard from since the riots began. Other rappers issued well-publicized statements and, *Nightline*'s May 5th coverage of the riots concluded with South Central rappers' comments. It was as if the rage that had exploded in South Central had finally validated rappers' nagging, seemingly exaggerated stories of race and class frustration. Overnight, such rappers as Chuck D and Ice Cube, who were once considered social menaces, became prophets and seeing eye dogs for a nation that had just realized it had gone blind. A few days later, black nationalist activist and rapper Sister Souljah was publicly criticized by Democratic presidential candidate Bill Clinton for her ambiguous, aggressive comments regarding the "logic" behind attacks on whites in Los Angeles; black leaders, save Jesse Jackson, said nothing. Finally, in the wake of South Central's rubble, Ice-T's fantasy heavy metal song "Cop Killer" (which had been released several weeks before the riots) provoked 60 congressmen to sign a letter of protest pronouncing the song "vile and despicable." George Bush chimed in, calling Ice-T's work "sick." Since then, Warner Records has recalled the original album, the song has been totally removed from the new pressings of the album, and Ice-T has been released from his recording contract. Calvin Butts, black minister of the Abyssynian Baptist Church in Harlem, has gone on a mission to rid the black community of rap music because of its harmful effects on today's youths. His was not a call for open social criticism of some of rap's lyrics; it was a call for censorship. His book-burning–style cassette-crushing publicity stunt was a disgraceful display of just how misguided black moral or political leadership is, and it certainly did more toward severing the fragile links between today's black working-class youths and black middle-class religious and political leadership and less toward discouraging consumption of "morally degraded" music.

Via commercial industries, new technologies and mass media outlets, rappers attempt to rewrite, rearticulate and revise popular, national, and local narratives. Rappers negotiate these narratives from a peculiarly contradictory position of social vulnerability and cultural clout. By this, I mean that, although rappers are some of the most prominent social critics in contemporary popular culture, they remain some of the most institutionally policed and stigmatized. Long after their emergence as prominent social critics, several male rappers continue to be stopped, searched, and questioned as if they were still just "regular young black urban men." Well-known female rappers continue to find themselves sexually degraded and marginalized by powerful and not so powerful members of the music industry.

Rap music is a social form that voices many of the class-, gender-, and race-related forms of cultural and political alienation, and it voices this alienation in the commercial spotlight. Each year rappers sell more records, develop new sonic and narrative hybrids, draw the attention of more listeners, and each year rappers are subjected to new forms of containment, ranging from sampling laws and limited insurance coverage to police targeting and direct congressional sanctions.

Black music has always been a primary means of cultural expression for African Americans, particularly during especially difficult social periods and transitions. In this way, rap is no exception; it articulates many of the facets of life in urban America for African Americans situated at the bottom of a highly technological capitalist society. Rap often takes on a deeply political character because of rappers' social, racial, and gender locations. Because, as Cornel West has said, they "face a reality that the black underclass *cannot not know*: the brutal side of American capitalism, the brutal side of American racism, the brutal side of sexism against black women."[1] As more and more of the disenfranchised and alienated find themselves facing conditions of accelerating deterioration, rap's urgent, edgy, and yet life-affirming resonances will become a more important and more contested social force in the world.

Rap is also a contemporary amalgam of key stylistic elements in several earlier black musics that were situated at other major points of social transition. It combines the improvisational elements of jazz with the narrative sense of place in the blues; it has the oratory power of the black preacher and the emotional vulnerability of Southern soul music. And yet, rap also speaks to the future of black culture in the postindustrial city and American culture in general. Its musical voice is achieved via the constant manipulation of high-tech equipment that will continue to have a profound effect on speech, writing, music, communication, and social relations as we approach the twenty-first century.

As Greg Tate has warned, "hip hop might be bought and sold like gold, but the miners of its rich ore still represent a sleeping-giant constituency."[2] Rappers and their young black constituency are the miners, they are the cultivators of communal artifacts, refining and developing the framework of alternative identities that draw on Afrodiasporic approaches to sound organization, rhythm, pleasure, style, and community. These cultivation processes are formally wedded to digital reproduction and life in an increasingly information-management–driven society. Rap is a technologically sophisticated project in African-American recuperation and revision. African-American music and culture, inextricably tied to concrete historical and technological developments, have found yet another way to unnerve and simultaneously revitalize American culture.

Notes

◆

1. Voices from the Margins (pp. 5–20)

1. See Kathy J. Ogren, *The Jazz Revolution: Twenties America and the Meaning of Jazz* (New York: Oxford University Press, 1989); Lewis A. Erenberg, *Steppin' Out: New York Night Life and the Transformation of American Culture, 1890–1930* (Chicago: University of Chicago Press, 1981); Nelson George, *The Death of Rhythm and Blues* (New York: Pantheon, 1988); Leroi Jones, *Blues People: The Negro Experience in White America and the Music That Developed from It* (New York: Morrow Quill, 1963), for discussions on the politics of black music in the United States.

2. Jones, *Blues People*, p. 181.

3. Russell Sanjek and David Sanjek, *American Popular Music Business in the 20th Century* (New York: Oxford University Press, 1991).

4. Reebee Garofalo, "Crossing Over: 1939–1989," in Janette L. Dates and William Barlow, eds., *Split Image: African Americans in the Mass Media* (Washington, D.C.: Howard University Press, 1990), pp. 57–121.

5. At the last three annual New Music Seminars in New York, panels were devoted to the issue of bootleg record sales and their effect on rap music sales.

6. Although some evidence suggests that more adults are buying rap music, rap is still predominantly consumed by teenagers and young adults. See Janine McAdams and Deborah Russell, "Rap Breaking Through to Adult Market," *Hollywood Reporter*, 19 September 1991, pp. 4, 20. Chuck D and Ice-T have claimed that white teenagers consume approximately 50 to 70 percent of rap music. Ice-T claims that "more than 50 percent are going to white kids. Black kids buy the records, but the white kids buy the cassette, the CD, the album, the tour jacket, the hats, everything. Black kids might just be buying the bootleg on the street. It's only due to economics." Alan Light, "Ice-T," *Rolling Stone*, 20 August 1992, pp. 31–32, 60. My research has yielded no source for these statistics other than speculation. Furthermore, these rappers may be specifically referring to their fan base; Ice-T and Public Enemy are both known for mixing rock and rap, making it more likely that white consumers would be drawn to their work.

7. Garofalo, "Crossing Over," p. 108. See also Serge Denisoff, *Inside MTV* (New Brunswick, N.J.: Transaction Books, 1987).

8. Jamie Malanowski, "Top Hip Hop," *Rolling Stone*, 13 July 1989, pp. 77–78.

9. Rose interview with Kevin Bray, 18 March 1993. Kevin Bray has directed

many rap videos, some of which are quite well-known and highly regarded, including: "Strobe Light Honey" and "Flavor of the Month" for Black Sheep; "All for One" for Brand Nubian; "Not Yet Free" for The Coup; "The Creator" and "Mecca and the Soul Brothers" for Pete Rock and C.L. Smooth; "I've Got the Power" for Chill Rob G; and "I Got To Have It" for Ed O.G. and the Bulldogs.

10. Of course, rap videos narrate other themes and situate rappers in other settings and locations. Probably, the next most frequent rap music video theme features the objectification of young women's bodies as a sign of male power. Some rap videos are explicit political and social statements, others are comic displacements of rappers from familiar surroundings, and increasingly, rap videos feature abstract props and images that deploy fewer location-specific settings. However, no other concept or location is as recurrent and emotionally significant as the depiction of one's home turf and posse.

11. Rose interview with Bray.

12. George F. Will, "Therapy from a Sickening Film," *Los Angeles Times*, 17 June 1993, p. B7. This article reviews the Hughes brothers' debut film, *Menace To Society*.

13. Rob Tannenbaum, "Sucker MC," *Village Voice*, 4 December 1990, p. 69. See Stephen Holden's "Pop Life" column, *New York Times*, 17 October 1990, p. C17, for published details of the fabricated biography. After the Perkins story and others, Ice's publicist significantly revised the bio, admitting that Vanilla Ice had actually grown up in both Miami and Dallas and deleted all references to Luther Campbell. Although fabricated artist biographies are not uncommon, Vanilla Ice's claims are particularly far from the truth and, as Tannenbaum points out, insulting to poor black communities.

14. John Shecter, "Chocolate Ties," *The Source*, July 1993, p. 18.

15. Special thanks to producer Gina Harrell for her help in explaining this process.

16. Interview with Charles S. Stone III, 15 July 1993. Stone, who has been directing music videos, especially rap music videos, for several years is especially known for his creative use of animation and humor in his video treatments and concepts. Some of his more prominent and well-respected videos include "The Choice is Yours" for Black Sheep (which won MTV's and *The Source's* best rap video awards for 1992); "911 is a Joke" for Public Enemy; "Bonita Applebum" and "I Left My Wallet In El Segundo" for A Tribe Called Quest; "Blackman" for Tashan; "Funny Vibe" for Living Color; and "Sassy" for Neneh Cherry (featuring Guru).

17. Rose interview with Gina Harrell, March 20, 1993. Harrell is an experienced video producer who has worked on dozens of music videos, commercials, and other projects.

18. Ibid.

19. See Tricia Rose interview with Carmen Ashhurst-Watson in Andrew Ross and Tricia Rose, eds., *Microphone Fiends: Youth Music & Youth Culture* (New York: Routledge, 1994).

20. Andrew Ross, *No Respect: Intellectuals and Popular Culture* (New York: Routledge, 1989), p. 71.

21. Cindi Katz and Neil Smith, "L.A. Infitada: Interview with Mike Davis," *Social Text*, no. 33, 19–33, 1993.

2. "All Aboard the Night Train" (pp. 21–60)

1. Grand Master Flash and the Furious Five, "The Message" (Sugar Hill Records, 1982).

2. I have adopted Mollenkopf and Castells use of the term *postindustrial* as a means of characterizing the economic restructuring that has taken place in urban America over the past twenty-five years. By defining the contemporary period in urban economies as postindustrial, Mollenkopf and Castells are not suggesting that manufacturing output has disappeared, nor are they adopting Daniel Bell's formulation that "knowledge has somehow replaced capital as the organizing principle of the economy." Rather, Mollenkopf and Castells claim that their use of postindustrial "captures a crucial aspect of how large cities are being transformed: employment has shifted massively away from manufacturing toward corporate, public, and nonprofit services; occupations have similarly shifted from manual worker to managers, professionals, secretaries, and service workers." John Mollenkopf and Manuel Castells, eds., *Dual City: Restructuring New York* (New York: Russel Sage Foundation, 1991), p. 6. Similarly, these new postindustrial realities entailing the rapid movement of capital, images, and populations across the globe have also been referred to as "post-Fordism" and "flexible accumulation." See David Harvey, *Social Justice and the City* (Oxford: Basil Blackwell, 1988). For an elaboration of Bell's initial use of the term, see Daniel Bell, *The Coming of Post-Industrial Society* (New York: Basic Books, 1973).

3. Houston Baker, *Blues, Ideology, and Afro-American Literature: A Vernacular Theory* (Chicago: University of Chicago Press, 1984), pp. 7, 11, 150. Baker's phrase "crossroads of lack and desire" is used in reference to the blues. I have appropriated it here in the context of hip hop.

4. My arguments regarding Afrodiasporic cultural formations in hip hop are relevant to African-American culture as well as Afrodiasporic cultures in the English- and Spanish-speaking Caribbean, each of which has prominent and significant African-derived cultural elements. Although rap music, particularly early rap, is dominated by English-speaking blacks, graffiti and breakdancing were heavily shaped and practiced by Puerto Ricans, Dominicans, and other Spanish-speaking Caribbean communities that have substantial Afrodiasporic elements. (The emergence of Chicano rappers took place in the late 1980s in Los Angeles.) Consequently, my references to Spanish-speaking Caribbean communities should in no way be considered inconsistent with my larger Afrodiasporic claims, particularly those that dominate future chapters devoted specifically to rap music. Substantial work has illuminated the continued significance of African cultural elements on cultural production in both Spanish- and English-speaking nations in the Caribbean. For examples, see Herbert S. Klein, *African Slavery in Latin America and the Caribbean* (New York: Oxford University Press, 1986); Ivan G. VanSertimer, *They Came before Columbus* (New York: Random House, 1976); and Robert Farris Thompson, *Flash of the Spirit* (New York: Random House, 1983).

5. See Allen J. Matusow, *The Unravelling of America: A History of Liberalism in the 1960s* (New York: Harper & Row, 1984).

6. In hip hop, the train serves both as means of interneighborhood communication and a source of creative inspiration. Big Daddy Kane says that he writes his best lyrics on the subway or train on the way to producer Marly Marl's house. See Barry Michael Cooper, "Raw Like Sushi," *Spin*, March 1988, p. 28. Similarly, Chuck D claims that he loves to drive; that he would be a driver if rap didn't work out. See Robert Cristgau and Greg Tate, "Chuch D All over the Map," *Village Voice Rock n Roll Quarterly*, vol. 4, no. 3, Fall 1991, pp. 12–18.

7. Morphing is a computer-based special effect that allows any image to transmutate into another apparently seamlessly.

8. Baker, *Blues, Ideology*; Hazel V. Carby, " 'It Jus Be's Dat Way Sometime': The Sexual Politics of Women's Blues," *Radical America*, vol. 20, no. 4, 9–22,

1986; George Lipsitz, "Cruising around the Historical Bloc: Postmodernism and Popular Music in East Los Angeles," in *Time Passages: Collective Memory and American Popular Culture* (Minneapolis: University of Minnesota Press, 1990). See also Jones, *Blues People*, for a polemical, yet groundbreaking analysis of the relationship between economic forces and black cultural formations.

9. Andre Craddock Willis, "Rap Music and the Black Musical Tradition: A Critical Assessment," *Radical America*, vol. 23, no. 4, 29–38, 1991. Willis only refers to rap music, he does not situate the music in hip hop culture. For an elaborate mapping of the links between black musical forms, see Portia K. Maultsby, "Africanisms in African-American Music," in Joseph E. Holloway ed., *Africanisms in American Culture* (Bloomington: Indiana University Press, 1990), pp. 185–210.

10. For a similar critique of Willis's romantic look at the blues see, Robin D. G. Kelley, "Kickin' Reality, Kickin' Ballistics: The Cultural Politics of Gangsta Rap in Postindustrial Los Angeles," in Eric Perkins, ed., *Droppin' Science: Critical Essays on Rap Music and Hip Hop Culture* (Philadelphia: Temple University Press, Fall, 1994).

11. See Stuart Hall, "Notes on Deconstructing 'the popular,'" in Raphael Samuel, ed., *People's History and Socialist Theory* (London: Routledge and Kegan Paul, 1981), p. 233.

12. See Lipsitz, *Time Passages*; William Barlow, *Looking up at Down: The Emergence of Blues Culture* (Philadelphia: Temple University Press, 1989); Baker, *Blues, Ideology*.

13. Garofalo, "Crossing Over," pp. 57–121.

14. For an analysis of signifying that explores gender as well as age considerations, see Claudia Mitchell-Kernan, "Signifying," in Alan Dundes, ed., *Mother Wit from the Laughing Barrel: Readings in the Interpretation of Afro-American Folklore* (New York: Garland, 1981), pp. 310–28. See also Henry Louis Gates, Jr., *The Signifying Monkey: A Theory of African-American Literary Criticism* (New York: Oxford University Press, 1988), pp. 80–88, for a treatment that explores the significance of Mitchell-Kernan's work and gently points out the gender limitations of a number of significant works on black oral practices.

15. See John H. Mollenkopf, *The Contested City* (Princeton, N.J.: Princeton University Press, 1983), especially pp. 12–46, for a discussion of larger twentieth-century transformations in U.S. cities throughout the 1970s and into the early 1980s. See also Mollenkopf and Castells, eds., *Dual City*.

16. I am not suggesting that New York is typical of all urban areas, nor that regional differences are insignificant. However, the broad transformations under discussion here have been felt in all major U.S. cities, particularly New York and Los Angeles—hip hop's second major hub city—and critically frame the transitions that, in part, contributed to hip hop's emergence. In the mid-1980s very similar postindustrial changes in job opportunities and social services in the Watts and Compton areas of Los Angeles became the impetus for Los Angeles gangsta rappers. As Robin Kelley notes: "The generation who came of age in the 1980s, under the Reagan and Bush era, were products of devastating structural changes in the urban economy that date back at least to the late 1960s. While the city as a whole experienced unprecedented growth, the communities of Watts and Compton faced increased economic displacement, factory closures, and an unprecedented deepening of poverty. . . . Developers and city and county government helped the process along by infusing massive capital into suburbanization while simultaneously cutting back expenditures for parks, recreation, and affordable housing in inner city communities." Kelley, "Kickin'

Reality, Kickin' Ballistics." See also Mike Davis, *City of Quartz: Excavating the Future of Los Angeles* (London: Verso, 1989).

17. Mollenkopf, *Contested City*, p. 213.

18. Frank Van Riper, "Ford to New York: Drop Dead," *New York Daily News*, 30 October 1975, p. 1.

19. Daniel J. Walkowitz, "New York: A Tale of Two Cities," in Richard M. Bernard, ed., *Snowbelt Cities: Metropolitan Politics in the Northeast and Midwest since WW II* (Bloomington: Indiana University Press, 1990), p. 204. Walkowitz goes on to point out that the "city banks and bondholders never lost a penny, and the banks profited more than they lost, selling bonds before the panic in 1974 and buying back into a deflated market in 1976." See also Eric Lichten, *Class Power and Austerity* (South Hadley, Mass.: Bergin and Garvey Press, 1986); William Tabb, *The Long Default* (New York: Monthly Review Press, 1982).

20. Philip Weitzman, *"Worlds Apart": Housing, Race, Ethnicity and Income in New York City* (New York: Community Service Society of New York, 1989). See also Terry J. Rosenberg, *Poverty in New York City: 1980–1985* (New York: Community Service Society of New York, 1987); Robert Neuwirth, "Housing after Koch," *Village Voice*, 7 November 1989, pp. 22–24.

21. Walkowitz, "New York," pp. 190–91.

22. Mollenkopf and Castells, eds., *Dual City*, p. 9. See also Parts 2 and 3 of the collection, which deal specifically and in greater detail with the forces of transformation, gender, and the new occupational strata.

23. Ben Bagdigian, *The Media Monopoly* (Boston: Beacon Press, 1987). Despite trends toward the centralization of news and media sources and the fact that larger corporate media outfits have proven unable to serve diverse ethnic and racial groups, a recent study on New York's media structure in the 1980s suggests that a wide range of alternative media sources serve New York's ethnic communities. However, the study also shows that black New Yorkers have been less successful in sustaining alternative media channels. See Mitchell Moss and Sarah Ludwig, "The Structure of the Media," in Mollenkopf and Castells, *Dual City*, pp. 245–65.

24. See Tom Forester, *High-Tech Society* (Cambridge, Mass.: MIT Press, 1988), and Herbert Schiller, *Culture, Inc., The Corporate Takeover of Public Expression* (New York: Oxford University Press, 1989).

25. See Mollenkopf, *Contested City*.

26. Similar strategies for urban renewal via slum clearance demolition took place in a number of major metropolises in the late 1960s and 1970s. See Mollenkopf, *Contested City*, especially Chapter 4, which describes similar processes in Boston and San Francisco.

27. Marshall Berman, *All That Is Solid Melts into Air* (New York: Simon & Schuster, 1982), pp. 290–92.

28. Robert D. McFadden, "Power Failure Blacks Out New York; Thousands Trapped in Subways; Looters and Vandals Hit Some Areas," *New York Times*, 14 July 1977, p. A1; Lawrence Van Gelder, "State Troopers Sent into City as Crime Rises," *New York Times*, 14 July 1977, p. A1; Charlayne Hunter-Gault, "When Poverty Is Part of Life, Looting Is Not Condemned," *New York Times*, 15 July 1977, p. A4; Selwyn Raab, "Ravage Continues Far into Day; Gunfire and Bottles Beset Police," *New York Times*, 15 July 1977, p. A1; Editorial, "Social Overload," *New York Times*, 22 July 1977, p. A22.

29. Lee Dembart, "Carter Takes 'Sobering' Trip to South Bronx," *New York Times*, 6 October 1977, p. A1, B18; Richard Severo, "Bronx a Symbol of America's Woes," *New York Times*, 6 October 1977, p. B18; Joseph P. Fried, "The

South Bronx USA: What Carter Saw in New York City Is a Symbol of Complex Social Forces on a Nationwide Scale," *New York Times*, 7 October 1977, p. A22.

30. Michael Ventura, *Shadow Dancing in the USA* (Los Angeles: Tarcher, 1986), p. 186. Other popular films from the late 1970s and early 1980s that followed suit included *1990: The Bronx Warriors* and *Escape from New York*. This construction of the dangerous ghetto is central to Tom Wolfe's 1989 best-seller and the subsequent film *Bonfire of the Vanities*. In it, the South Bronx is constructed as an abandoned lawless territory from the perspective of substantially more privileged white outsiders.

31. Rose interviews with all artists named except Futura, whose printing trade school experience was cited in Steve Hager, *Hip Hop: The Illustrated History of Breakdancing, Rap Music, and Graffiti* (New York: St. Martin's Press, 1984), p. 24.

32. Rose interview with Crazy Legs, 6 November 1991. *Piecing* means drawing a mural or masterpiece.

33. See Gates, *Signifying Monkey*, pp. 55, 87. Gates's suggestion that naming be "drawn upon as a metaphor for black intertextuality" is especially useful in hip hop, where naming and intertextuality are critical strategies for creative production.

34. Dick Hebdige, *Subculture: The Meaning of Style* (London: Routledge, 1979), see, especially pp. 17–19, 84–89.

35. For an interesting discussion of time, the clock, and nationalism in hip hop, see Jeffrey L. Decker, "The State of Rap: Time and Place in Hip Hop Nationalism," *Social Text*, no. 34, 53–84, 1993.

36. *Hoodies* are hooded jackets or shirts, *snooties* are skull caps, and *tims* are short for Timberland brand boots.

37. Cited in Nelson George et al., eds., *Fresh: Hip Hop Don't Stop* (New York: Random House, 1985), p. 111.

38. Although I had isolated some general points of aesthetic continuity between hip hop's forms, I did not identify these three crucial organizing terms. I am grateful to Arthur Jafa, black filmmaker, artist, and cultural critic, who shared and discussed the logic of these defining characteristics with me in conversation. He is not, of course, responsible for any inadequacies in my use of them here.

39. For a brilliant example of these moves among recent hip hop dances, see "Reckin' Shop in Brooklyn," directed by Diane Martel (Epoch Films, 1992). Thanks to A. J. for bringing this documentary film to my attention.

40. Some examples of explicit attention to flow are exhibited in Queen Latifah's *Ladies First*: "Some think that we can't flow, stereotypes they go to go"; Big Daddy Kane's *Raw*: "Intro I start to go, my rhymes will flow so"; in Digital Underground's *Sons of the P (Son's of the Flow)*: "Release your mind and let your instincts flow, release your mind and let the funk flow."

41. Hebdige, *Subculture*, pp. 94–95.

42. Ibid. Published in 1979, *Subculture: The Meaning of Style* concludes at the point of dominant British culture's initial attempts at incorporating punk. The remaining chapters in this project focus on the moments after the first stabs at incorporation and more specifically attend to the various thematic, creative, and discursive responses to these ongoing processes. In this way, the following chapters examine the points of incorporation and responses that come after the initial moment of incorporation to which Hebdige's study is devoted.

43. Martha Cooper and Henry Chalfant, *Subway Art* (New York: Holt, Rinehart & Winston, 1984), p. 14. Other accounts of the early years in New

York graffiti consider Taki one of several early taggers, along with Chew 127, Frank 207, and Julio 204. Taki was the first to receive media notoriety.

44. The expansion of graffiti art was significantly aided by technological advances in permanent markers and spray paint formulas. In both tools, product improvement allowed writers to apply colors more smoothly, with greater precision and technique. Furthermore, technique is not limited to these formal advances; writers used these advances in new ways to make them respond to artistic impulses. For example, according to Cooper and Chalfant, writers customized these new products, fitting "nozzles from household products on spray-cans to vary the width of the spray." See *Subway Art*, pp. 14, 33.

45. Craig Castleman, *Getting Up: Subway Graffiti in New York* (Cambridge, Mass.: MIT Press, 1982), p. 50. Other academic profiles and histories of graffiti include: Nancy Guevara, "Women Writin' Rappin' Breakin'," in Mike Davis et al., eds., *The Year Left 2: An American Socialist Yearbook* (London: Verso, 1987); Atlanta and Alexander, "Wild Style: Graffiti Painting" in Angela McRobbie, ed., *Zoot Suits and Second-Hand Dresses: An Anthology of Fashion and Music* (Boston: Unwin Hyman, 1988), pp. 156–68. Notable film and video histories include *Style Wars*, produced by Tony Silver and Henry Chalfant, directed by Tony Silver (1983), and *Wild Style*, produced and directed by Charlie Ahern.

46. Castleman, *Getting Up*, p. 114.

47. Guevara, "Women Writin'," pp. 161–75. It is important to point out that Castleman's research suggests that there have probably been much larger numbers of female writers than we are aware of, because women writers often used male names as tags. In his work on graffiti writing gangs in the early 1970s, a male writer/gang member claimed that upward of twenty-five women were a part of the writing crews for the Ex-Vandals, and many of them used boys' names for tags. See Castleman, *Getting Up*, pp. 100–101.

48. Guevara refers to the differences between female and male writers as stylistic differences, when in fact I think the differences are better described as gender-based strategies for individualization that are articulated at the level of style but do not deviate from the larger stylistic parameters and approaches to line, motion, and rupture that I have discussed. Furthermore, the same categories of "stylistic" differences (e.g., colors and themes) that Guevara notes between males and females can be identified among male writers.

49. See Nathan Glazer, "On Subway Graffiti in New York," *The Public Interest*, (Winter, 1979, pp. 11–33. In this article, Glazer argues that the significance of the graffiti "problem" was in fact its symbolic power. According to Joe Austin and Craig Castleman, Glazer's "out of control" rhetoric was instrumental in solidifying the image of graffiti writers as the source of New York's civic disorder and tarnished image, effectively displacing the more substantial and complex factors for New York's decline onto an unidentified band of black and Hispanic marauders. This move justified treating graffiti writers as dangerous criminals who threatened social order and contributed to the social tenor that resulted in the fatal beating of graffiti writer Michael Stuart at the hands of the transit police in 1982.

50. Hager, *Hip Hop*, p. 60.

51. For an extended description of TA expenditures and an insightful reading of the institutional discourse that surrounded the war on graffiti, see Joe Austin, "A Symbol That We Have Lost Control: Authority, Public Identity, and Graffiti Writing," unpublished paper in possession of the author at the University of Minnesota, Department of American Studies. See also, Castleman, *Getting Up*, especially Chapters 7, 8, 9. Although Castleman offers substantial

data, he unfortunately does not offer sufficient critique or analysis either of the graffiti itself or of the institutional discourse that surrounds it.

52. Jean Michel Basquiat was one of the only graffiti artists to make a successful transition into the "legitimate art world" and was quite celebrated until his drug-related death in 1985. He has been noted particularly for his ability to play on white gallery owners' stereotypes of him as a wild, animallike talent—using the myth of black bestiality as a means of manipulation. Another artist who was able to remain in the art world, Rammelzee, continues to draw and develop performance art in the United States, Europe, and Japan. Both of these writers also produced rap records.

53. This aspect of the contemporary graffiti scene emerged in discussions following the presentation of his paper, "A Symbol That We Have Lost Control: Authority, Public Identity, and Graffiti Writing," which was delivered at the 1991 American Studies Association meeting.

54. The break is a point in a song or performance where the rhythmic patterns established by the bass, drums, and guitar are isolated from the harmonic and melodic elements and extended. In jazz, the break refers to the soloist's improvised bridge between stanzas.

55. George et al., *Fresh*, p. 79.

56. Electric boogie is a robotic, mimelike dance that began in California and was most popular there and in parts of the South. The Lockers, a Los Angeles–based dance troupe (that evolved from the Soul Train dancers) used many electric boogie moves, in more fluid patterns. *Up-rock* is a very acrobatic, confrontational, and insulting gesture or move that is specifically directed at an opponent.

57. George et al., *Fresh*, p. 90.

58. Ibid., p. 96.

59. Interview with Crazy Legs and Wiggles, 6 November 1991. The fact that fights were and remain common in and around hip hop is important, because it stands in contrast to one of the central media depictions of hip hop as a form that redirected gang-related energies into peaceful creative outlets. In fact, the "celebratory" media discourse regarding hip hop relied on this myth to justify its celebration. Although it is quite possible that breaking, rapping, and graffiti writing absorbed time that might have otherwise been spent fighting or stealing, fighting and stealing remain common.

60. Guevara, "Women Writin," p. 171.

61. Rose interview with Crazy Legs and Wiggles, 6 November 1991.

62. This connection was made in Gray's unpublished paper presented at the 1990 American Studies Association meeting; Marcus Reeves, "Ear to the Street," *The Source*, March 1993, p. 18. For discussions on black dance and movement see Robert Farris Thompson, "Kongo Influences on African-American Artistic Culture," in Holloway, ed., *Africanisms in American Culture*, pp. 148–84, and "Hip Hop 101," *Rolling Stone*, 27 March 1986, pp. 95–100; Elizabeth C. Fine, "Stepping, Saluting, Cracking and Freaking: The Cultural Politics of Afro-American Step Shows," *The Drama Review*, vol. 35, no. 2, 39–59, Summer 1991; and Katrina Hazzard, *Jookin'* (Philadelphia: Temple University Press, 1991).

63. Sally Banes, "Breaking Is Hard to Do," *Village Voice*, 22–28 April 1981, pp. 31–33; Wesley G. Hughes, "Putting the Breaks on Break Dancing?," *Los Angeles Times*, 5 March 1984, Part II, p. 1; "C'mon Gimme a Break," *Newsweek*, 14 May 1984, p. 28; Laura Castaneda, "Annapolis Banishes Breakdancers from City Dock," *Washington Post*, 3 August 1984, p. C13.

64. Cathleen McGuigan et al., "Breaking Out: America Goes Dancing," *Newsweek*, 2 July 1984, pp. 46–52. This cover story is an exploration into the

discovery of breaking among middle-class Americans, particularly the "urban chic" who frequent posh clubs. These clubs may let in breakers for "color" but will not generally permit their black and Latino peers. See advertisements for breakdance workshops, *Village Voice*, 4 December 1984, p. 100.

65. Interview with Crazy Legs and Wiggles, 6 November 1991.

66. See Peter Watrous, "It's Official: Rap Music Is in the Mainstream," *New York Times*, 16 May 1988, p. C11; After expressing frustration over the coverage of "Walk This Way" as a crossover strategy, Run describes his motivation: "I made that record because I used to rap over it when I was twelve. There were lots of hip-hoppers rapping over rock when I was a kid." Ed Kierch, "Beating the Rap," *Rolling Stone*, 4 December 1986, pp. 59–104.

67. Cited in Jon Young, "P.M. Dawn Sample Reality," *Musician*, June 1993, p. 23.

68. According to Hager, the Hurculords were two Shure brand speaker columns aided by a Macintosh amplifier. Hager, *Hip Hop*, p. 33. It is also interesting to note that, even though the equipment and Herc's style were heavily influenced by Jamaican sound systems and dub, Herc claims that he could not get the crowd to respond to Jamaican music. This is one of many interesting points of diasporic hybridity in which the influences move bidirectionally.

69. MTV, *Rapumentary* (1990).

70. Interview with Red Alert, 8 May 1990.

71. Not long after his rise to local fame, Kool Herc was stabbed multiple times during one of his shows. After this incident, he dropped out of the hip hop scene.

72. George et al., *Fresh*, pp. 6–7. I explore the technical and artistic practices in rap music production in Chapter 3.

73. According to Flash and Red Alert, a still crowd seemed to be more prone to fighting and confrontations.

74. Hager, *Hip Hop*, p. 48. *Hustler's Convention* is the 1973 album written and performed by Jalal Uridin, leader of the black militant ex-convicts, The Last Poets. *Hustler's Convention* (and the related blaxsploitation genres of the late 1960s and early 1970s) are clear predecessors to contemporary gangsta rap's thematic and stylistic preference for violence, drugs, sex, and sexism. The critical formal difference is rap's emphasis on danceable beats and its musical complexity.

75. Interview with Kid, from Kid-N-Play, 11 January 1990.

76. Rap's roots in black oral practices are extensive, and research on black oral practices is equally so. Some major texts that explore the history of black oral practices are listed here: Houston Baker, *Long Black Song: Essays in Black American Literature and Culture* (London: University Press of Virginia, 1972, 1990); Gates, *The Signifying Monkey*; Dennis Wepman, Ronald Newman, and Murry Binderman, *The Life The Lore and Folk Poetry of the Black Hustler* (Philadelphia: University of Philadelphia Press, 1976); Dundes, ed., *Mother Wit from the Laughing Barrel*; Daniel Crowley, *African Folklore in the New World* (Austin: University of Texas Press, 1977); Lawrence Levine, *Black Culture and Black Consciousness: Afro-American Folk Thought from Slavery to Freedom* (New York: Oxford University Press, 1977); Roger D. Abrahms, *Deep Down in the Jungle: Negro Narrative Folklore from the Streets of Philadelphia* (Chicago: Aldine, 1970); Geneva Smitherman, *Talkin' and Testifyin': The Language of Black America* (Boston: Houghton Mifflin, 1977).

77. Eric B. & Rakim, "Microphone Fiend," in *Follow the Leader* (Uni Records, 1988). In Chapter 3 I explore the relationship between technology and orality in rap in much greater depth.

78. There is a great deal of controversy regarding the Sugar Hill Gang's sud-

den, albeit short-lived success. According to a number of rappers and DJs from this period, the three members of Sugar Hill Gang were not local performers. One of the members, Hank was a doorman/bouncer at a rap club in New York and had access to bootleg tapes that he played back in northern New Jersey, an area that at this point had no local rap scene. Sylvia Robinson heard one of Hank's tapes and approached him about recording a rap single. According to Hager's *Hip Hop*, Hank borrowed Grandmaster Caz's rhyme book and used his rhymes in "Rapper's Delight." Kool Moe Dee, Red Alert, and others explained to me that when they heard the record, they were shocked. Not only had they never heard of the Sugar Hill Gang, but they could not believe that a rap record (even one that they thought was so elemental) could become commercially successful.

79. Rose interview with Salt, 22 May 1990.

80. "Rapper's Delight" sold over two million copies in the United States, and "The Breaks" sold over 500,000 copies. These record sales were primarily the result of word of mouth and hip hop club play.

81. Shante's single "Roxanne's Revenge" (Pop Art Records, 1984) sold over two million copies.

82. Women rappers are the subject of Chapter 5, in which their contributions and an analysis of rap's sexual politics are explored in greater depth.

83. Watrous, "Rap Music in the Mainstream."

84. The purpose of this chapter is not to give a chronological history of all the developments in hip hop. As stated, I have focused on the context for creativity and hip hop's links to Afrodiasporic styles and practices. For more background on hip hop artists and commercial developments, see Havelock Nelson and Michael A. Gonzales, *Bring the Noise: A Guide to Rap Music and Hip Hop Culture* (New York: Crown, 1991); Joseph D. Eurie and James G. Spady, *Nation Conscious Rap: The Hip Hop Version* (New York: PC International, 1991); David Toop, *Rap Attack 2* (Boston: Consortium Press, 1992); Bill Adler, *Tougher Than Leather: Run DMC* (New York: Penguin, 1987); Bill Adler, *Rap: Portraits and Lyrics of a Generation of Black Rockers* (New York: St. Martin's Press, 1991). For a sobering look at how independent labels (where almost all rappers contracts are negotiated) have been maneuvered into a subcontractor's position in relation to the large music companies, see Frederic Dannen, *Hit Men: Powerbrokers and Fast Money inside the Music Business* (New York: Random House, 1990), especially Chapter 17.

85. For examples, see Gang Starr, *Step in the Arena* (Chrysalis, 1990); Guru, *Jazzamatazz* (Chrysalis, 1993); MTV, *Rap Unplugged* (Spring 1991); Basehead, *Play with Toys* (Image, 1992); Disposable Heroes of Hiphoprisy, *Disposable Heroes of Hiphoprisy* (Island, 1992); P.M. Dawn, *Of the Heart, Of the Soul and Of the Cross* (Island, 1991); and Me Phi Me, *One* (RCA, 1992); Arrested Development, *3 Years, 5 Months and 2 Days in the Life Of* (Chrysalis, 1992).

86. See Duncan Smith, "The Truth of Graffiti," *Art & Text*, no. 17, 84–95, April 1985.

87. For example, Kurtis Blow's "The Breaks" (1980) was both about the seeming inevitability and hardships of unemployment and mounting financial debt and the sheer pleasure of "breaking it up and down," of dancing and breaking free of social and psychological constrictions. Regardless of subject matter, elaborate graffiti tags on train facades always suggested that the power and presence of the image was possible only if the writer had escaped capture.

88. See Bob Mack, "Hip-Hop Map of America," *Spin*, June 1990.

3. Soul Sonic Forces (pp. 62–95)

1. Sister Souljah speaking at "We Remember Malcolm Day" held at Abyssinian Baptist Church in Harlem, New York, 21 February 1991.

2. Cited in Mitch Berman and Susanne Wah Lee, "Sticking Power," *Los Angeles Times Magazine*, 15 September 1991, pp. 23–50.

3. Leopold Sendar Senghor, "Standards critiques de l'art Africain," *African Arts/Arts d'Afrique*, vol. 1, no. 1, (Autumn 1967), excerpted in John Miller Chernoff, *African Rhythm and African Sensibility: Aesthetics and Social Action in African Musical Idioms* (Chicago: University of Chicago Press, 1979), p. 22.

4. Rose interview with female rapper Harmony, 14 June 1991.

5. Gang Starr, "Step in the Arena," *Step In The Arena* (Chysalis, 1990).

6. Jeep beats are rap songs with especially heavy bass and drum sounds that are intended for play in automobiles, preferably with customized stereo systems. Album titles such as *Terminator X & The Valley of the Jeep Beats* (Columbia Records, 1991) and Marley Marl, *In Control: Volume 1*, advertised as an album designed "for your steering pleasure," illustrate the centrality of heavy prominent beats in rap production. The August 1991 issue of *The Source*, a popular magazine that covers hip hop music culture and politics, also featured a Jeep slammers section that reviewed recent releases based in part on their value as jeep beats. Favored albums received comments such as, "fatter beats, thunderous beats, and street feel."

7. Chernoff, *African Rhythm*; Dick Hebdige, *Cut n Mix: Culture, Identity and Caribbean Music* (London: Methuen, 1987); Levine, *Black Culture, Black Consciousness*; Maultsby, "Africanisms"; Eileen Southern, *The Music of Black Americans* (New York: Norton, 1971).

8. Christopher Small, *Music, Society, Education: An Examination of the Function of Music in Western, Eastern and African Cultures with its Impact on Society and Its Use in Education* (New York: Schirmer, 1977), pp. 20–21. See also Christopher Small, *Music of the Common Tongue* (New York: Riverrun Press, 1987).

9. Small, *Music, Society, Education*, pp. 9–10. See also John Storm Roberts, *Black Music of Two Worlds* (New York: William Morrow, 1974).

10. Rap's "human beat box" shares many vocal sounds found in African vocal traditions. Marc Dery describes this link: "The hums, grunts and glottal attacks of Central Africa's pygmies, the tongue clicks, throat gurgles and suction stops of the Bushmen of the Kalahari Desert, and the yodeling, whistling vocal effects of Zimbabwe's m'bira players all survive in the mouth percussion of such "human beat box" rappers as Doug E. Fresh and Darren Robinson of the Fat Boys." Marc Dery, "Rap!," *Keyboard*, November 1988, p. 34.

11. Small, *Music, Society, Education*, pp. 54–55.

12. See also Ben Sidran, *Black Talk* (New York: Holt, Reinhart & Winston, 1971), and Olly Wilson, "Black Music as Art," *Black Music Research Journal*, no. 3, 1–22, 1983.

13. Poor Righteous Teachers, "Rock Dis Funky Joint," *Holy Intellect* (Profile, 1990). See also Ice Cube, "The Bomb," *AmeriKKKa's Most Wanted* (Profile, 1990), and the Fu-schnickens, *Take It Personal* (Jive, 1992). Bear in mind that not all rap music deploys these characteristics equally. In particular, some of the earliest rap recordings used the instrumental side of a disco single verbatim as the sole musical accompaniment. This may, in part, be due to limited musical resources, as disc jockey performances that predate these recordings demonstrate substantial skill and complexity in rhythmic manipulation.

14. A Tribe Called Quest, "Youthful Expression," *People's Instinctive Travels and the Paths of Rhythm* (Jive Records, 1989/1990).

15. James A. Snead, "On Repetition in Black Culture," *Black America Literature Forum*, vol. 15, no. 4, 153, 1981. Special thanks to AJ for this reference.

16. Snead, "Repetition," 146–47. Culture is one of the most complex words in the English language. Culture, as I use it and as Snead uses it, is both a "whole way of life, which is manifest over the whole range of social activities but is most evident in 'specifically cultural' activities—a language, styles of art, kinds of intellectual work; and an emphasis on a 'whole social order' within which a specifiable culture, in styles of art and kinds of intellectual work, is seen as the direct or indirect product of an order primarily constituted by other social activities." From Raymond Williams, *The Sociology of Culture* (New York: Schocken, 1981), pp. 11–12. See also Raymond Williams, *Keywords* (Glasgow: Fontana, 1976).

17. Snead, "Repetition," p. 152, my italics; Susan McClary, *Feminine Endings* (Minneapolis: University of Minnesota Press, 1991), p. 155.

18. Snead also demonstrates that the recovery of repetition in twentieth-century European literature (e.g., Joyce, Faulkner, Woolf, Yeats, and Eliot) suggests that the dominance of nineteenth-century repression of European traditions that favored privileged uses of repetition and verbal rhythm in the telling "in favor of the illusion of narrative verisimilitude" may have "begun to ebb somewhat." Ibid., p. 152. For a range of discussions on form and meaning in black music and culture, see Graham Lock, *Forces in Nature: The Music and Thoughts of Anthony Braxton* (New York: Da Capo Press, 1988); Wole Soyinka, *Myth, Literature and the African World* (New York: Cambridge University Press, 1990); and Gates, *The Signifying Monkey*. Gates affirms Snead's argument regarding the centrality of repetition in black culture: "repetition and revision are fundamental to black artistic forms from painting and sculpture to music to language use," p. xxiv.

19. Snead, "Repetition," p. 150.

20. Susan McClary and Richard Leppert, eds., *Music and Society: The Politics of Composition, Performance and Reception* (New York: Cambridge University Press, 1989), and McClary, *Feminine Endings*; Small, *Common Tongue*, and *Music, Society, Education*; Jacques Attali, *Noise: The Political Economy of Music* (Minneapolis: University of Minnesota Press, 1985).

21. Attali, *Noise*, p. 88.

22. Theodore W. Adorno (with the assistance of George Simpson), "On Popular Music," in Simon Frith and Andrew Goodwin, eds., *On Record: Rock, Pop and the Written Word* (New York: Pantheon, 1990), p. 313. Also see T.W. Adorno, "On the Fetish-Character in Music and the Regression of Listening," in Andrew Arato and Eike Gebhardt, eds., *The Essential Frankfurt School Reader* (New York: Continuum, 1982), pp. 288–89.

23. Frederic Jameson, "Reification and Utopia in Mass Culture," *Social Text*, Winter, 137, 1979.

24. Richard Middleton's *Studying Popular Music* (Philadelphia: Open University Press, 1990) attempts to grapple with the question of repetition in popular music in his chapter on pleasure, value, and ideology in popular music (see esp. pp. 267–93). He finds that "popular common sense tends to see repetition as an aspect of mass production and market exploitation but often also associates it with the phenomenon of being 'sent,' particularly in relation to 'hypnotic' rhythmic repetitions and 'primitive' audience trance. . . . How can we square a psychology of repetition and the historically specific Adornian notion of repetition as a function of social control?" (pp. 286–87). Middleton suggests that multiple determinations are operative at once. To illustrate his point, he compares Freud, Barthes, Deleuze, and Guattari, Jameson, Rosolato, and Lacan on

the question of repetition. The multiple determinations he offers cannot accommodate the kind of black approach to repetition as articulated by Snead and Small. In fact, none of the approaches he offers ground black practices in African traditions. Although he is quite aware of black cultural influences in popular music, in his mind these influences do not reflect an alternative approach to cultural production; they are discrete black practices that are not constructed as part of a larger approach. So, although he agrees that black musics privilege repetition (although not rhythmically complex uses of repetition, but "riffs, call-and-response, short unchanging rhythmic patterns"), it is a technique, not a manifestation of an alternative approach.

25. Stetsasonic, "Talkin' All That Jazz," *In Full Gear* (Tommy Boy, 1988).

26. See Charles Aaron, "Gettin' Paid: Is Sampling Higher Education or Grand Theft Auto?," *Village Voice Rock 'n' Roll Quarterly*, Fall, pp. 22–23, 1989; Jeff Bateman, "Sampling: Sin or Musical Godsend?," *Music Scene*, September/October, pp. 14–15, 1988.

27. Harry Allen, "Invisible Band," *Village Voice*, 18 October 1988, p. 10 (eletromag section).

28. Phone conversation with Tricia Rose, 14 August 1991. There is quite a large underground market for break beat records. These LP records are comprised of several rerecorded break beats compiled from other albums. I am aware of at least twenty-five to thirty volumes of such break beat records.

29. Tricia Rose interview with Bomb Squad producer Eric (Vietnam) Sadler, 4 September 1991.

30. Decades ago, blues musicians jimmied amplifiers and guitars to get desired sounds, and punk musicians have ignored the official limitations of musical equipment to achieve sought-after effects. For other examples, see Kyle Gann, "Sampling: Plundering for Art," *Village Voice*, 1 May 1990, p. 102; Andrew Goodwin, "Sample and Hold: Pop Music in the Age of Digital Production," in Simon Frith and Andrew Goodwin, eds., *On Record: Rock, Pop and the Written Word* (New York: Pantheon, 1990), pp. 258–73.

31. See Hebdige, *Cut n Mix*, especially Chapter 10. Rap music is heavily indebted to Jamaican musical practices. As mentioned in Chapter 2, such early rap DJs in the Bronx as DJ Kool Herc were recent Caribbean immigrants and brought with them black Caribbean sound system practices, including sound system wars between DJs. It is also important to stress Jamaican sound systems' emphasis on bass tones. This cross-fertilization is even more complex than immigration patterns suggest. Hebdige demonstrates that reggae's roots are actually in Post–WW II black American music. He claims that large powerful sound systems became a popular means by which black American R&B music could be played to large numbers of Jamaicans. See *Cut n Mix*, Chapter 7.

32. Mark Dery and Bob Doerschuk, "Drum Some Kill: The Beat behind the Rap," *Keyboard*, November 1988, pp. 34–36.

33. Cited in Ibid., p. 34 (my italics).

34. For a discussion of the transformation of the role of recording engineers and their relationship to musicians, see Edward R. Kealy, "From Craft to Art: The Case of Sound Mixers and Popular Music," in Frith and Goodwin, eds., *On Record*, pp. 207–20.

35. Cited in Dery and Doerchuk, "Drum Some Kill," pp. 34–35 (my italics).

36. Hank Shocklee is a member of the Bomb Squad rap production team, which also includes Keith Shocklee, Carl Ryder (Chuck D), and Eric (Vietnam) Sadler. Also, note that house music, a contemporary dance music similar to disco, has been combined with rap to produce Hip House, a popular dance music with rap lyrics.

37. Cited in Mark Dery, "Hank Shocklee: 'Bomb Squad' Leader Declares War on Music," *Keyboard*, September 1990, pp. 82–83, 96.

38. Shocklee's passion for the cut can be best observed in the work of Public Enemy. See especially "Don't Believe the Hype," "Bring the Noise," "Terminator X to the Edge of Panic," and "Night of the Living Baseheads," *It Takes a Nation of Millions To Hold Us Back* (Def Jam Records, 1988). Similarly, see Eric Sadler and DJ Jinx's work on Ice Cube's "The Bomb," *AmeriKKKa's Most Wanted* (Priority Records, 1990).

39. Rose interview with Eric Sadler. For a transcription and interpretation of "The Titanic," see, Bruce Jackson, *Get Your Ass in the Water and Swim Like Me* (Cambridge, Mass.: Harvard University Press, 1974). For a provocating reading of the cultural and psychological significance of the sinking of *The Titanic* particularly as a symbolic representation of the death of civilized European culture, see Doane's reference to Slavoj Zizek in Mary Anne Doane, "Information, Crisis and Catastrophe," in Patricia Mellencamp, ed., *Logics of Television* (Bloomington: Indiana University Press, 1990), pp. 229–39.

40. Cited in Dery and Doerchuk, "Drum Some Kill," p. 35. Although Stephney suggests that rappers do not use live drummers with desired success, many albums do feature live drummers in the credits.

41. Sampling attorney Micheline Wolkowicz, who investigates and clears rap samples for Berger, Steingut, Tarnoff, and Stern (a firm that counsels and clears samples for Marly Marl, DJ Jazzy Jef and the Fresh Prince, the Beastie Boys, and other artists), states that the vast majority of samples cleared by rap musicians are taken from black music performed and created by black musicians. Interview with Rose, September 1991.

42. A Tribe Called Quest, "Verses from the Abstract," *The Low End Theory* (Jive Records, 1991). The title of this album is an obvious affirmation of the importance of low-frequency sounds. Pete Rock and C.L. Smooth, *Mecca and the Soul Brother* (Elektra, 1992); Guru, *Jazzamatazz* (Chrysalis, 1993). See also Ed O.G. and the Bulldogs, "Be a Father to Your Child," *Life of a Kid in the Ghetto* (Polygram Records, 1991).

43. Cited in Jon Young, "P.M. Dawn Sample Reality," *Musician*, June 1993, p. 23.

44. Cited in Havelock Nelson, "Soul Controller, Sole Survivor," *The Source*, October 1991, p. 38. According to Marley Marl: "'Marley's Scratch' was the first record to use sampled drums, but the innovation really got noticed when it appeared on MC Shan's 'The Bridge' (1986) and Eric B. & Rakim's 'Eric B. Is President' (1986)." Both of these raps were critical successes among hip hop fans and were produced or remixed by Marley Marl.

45. Hebdige, *Cut n Mix*, p. 14.

46. Cited in Aaron, "Gettin Paid," p. 26.

47. Bill Stephney, cited in Dery and Doerchuk, "Drum Some Kill," p. 36.

48. Rose interview with Sadler, 4 September 1991.

49. Cited in Mitch Berman and Susanne Wah Lee, "Sticking Power," *Los Angeles Times Magazine*, 15 September 1991, p. 50.

50. David Samuels, "The Real Face of Rap," *New Republic*, 11 November 1991, pp. 24–29 (my italics); J. D. Considine, "Fear of a Rap Planet," *Musician*, February 1992, p. 35; Jon Parales, "On Rap, Symbolism and Fear," *New York Times*, 2 February 1992, Section 2, pp. 1, 23; letters to the editor, *New York Times*, 16 February 1992. I presume that a lengthy reminder of the power of editorial decision making in legitimating and simultaneously refusing to legitimate ideas and sentiments is not needed.

51. Dery, "Hank Shocklee," p. 82. Little has been published on the sound of and process involved in creating rap music. In attempting to garner respect for rap among traditional musicians, Dery supports his technical description of rap's style with a criticism of the rock establishment for considering rap musicians "musical illiterates."

52. Ibid., p. 83.

53. Cited in Frank Tirro, *Jazz: A History* (New York: Norton, 1977), pp. 306–307; Jason Berry, et al., *Up from the Cradle of Jazz* (Athens: University of Georgia Press, 1986), p. 5; Dery, "Hank Shocklee," p. 83.

54. Except for those discussions that focus on rap's use of technology as a postmodern technique rather than a black practice. For discussions that make this distinction and focus on the former, see Frith and Goodwin, eds., *On Record*; Simon Frith, ed., *Facing the Music* (New York: Pantheon, 1988); Bruce Tucker, "Tell Tchaikovsky the News: Postmodernism, Popular Culture and the Emergence of Rock n Roll," *Black Music Research Journal*, vol. 9, no. 2, 271–94, 1989.

55. Frith and Goodwin, eds., *On Record*, p. 263. It should be mentioned that in this large collection on popular music, there is no discussion of black popular forms, nor is there any consideration of race as a category of analysis in relation to the category popular music. Although the collection is not limited to American popular forms, it focuses a great deal on American and British popular music.

56. Mead Hunter, "Interculturalism and American Music," *Performing Arts Journal*, vols. 33/34, 186–202, 1989.

57. The quote in the heading is from Ice Cube, "Parental Discretion Is Advised," *AmeriKKKa's Most Wanted* (Profile Records, 1990).

58. David Toop, *The Rap Attack: African Jive to New York Hip Hop* (London: South End Press, 1984), p. 19. (my italics). For other analyses regarding rap's use of black oral traditions, see Charles P. Henry, *Culture and African American Politics* (Bloomington: Indiana University Press, 1990); Wheeler Winston Dixon, "Urban Black American Music in the Late 1980s: The Word as Signifier," *Midwest Quarterly*, vol. 30 (Winter), 229–41, 1989; Cheryl L. Keyes, "Verbal Art Performance in Rap Music: The Conversation of the 1980s," *Folklore Forum*, vol. 17 (Fall) 143–52, 1984; and Jon Michael Spencer, ed., *The Emergency of Black and the Emergence of Rap*, Special Issue of *Black Sacred Music*, vol. 5, no. 1 (Spring), 1991.

59. Allen, "Invisible Band," p. 10 (electromag section).

60. Walter Ong, *Orality and Technology: The Technologizing of the Word* (London: Methuen, 1982), p. 42.

61. See Jackson, *Get Your Ass in the Water*, for transcriptions of Signifying Monkey and other Afro-American oral folktales. See also Hebdige, *Cut n Mix*, in which he notes that Caribbean artist Wayne Smith's "Under Mi Sleng Teeng" prompted no fewer than 239 versions of the song.

62. Kool Moe Dee, "How Ya Like Me Now," *How Ya Like Me Now* (Jive Records, 1987).

63. Salt 'N' Pepa, "Get Up Everybody (Get Up)," *Salt with a Deadly Pepa* (Next Plateau Records, 1988).

64. Eric B. & Rakim, "Follow The Leader," *Follow The Leader* (UNI Records, 1988).

65. L. L. Cool J., "I'm Bad," *Bad* (Def Jam Records, 1987).

66. Ong, *Orality*, p. 35.

67. Ibid., p. 42.

68. Rose interview with Sadler, 4 September 1991.

69. Stetsasonic, "Talkin' All That Jazz," *In Full Gear* (Tommy Boy Records, 1988). For an in-depth reading of poetic and narrative complexity in "Talkin All That Jazz," see Richard Shusterman, "The Fine Art of Rap," *New Literary History*, vol. 22, no. 3 (Summer), 613–32, 1991. Not only have records been reprinted, but artists such as Parliament and Chic are touring and drawing crowds too young to have heard their music when it was first released. A recent Parliament concert at the Apollo was heavily attended by young hip hop fans who were familiar with De La Soul's use of their bass lines.

70. Hebdige, *Cut n Mix*, p. 14.

71. Simon Frith, "Picking Up the Pieces," in Simon Frith, ed., *Facing the Music*, pp. 121–22 (my italics).

72. Under the U.S. Copyright Act, authors of copyrighted compositions and copyright holders of sound recordings control usage of their materials. The Act has schedules of royalty rates for use of compositions, but no such schedule for sound recordings. As Charles Aaron explains: "If permission is granted to appropriate a composition or sound recording—to cover a tune or to sample one—the artists doing the appropriating receives a compulsory royalty license under section 115. With a mechanical license for a composition, the rate for a cover version is 5.25 cents per record sold, or one cent per minute, whichever is larger. No rate scale exists for sampling compositions or for sampling sound recordings." Aaron, "Gettin' Paid," p. 23.

73. This recent settlement has accelerated the process of legally defining the terms of sample use. Rapper Biz Markie used an uncleared sample of Gilbert O'Sullivan's "Alone Again Naturally," and a Federal judge in New York ruled that it was a case of copyright infringement rather than an example of fair use for artistic or educational purposes. It is expected that this ruling will have a significant effect on sampling use and clearance. Chuck Phillips, "Songwriter Wins Large Settlement in Rap Suit," *Los Angeles Times*, 1 January 1992, pp. F1, F12. See also Melinda Newman and Chris Morris, "Sampling Safeguards Follow Suit," *Billboard*, 23 May 1992, pp. 1, 80; and Robert G. Sugarman and Joseph P. Salvo, "Sampling Case Makes Music Labels Sweat," *National Law Journal*, 15 March 1991, vol. 14, no. 28, 34.

74. In my interview with Micheline Wolkowitz, she pointed out the increasing complexity of sampling uses and fee determination. When a rap artist gives away a percentage of his or her royalty fee for the usage of a sample, that percentage must be multiplied by their royalty rate and prorated by the ten-song standard contract limit. This is in the case of *one* sample usage. Increasing legal fees for production, limited access to actual sales figures for the artists, and the introduction of a myriad of publishing companies and sampled artists add a great deal of confusion to an already complex, heavily commodified, and legally managed process. Interview with Rose, September 1991.

75. "Rock Beat," *Village Voice*, 6 July 1993, p. 75.

76. Aaron, "Gettin' Paid," p. 23.

77. Successful attempts include NWA *Niggaz4life* (Priority, 1991) and Tim Dog's "Fuck Compton," *Penicillin on Wax* (Ruffhouse, 1991).

78. Eric B. & Rakim, "Paid in Full," *Paid in Full* (Island Records, 1986). "Dead Presidents" refer to U.S. currency that feature dead presidents. I wouldn't be surprised if righteous secret service types assumed it meant assassinating presidents, given that some progressive activists frequently misinterpreted "homie" as an anti-gay epithet rather than an affectionate term for a friend from the "hood."

79. The music video for "Paid in Full" supports this interpretation of what

happened to "peace" rather than "piece" by showing a peace sign during that lyrical passage.

80. See *Spin* (October 1988) for a hip hop slang dictionary.

4. Prophets of Rage (pp. 99–144)

1. Public Enemy, "Prophets of Rage," *It Takes a Nation of Millions to Hold Us Back* (Def Jam Records, 1988).

2. James C. Scott, *Domination and the Arts of Resistance: Hidden Transcripts* (New Haven: Yale University Press, 1990).

3. Ibid., p. xiii.

4. Ibid., p. 5. Although Scott's study is based on observations about power relationships and discourse in peasant societies, he has used his research to examine "more systematically what it can teach us about power, hegemony, resistance and subordination" in general. His observations about discursive and ideological exercises of power have important bearing on my work here. See also Joan W. Scott, *Gender and the Politics of History* (New York: Columbia University Press, 1988).

5. In *Subculture*, Hebdige uses the term incorporation to describe the ways in which punk identities and meanings were manipulated and absorbed by dominant institutions, particularly the media.

6. Antonio Gramsci, *Selections from the Prison Notebooks* (New York: International Universities Publishers, 1971), pp. 229–35, 238–39.

7. George Lipsitz, "The Struggle for Hegemony," *Journal of American History*, vol. 75, no. 1, 147, 1988.

8. Gramsci, *Selections*, pp. 229–35, 238–39.

9. Paris, "The Devil Made Me Do It," *The Devil Made Me Do It* (Tommy Boy Records, 1989/1990).

10. Paris, "The Devil Made Me Do It."

11. Paris is the first and possibly the only rapper to perform in a socialist country. In December 1990, Paris performed in the Karl Marx auditorium in Havana, Cuba. The arena was sold-out and the crowd response to his English-language performance was overwhelming. Black Liberation Army exile Joanne Chessamard (Assata Shakuur) sat on the stage as he performed. During a break in his performance, Paris read a prepared speech that was translated into Spanish simultaneously. In his speech, he called for Third World unity and the need to contain capitalism. He saluted Fidel and criticized the Bush administration on its treatment of minorities, Third World nations, and the brewing confrontation with Iraq (Gulf War).

12. See Paul Willis, *Learning to Labor: How Working-Class Kids Get Working-Class Jobs* (England: Saxon House, 1977), and Michael Katz, *The Irony of Early School Reform* (Cambridge, Eng.: Cambridge University Press, 1968).

13. This is not to say that women have never leveled critiques of the government, police, or media. Queen Latifah's "The Evil That Men Do" describes government-sponsored oppression and inequality, critiquing men in power and the effect of government policies on poor and black people. Female rapper Nefertitti, whose vocal style and subject matter is more like those of Chuck D than any other female rapper, renders similar political commentary. (She does not yet have any recorded material, however, I have seen her perform in a "Sisters in Rap" showcase.) And female rap group BWP (Bytches with Problems) discusses both sexual exploitation and police brutality in "Wanted" (No Face Records, 1991). Yet, examples such as these are relatively scarce. Women rappers may focus on police brutality less frequently, because black women are not

the primary target of street-based anticrime efforts. Young black men are much more likely to be harassed by police officers on the street. In regard to the question of media critiques, media coverage of women rappers has been far more favorable than coverage devoted to male rappers. Positioned as a countervailing voice in hip hop against sexism in rap music, women rappers are rarely criticized overtly in the press. These gender-based factors help to explain why the police and media are not central points of contestation for female rappers, but it does *not* explain why other forms of institutional discrimination and oppression to which black women are more directly subjected. State welfare, economic discrimination, and limited education are not central sites of contestation in black women's rap lyrics. See Linda Gordon, ed., *Women, the State and Welfare* (Madison: University of Wisconsin Press, 1990), for a gendered reading of state institutional oppression. As it currently stands, women rappers refer indirectly to gender and racially based institutional oppression through private, sexual, and domestic space narratives as well as identity-based politics. See also Lisa Lewis, *Gender Politics and MTV* (Philadelphia: Temple University Press, 1990), and Leslie G. Roman and Linda K. Christian-Smith, eds., *Becoming Feminine: The Politics of Popular Culture* (London: Falmer Press, 1988), for other examples of women's social space contestation in popular music. In Chapter 5 I provide an extended reading of women's narrative focus in rap narratives with particular attention given to black sexual politics.

14. The literature on black urban America and social control agencies as institutional arms of racism and of the maintenance of inequality is vast. Suffice it to say that African Americans are suspicious of and remain in an antagonistic relationship with the police. Of course, key civil rights victories have been facilitated by police forces. However, these efforts were conducted as a direct result of pressure against the state and are not frequent enough to counteract the daily and consistent tensions that comprise police-black relations. A short sampling of some studies that include police community relations follows: Ellis Cashmore and Eugene McLaughlin, eds., *Out of Order? Policing Black People* (London: Routledge, 1991); Richard Thomas and Homer Hawkins, "White Policing of Black populations: A History of Race and Social Control in America," in Cashmore and McLaughlin, eds., *Out of Order?*, pp. 65–86; Charles E. Cobb, "The People Have Spoken," *The Crisis*, November 1983, p. 28; Kenneth B. Clarke, *Dark Ghetto* (New York: Harper & Row, 1965); George Lipsitz, *A Life in the Struggle: Ivory Perry and the Culture of Opposition* (Philadelphia: Temple University Press, 1988).

15. Women rappers do not address questions of police brutality to any great extent. Because street crime is predominantly a male phenomenon, the experience of being assumed guilty of a street crime and the harassment that often accompanies it is more often experienced by men than by women. Similarly, the experience of being sexually objectified and sexually oppressed is much more often experienced by women and therefore more frequently articulated by women rappers.

16. See Davis, *City of Quartz*, especially Chapter 5, "The Hammer and the Rock," for a complex analysis of the role of police in black and Latino communities in Los Angeles and the Bush administration's war on drugs. See also Jerry G. Watts, "It Just Ain't Righteous: On Witnessing Black Crooks and White Cops," *Dissent*, vol. 90, 347–53, 1983; H. Bruce Pierce, "Blacks and Law Enforcement: Towards Police Brutality Reduction," *Black Scholar*, vol. 17, 49–54, 1986.

17. Boogie Down Productions, "Who Protects Us from You?," *Ghetto Music: The Blueprint of Hip Hop* (Jive/Zomba Records, 1989).

18. See Sterling Stuckey, *Slave Culture: Nationalist Theory and the Founda-*

tions of Black America (New York: Oxford University Press, 1977); Paul Gilroy, *There Ain't No Black in the Union Jack* (London: Hutchinson, 1987); and Stephen Davis, *Reggae Bloodlines* (New York: DeCapo Press, 1977). KRS-One has a number of reggae/rap songs on his own albums, he performs regularly with reggae artists Sly and Robbie and others, and he produces reggae music for various artists in the Caribbean and the United States.

19. Gil Scott-Heron, "No Knock," *The Revolution Will Not Be Televised* (Fly and Dutchman Records, 1969).

20. Scott, *Domination*, p. 11. See also Chapters 3, "Public Transcripts as Respectable Performance," and 5, "Making Social Space for a Dissident Subculture."

21. It is interesting to note that L.L. Cool J. has a long-standing reputation as a storytelling boasting rapper rather than as a political rapper. Also, for other especially pointed critiques of the police in rap music, see: NWA " ___ the Police," *Straight Outta Compton* (Priority Records, 1988), and Ice Cube, "Endangered Species," *AmeriKKKa's Most Wanted* (Priority Records, 1990); Ice-T, "Squeeze the Trigger," *Rhyme Pays* (Sire Records, 1987); Ice-T, "Escape From the Killing Fields," *O.G. Original Gangster* (Sire Records, 1991); W.C. and the MAAD Circle, "Ain't a Damn Thing Changed," and "Behind Closed Doors," *Ain't a Damn Thing Changed* (Priority, 1991).

22. L.L. Cool J., "Illegal Search," *Mama Said Knock You Out* (Def Jam/ Columbia Records, 1990).

23. Naus, cited in "Man in Police Bias Case May Get Troopers' Files," *New York Times*, 24 February 1990, L28. According to the national newspaper index, no further information was published regarding this case or the larger issue of racially discriminatory profile arrests. The first article includes the issue of gay discrimination and targeting and provides interviews with blacks who claim to have been harassed and forced to exit the turnpike for no apparent reason.

24. See Joe R. Feagin, "The Continuing Significance of Race: Antiblack Discrimination in Public Places," *American Sociological Review*, vol. 56, no. 101– 16, 1991, for an extended discussion on the contemporary character of discrimination against blacks, the nature of responses, and the significance of class in determining such responses. See also Patricia J. Williams, *The Alchemy of Race and Rights* (Cambridge, Mass.: Harvard University Press, 1991). For a dissenting view, see William J. Wilson, *The Truly Disadvantaged* (Chicago: University of Chicago Press, 1987), Wilson claims that police arrest more blacks because blacks commit more crimes. See Adolph L. Reed, Jr., "The Liberal Technocrat," *The Nation*, 6 February 1988, pp. 167–70, for a critique of Wilson's argument and its underpinnings.

25. Angus Gillespie and Michael Rockland, *Looking for America on the New Jersey Turnpike* (New Brunswick, N.J.: Rutgers University Press, 1989), p. 67.

26. Joseph F. Sullivan, "New Jersey Police Are Accused of Minority Arrest Campaigns," *New York Times*, 19 February 1990, B3.

27. Scott, *Domination*, p. 9.

28. As quoted in Peggy Dye, "High Tech Ballroom," *Village Voice*, 5 December 1989, pp. 10–12.

29. I will be discussing the video and lyrics together. Taken alone, the lyrics specifically address drugs, whereas the video interweaves several narratives.

30. Public Enemy, "Night of the Living Baseheads," *Nation of Millions* (Def Jam Records, 1988).

31. *Ballistics* means facts, truth, information, and *G* is an expression for a friend or associate.

32. Public Enemy, "Baseheads," *Nation of Millions* (Def Jam Records, 1988).

33. D.J. Red Alert was one of the early New York club-based rap DJs, along with Grand Master Flash, Cool DJ Herc, Marley Marl, and Mr. Magic. He has produced music for The Jungle Brothers and has been producing the WBLS rap show in New York City since at least 1985. In the video, Red Alert brings the red alert news flash on the status of Chuck D.

34. "Baseheads" also suggests a reference to Michael Jackson's reworking of "Night of the Living Dead" in his landmark video film for "Thriller." See Kobena Mercer, "Monster Metaphors: Notes on Michael Jackson's 'Thriller'," in McRobbie, ed., *Zoot Suits and Second-Hand Dresses*, pp. 50–73.

35. Some of this discrepancy is a product of BET's limited resources. On MTV there is little time lag between an event and its airing on the "Week in Rock." MTV has a much larger staff and a great deal more money with which to produce programming. However, BET's attitude toward rap music and black youth culture is a critical issue. For example, although BET programs black music almost exclusively, MTV offered the first all-rap video show, "Yo MTV Raps." BET has consistently aired rap videos, but it did not offer a rap show (Rap City) until after the MTV success story. Video Soul, Video Vibrations, Gospel, and Love Song programming have been staples. These musical genres, although popular among a wide range of black Americans and others, are not as heavily associated with poor black inner-city youths and can more easily serve as representative genres for the upwardly mobile black bourgeoisie that BET cultivates as its preferred audience. Rap music, which dominates the black music charts and is clearly the music of choice for black urban teenagers, is relatively marginalized on BET.

36. Style and inventiveness are critical measures of prowess in black aesthetics, so that naming this ultra hyper group the Brown Bags is intended to mock their lack of power via rigidity, blandless, and lack of creativity. See Albert Murray, *Stompin the Blues* (New York: Random House, 1976), for a discussion on the centrality of style and individuality in black cultural aesthetics.

37. PE's target, which is an effective strategy for reappropriating the rifle sight (used here to focus attention on oppression and violence against African Americans), also fuses racial targeting with gender targeting. The issue of black males as an endangered species is ongoing on black talk shows (e.g., New York WLIB) and in the black press (such as the *City Sun* and the *Amsterdam News*). However, such arguments are not without significant sexist assumptions. The Nation of Islam is especially guilty (although not alone) is using these arguments in an overtly patriarchal context. The "genocide" against black males is used as an explanation for the lack of masculine authority that has contributed significantly to the breakdown of the black family. This argument is uncomfortably close to suggesting that black progress hinges on the reestablishment of black patriarchy and that black female single-headed households are a problem, not as a consequence of economic discrimination against women but as a result of discrimination against black men. For a concise critique of similar arguments, see Reed, "The Liberal Technocrat," pp. 167–70, "The Rise of Louis Farrakhan," *The Nation*, 21 January 1991 and 28 January 1991 (two-part article), and Reed and Julian Bond, eds., special issue of *The Nation* on "Equality: Why We Can't Wait," *The Nation*, 9 December 1991, pp. 733–37.

38. Dye, "High Tech," p. 11.

39. Darrell M. McNeill, "Demand Malcolm X Memorial," *Village Voice*, 13 March 1990, p. 13.

40. Dye, "High Tech," p. 12.

41. Venues are clubs, theaters, and other performance spaces. I am con-

cerned specifically with large venues, such as the Capital Center, Nassau Coliseum, and Madison Square Garden. Larger venues constitute the most significant public arena contestations, because they are located in urban development zones, outside black areas and because they can house the largest numbers of people. I am particularly interested in accounts of rap music in major newspapers. Music periodicals are not the focus here.

42. A Tribe Called Quest, "Youthful Expressions," *People's Instinctive Travels and the Paths of Rhythm* (Jive Records, 1989/1990).

43. At a 1988 rap concert in New Haven, Connecticut, a young African-American male protested the weapon search shouting, "Fuck it! I'm not going through the search." But after a short protest, realizing that he would have to forfeit his ticket, he entered the lines and proceeded through the search station. In the summer of 1990, outside the San Diego Sports Arena, a young woman wanted to go inside to see if her friend had already arrived and was waiting inside, but she said that she would rather wait outside a bit longer instead of having to go through the search twice if it turned out that her friend was not in fact inside.

44. Public space discrimination and the public injury to dignity it creates is not limited to black teenagers. Feagin's "Continuing Significance of Race" illustrates that in post–Civil Rights America, discriminatory practices against blacks of all ages and classes remain a significant part of public space interaction with whites. He points out a number of critical public spaces in which black men and women are likely to be humiliated and discriminated against. His findings are in keeping with my experiences and observations and the context within which they took place.

45. Dave Marsh and Phyllis Pollack, "Wanted for Attitude," *Village Voice*, 10 October, 1989, pp. 33–37.

46. Ibid., pp. 33–37.

47. NWA, "—— The Police," *Straight Outta Compton* (Priority, 1988).

48. See Robert Walser, *Running with the Devil: Power, Gender and Madness in Heavy Metal Music* (Hanover: University Press of New England, 1993). See also Marsh and Pollack, "Wanted," and *Rock and Roll Confidential*, (*RRC*), especially their special pamphlet "You've Got a Right to Rock: Don't Let Them Take It Away." This pamphlet is a detailed documentation of the censorship movements and their institutional bases and attacks. The *RRC* is edited by David Marsh and can be subscribed to by writing to *RRC*, Dept. 7, Box 341305, Los Angeles, CA 90034. See also Linda Martin and Kerry Seagrave, *Anti-Rock: The Opposition to Rock n Roll* (Hamden, Ct.: Archon Books, 1988).

49. In fact, the attacks on earlier popular black expressions such as jazz and rock 'n' roll, were grounded in fears that white youths were deriving too much pleasure from black expressions and that these primitive, alien expressions were dangerous to their moral development. See Steve Chapple and Reebee Garofalo, *Rock 'n' Roll Is Here to Pay* (Chicago: Nelson, 1979); Lewis A. Erenberg, *Steppin' Out*; Jones, *Blues People*; Ogren, *Jazz Revolution*; Lipsitz, *Time Passages*.

50. Cited in Light, "Ice-T."

51. Bruce Haring, "Many Doors Still Closed to Rap Tours," *Billboard*, 16 December 1989, p. 1. Obviously, Haring means building *owners*. Writers and venue representatives consistently refer to the buildings, not their owners, as the point of power. This language renders invisible the powerful people who control public space access and make discriminatory bureaucratic decisions.

52. "1500 Hurt at Jackson Concert," *New York Post*, 12 September 1988, p. 9.

53. Carl J. Pelleck and Charles Sussman, "Rampaging Teen Gang Slays 'Rap'

Fan," *New York Post*, 12 September 1988, p. 9. See the January 1991 issue of *The Source*, p. 24, for a discussion on bans on rap concerts and on rap-related violence.

54. It is deliberate and significant that the race of the suspects was not actually mentioned. As Timothy Maliqualim Simone points out: "In the aftermath of the civil rights movement of the sixties and seventies, American culture has discovered that racial effects are more efficiently achieved in a language cleansed of overt racial reference. . . . Instead they employ more subtle signifiers: 'Street youths,' 'welfare mothers,' 'inner-city residents'." Timothy Maliqualim Simone, *About Face: Race in Postmodern America* (New York: Autonomedia, 1989), p. 17. Given this astute observation, the picture that accompanied the text was unnecessary and might be considered gratuitous overkill.

55. Michel Marriott, "9 Charged, 4 with Murder, in Robbery Spree at L.I. Rap Concert," *New York Times*, 19 September 1988, B3.

56. James W. Messerschmidt, *Capitalism, Patriarchy and Crime: Toward a Socialist Feminist Criminology* (Savage, Md.: Rowman & Littlefield, 1986). See especially pp. 54–58.

57. Haring, "Many Doors Still Closed," p. 80.

58. See Messerschmidt, "*Capitalism*," especially Chapter 3, "Powerless Men and Street Crime." Messerschmidt notes that, "Public perception of what serious violent crime is—and who the violent criminals are—is determined first by what the state defines as violent and the types of violence it overlooks. . . . The criminal law defines only certain kinds of violence as criminal—namely, one-on-one forms of murder, assault, and robbery, which are the types of violence young marginalized minority males primarily engage in. The criminal law excludes certain types of avoidable killings, injuries and thefts engaged in by powerful white males, such as maintaining hazardous working conditions or producing unsafe products" (p. 52).

59. Mark Kruggel and Jerry Roga, "L.I. Rap Slayer Sought," New York *Daily News*, 12 September 1988, p. 3; David Gates et al., "The Rap Attitude," *Newsweek*, 19 March 1990, pp. 56–63.

60. Stuart Hall et al., *Policing the Crisis* (London: Macmillan, 1977), p. 19.

61. Interview with "Richard," a talent agency representative from a major agency that represents dozens of major rap groups, October 1990.

62. Paul Chevigny, *Gigs: Jazz and the Cabaret Laws in New York City* (London: Routledge, 1991). See also Ogren, *Jazz Revolution*.

63. Rose interview with "Richard." I have decided not to reveal the identity of this talent agency representative, because it serves no particular purpose here and may have a detrimental effect on his employment.

64. Roxbury is a poor, predominantly black area in Boston.

65. Ice Cube, "The Nigga You Love to Hate," *AmeriKKKa's Most Wanted* (Priority Records, 1990).

66. Gilroy, *There Ain't No Black*, p. 110. See also, Gilroy, "Police and Thieves," in Center for Contemporary Cultural Studies, ed., *The Empire Strikes Back* (London: CCCS Hutchinson University Library, 1982).

67. In the Howard Beach case, vicious racism was the only reasonable explanation for the brutal attack against three black men (one of whom was murdered) whose car had broken down. Yet, a question that preoccupied the defense was whether they had a "good reason" to be in the solidly white neighborhood. This question was established by pointing out that they had passed a number of gas stations and pizza parlors before stopping to call for help with their automobile. (Of course, they might have passed by establishments that seemed hostile, hoping the next might seem less threatening, or have some patrons of color

in them.) My point here is that if they hadn't had a disabled car as an excuse, they would have had significantly less moral leverage with white New Yorkers. As it was, the press was counting phone booths and open restaurants in the area to "explain" why they walked as far as they did. These three black men had transgressed across the boundaries that circumscribe black mobility, a transgression that makes sense within the social control discourse, explains white fear, and renders violence against blacks logical and understandable. See Williams, *The Alchemy of Race and Rights*, for an extended and important reading of the Howard Beach case and of several other recent racially motivated crimes.

68. Ice Cube, "Endangered Species," *AmeriKKKa's Most Wanted* (Priority Records, 1990).

69. Boogie Down Productions, "Necessary," *By All Means Necessary* (Jive Records, 1988).

70. See especially David Samuel, "The Real Face of Rap," *The New Republic*, 11 November 1991, and Gates et al., "The Rap Attitude." In contrast, Jon Parales and Peter Watrous, the primary popular music critics for the *New York Times*, have made noteworthy attempts to offer complex and interesting critiques of rap music. In many cases, a significant number of letters to the editor appeared in following weeks complaining about the appearance and content of their reviews and articles.

71. John D'Agostino, "Rap Concert Fails to Sizzle in San Diego," *Los Angeles Times* (San Diego edition), 28 August 1990, pp. F1, F5. This review is accompanied by subsequent short articles about charges brought against rappers for "obscene conduct" while on stage—fully clothed—during this concert and the massive coverage of the 2 Live Crew controversy regarding obscene lyrics. For example, Michael Granberry, "Digital Underground May Face Prosecution," *Los Angeles Times*, 17 November 1990, F9; "2 Rap Beat, Must Beat Rap," *New York Daily News*, 4 August 1990, p. 3. It is also quite important to point out how much D'Agostino's description of rap music is modeled after arguments made by T. W. Adorno regarding jazz music in the 1940s. In "On Popular Music," Adorno refers to rhythms in jazz as a sign of obedience to domination of the machine age: "The cult of the machine which is represented by unabating jazz beats involves a self-renunciation that cannot but take root in the form of a fluctuating uneasiness somewhere in the personality of the obedient." See Frith and Goodwin, eds., *On Record*, p. 313.

72. See Lipsitz, *Time Passages*, for an extended analysis of this process.

73. See Ray Pratt, "Popular Music, Free Space, and the Quest for Community," *Popular Music and Society*, vol. 13 no. 4, 59–76, 1989, on the question of public space moments of community experiences, and see Snead, "On Repetition."

74. D'Agostino, "Rap Concert," p. F5.

75. Nelson George, ed., *Stop the Violence: Overcoming Self-Destruction* (New York: Pantheon, 1990), p. 12.

76. "Self-Destruction," *Stop the Violence* (Jive, 1990).

77. Michael Parenti, *Inventing Reality: The Politics of the Mass Media* (New York: St. Martin's Press, 1986), p. 12.

78. Congressman John Conyers, "Main Solution Is National Plan Correcting Economic Injustice," *Ebony*, August 1979.

79. Bernard D. Headley, "'Black on Black' Crime: The Myth and the Reality," *Crime and Social Justice*, vol. 20, 50–62, 52, 1983.

80. Boogie Down Productions, "Stop the Violence," *By All Means Necessary* (Jive Records, 1988).

81. For a critique of the discourse on the underclass, its relationship to

the culture of poverty literature, and the rightward political shift over the 1980s, see Adolph L. Reed, Jr., "The 'Underclass' as Myth and Symbol: The Poverty of Discourse about Poverty," *Radical America*, vol. 24, no. 1 20–40, 1991; Michael Katz, *The Undeserving Poor* (New York: Pantheon, 1989); and Raymond S. Franklin, *Shadows of Race and Class* (Minneapolis: University of Minnesota Press, 1991).

82. bell hooks, *Yearning: Race, Gender and Cultural Politics* (Boston: South End Press, 1990).

83. David Brion Davis, *The Problem of Slavery in Western Culture* (Ithaca, N.Y.: Cornell University Press, 1966).

5. Bad Sistas (pp. 146–82)

1. Queen Latifah, "Ladies First," *All Hail the Queen* (Tommy Boy Records, 1989).

2. Harmony has not yet named the rap song from which these lyrics were excerpted.

3. Rose interview with Kid, 11 January 1990.

4. Jon Parales, "Female Rappers Strut Their Stuff in a Male Domain," *New York Times*, 5 November 1989, p. C19; Jon Parales, "The Women Who Talk Back in Rap," *New York Times*, 21 October 1990, p. C33; Marcus B. Marbry, "Rap Gets a Woman's Touch," *Emerge*, February 1990, pp. 62–65; David E. Thigpen, "Not for Men Only," *Time*, 27 May 1991, pp. 71–72. See Footnote 15 for further citations.

5. Lipsitz, *Time Passages*, p. 99. See also Mikhail Bakhtin, *Speech Genres and Other Late Essays* (Austin: University of Texas Press, 1986).

6. This refers to my use of Jim Scott's work in the preceding chapter.

7. Anders Stephanson, "Interview with Cornel West," in Andrew Ross, ed., *Universal Abandon: The Politics of Postmodernism* (Minneapolis: University of Minnesota Press, 1988), pp. 269–86.

8. Paula Ebron, "Rapping between Men: Performing Gender," *Radical America*, vol. 23, no. 4, 1991, 23–27. Although she is primarily concerned with gendered discourse in Public Enemy—even when such discourse does not refer to black women—she does cite women rappers as respondents to sexism who "contest the most regressive ideas about the role of Black women in the process of cultural production." p. 26. What is more interesting about the piece, how-ever, is her exploration of the way black men are in dialogue with white men, particularly in regard to women as sexual property.

9. Michelle Wallace, "When Black Feminism Faces the Music and the Music Is Rap," *New York Times*, 29 July 1990, p. 12. This kind of generalized character-ization of sexism in rap is also made glaringly apparent in the misquotation of my reference to sexism in the work of 2 Live Crew. In the interview she con-ducted with me for the article, I told Wallace that the 2 Live Crew's lyrics are basically male locker-room discourse with a beat. In the article, I was quoted as saying that *rap music* is basically locker-room with a beat.

10. Notes from the *New Music Seminar* conferences July 1990 and 1991; *Hip Hop at the Crossroads*, Howard University conference February 1991; Rose interviews with MC Lyte and Salt, 7 September 1990.

11. In her piece, "Beyond Racism and Misogyny: Black Feminism and the 2 Live Crew," Kimberle Crenshaw stakes out a position that addresses similar concerns regarding black feminists who are asked to respond to cases of sexism that have been selected for larger social scrutiny. She interrogates the single-axis opposition between race and gender as "the" most important aspect of the

2 Live Crew issue. She explores from a legal perspective the politics of selective prosecution and definitions of pornography. I raise her work here to point out the wide range of black women who find themselves in this difficult bind and to suggest that black women rappers' refusal to roundly condemn 2 Live Crew may be based in a larger, more complex dynamics regarding black female subjectivity. *Boston Review*, vol. 16, no. 6, 6–33, 1991.

12. There are also similar examples of homophobic lyrics by male rappers, but I have not enumerated them because they do not pertain to the point I am making here.

13. Houston A. Baker, "Hybridity, the Rap Race, and Pedagogy for the 1990s," in Andrew Ross and Constance Penley, eds., *Technoculture* (Minneapolis: University of Minnesota Press, 1991), pp. 197–209. In addition, disco's relationship to rap was not one of resentment—rap music was based on disco music and culture. Although some of the more upscale downtown New York clubs excluded black and Latino teenage b-boys, this was not a break from traditional class and racial hierarchies in New York nightlife, and plenty of uptown disco clubs were in operation. Instrumental disco singles served as the musical accompaniment for several early raps, and disco's transformation of the role of the DJ into a "master of musical ceremonies" set the stage for rap's DJs' providing much of the inspiration for rap's collage-oriented mixes. For a discussion of the substantial link between disco and rap, see Nelson George, *The Death of Rhythm and Blues*, pp. 188–91. For a discussion of disco as a black and a black gay musical culture, see Garofalo, "Crossing Over."

14. Nelson George, "Rap's Tenth Birthday," *Village Voice*, 24 October 1989, p. 40.

15. Dominique Di Prima and Lisa Kennedy, "Beat the Rap," *Mother Jones*, September–October 1990, pp. 32–35; Jill Pearlman, "Rap's Gender Gap," *Option*, Fall 1988, pp. 32–36; Marisa Fox, "From the Belly of the Blues to the Cradle of Rap," *Details*, July 1989, pp. 118–124; Judith Halberstam, "Starting from Scratch: Female Rappers and Feminist Discourse," *Revisions*, vol. 2, no. 2 (Winter), 1–4, 1989.

16. Guevara, "Women Writing'," pp. 160–75.

17. Angela Davis, "Black Women and Music: A Historical Legacy of Struggle," in Joanne M. Braxton and Andree Nicola McLaughlin, eds., *Wild Women in the Whirlwind: Afro-American Culture and the Contemporary Literary Renaissance* (New Brunswick, N.J.: Rutgers University Press, 1990), pp. 3–21.

18. Carby, "It Jus Be's Dat Way," pp. 9–22.

19. Roxanne Shante was the first commercial breakthrough female artist. Her basement-produced single was "Roxanne's Revenge" (1985). See also more recent works by Yo-Yo, Monie Love, Ms. Melodie, Harmony, Antoinette, Oaktown 3-5-7, and Shazzy.

20. Cited in Pearlman, "Rap's Gender Gap," p. 34.

21. Cited in Di Prima and Kennedy, "Beat the Rap," p. 34.

22. Pearlman, "Rap's Gender Gap," p. 34.

23. Salt 'N' Pepa, "Tramp," *Cool, Hot and Vicious* (Next Plateau Records, 1986).

24. MC Lyte, "Paper Thin," *Lyte as a Rock* (First Priority Records, 1988).

25. See Atlantic Records, *Rhythm and Blues Collection 1966–1969*, vol. 6. In the liner notes for this collection, Robert Pruter refers to "Tramp" as a dialogue between Carla and Otis, in which Carla's "invectives" are insufficiently countered by Otis. It should be pointed out the Otis and Carla "Tramp" is a remake of (an answer to?) Lowell and Fulsom's version made popular in 1966.

26. Laura Berlant, "The Female Complaint," *Social Text*, Fall, 237–59, 1988.

27. Queen Latifah, "Ladies First," *All Hail the Queen* (Tommy Boy Records, 1989).

28. Rose interview with Queen Latifah, 6 February 1990.

29. The melody, lyrical chorus, and rhythm section for "Shake Your Thang" is taken from the Isley Brothers single "It's Your Thang," which was on Billboards Top Forty charts in the winter of 1969.

30. Salt 'N' Pepa, "Shake Your Thang," *A Salt with a Deadly Pepa* (Next Plateau Records, 1988).

31. Salt 'N' Pepa's video for "Expression" covers similar ground but focuses more on fostering individuality and self-confidence in young women.

32. bell hooks, *Black Looks: Race and Representation* (Boston: South End Press, 1992), pp. 61–64.

33. See Susan Willis, *A Primer for everyday Life* (London: Routledge, 1991), especially, Chapter 6, and Wendy Chapkis, *Beauty Secrets: Women and the Politics of Appearance* (Boston: South End Press, 1986).

34. Hortense Spillers, "Interstices: A Small Drama of Words," in Carol Vance, ed., *Pleasure and Danger: Exploring Female Sexuality* (Boston: Routledge, Kegan Paul, 1984), pp. 73–100.

35. Other examples include L.L. Cool J., "Big Ole Butt"; 95 South, "Whoot, There It Is"; and Duice, "Dazzey Duks."

36. Cited in Laurie Pike, "Bad Rap," *Us*, 10 December 1990, p. 15.

37. Kelley, "Kickin' Reality."

38. Greg Tate, "Manchild at Large: One on One with Ice Cube, Hip Hop's Most Wanted," *Village Voice*, 11 September 1990, p. 78.

39. Rose interview with MC Lyte, 7 September 1990.

40. Boss, *Born Gangstaz* (Sony/Def Jam, 1993); dream hampton, "Hard to the Core," *The Source*, June 1993, p. 34.

41. Rose interview with Salt from Salt 'N' Pepa, 17 August 1990.

42. Salt 'N' Pepa, *Black's Magic* (Next Plateau Records, 1990).

43. Disposable Heroes of Hiphoprisy, "Music and Politics," *Disposable Heroes of Hiphoprisy* (Island Records, 1992).

44. Paula Giddings, *When and Where I Enter: The Impact of Black Women On Race and Sex in America* (New York: Bantam, 1984).

45. Rose interview with MC Lyte, 7 September 1990

46. See Susan Faludi, *Backlash: The Undeclared War against American Women* (New York: Crown), 1991).

47. Rose interview with Queen Latifah, 6 February 1990.

48. Rose interview with Salt, 17 August 1990.

49. See bell hooks, *Ain't I a Woman: Black Women and Feminism* (Boston: South End Press, 1982), and *Feminist Theory: From Margins to Center* (Boston: South End Press, 1984); Barbara Smith, ed. *Home Girls: A Black Feminist Anthology* (New York: Kitchen Table, 1983); Cheryl A. Wall, ed., *Changing Our Own Words: Essays on Criticism, Theory and Writing by Black Women* (New Brunswick, N.J.: Rutgers University Press, 1989).

50. Revolutionary Rhythms, "If You're Dissin' the Sisters You're Not Fightin' the Power," WBAI radio show, 20 March 1991.

51. Alan Light, "Beating Up the Charts," *Rolling Stone*, 6 August 1991, p. 66.

52. Kimberle Crenshaw, "Demarginalizing the Intersection of Race and Sex: A Black Feminist Critique of Antidiscrimination Doctrine, Feminist Theory and Antiracist Politics," in *University of Chicago Legal Forum*, vol. 139, 139–67, 1989.

53. Rose interview with MC Lyte, 7 September 1990.

54. Rose interview with Salt, 17 August 1990.

Epilogue (pp. 184–85)

1. Anders Stephanson, "Interview with Cornel West," in Ross ed., *Universal Abandon?*, p. 281.

2. Greg Tate, "It's Like This Y'all," *Village Voice*, 19 January 1988, p. 22.

Background Sources

✦

Interviews

Bray, Kevin, 18 March 1993.
Crazy Legs and Wiggles (breakdancers), 6 November 1991.
Daddy-O (from Stetsasonic), 9 August 1990.
Harmony, 14 June 1991.
Harrell, Gina, 20 March 1993.
Hunt, Rick (artist and repertoire), October 1989.
Kid (from Kid 'N Play), 11 January 1990.
Kool Moe Dee, September 1990.
Kriedman, Ron (entertainment attorney), 26 December 1989.
MC Lyte, 7 September 1990.
Paris, 18 September 1990.
Queen Latifah, 6 February 1990.
Red Alert (disc jockey/producer), 8 May 1990.
"Richard" (talent agency representative), October, 1990.
Sadler, Eric "Vietnam" (producer), 4 September 1991.
Salt (from Salt 'N' Pepa), 22 May 1990, and 17 August 1990.
Stone, Charles S. III, 15 July 1993.
Wolkowicz, Micheline (entertainment and sampling clearance attorney), September 1991.

Speeches and Conferences

"New Music Seminar" conferences, New York City, July 1990, and July 1991.
"Hip Hop at the Crossroads" conference, Howard University, Washington, D.C., 21–23 February 1991.
"We Remember Malcolm Day," Abyssinian Baptist Church, New York City, 21 February 1991.
WLIB "Rap Forum," New York City, 2–3 January 1990.
WLIB "Revolutionary Rhythms: If You're Dissin' the Sisters You're Not Fightin' the Power," New York City, 20 March 1991.

Magazines

Billboard	*Ebony*
Details	*Emerge*

Keyboard	Option
Mother Jones	Rock and Roll Confidential
Musician	Rolling Stone
Music Scene	The Source
New Republic	Spin
Newsweek	Time

Newspapers

Amsterdam News (New York)	New York Post
City Sun (New York)	New York Times
Los Angeles Times	Village Voice (New York)
New York Daily News	Washington Post

Partial Discography

Antoinette, *Who's the Boss?* (Next Plateau, 1989).

Atlantic Records, *Rhythm and Blues Collection, 1966–1969*, Vol. 6 (Atlantic, 1985).

Big Daddy Kane, *It's a Big Daddy Thing* (Cold Chillin', 1989).

Big Daddy Kane, *Long Live the Kane* (Cold Chillin', 1988).

Big Daddy Kane, *Taste of Chocolate* (Cold Chillin', 1990).

Boogie Down Productions, *By All Means Necessary* (Jive, 1988).

Boogie Down Productions, *Ghetto Music: The Blueprint of Hip Hop* (Jive/Zomba, 1989).

Boss, *Born Gangstaz* (Def Jam, 1993).

Bytches with Problems, "Wanted," *The Bytches* (No Face, 1991).

Cypress Hill, *Cypress Hill* (Ruffhouse, 1991).

D-Nice, *Call Me D-Nice* (Jive, 1990).

De La Soul, *De La Soul Is Dead* (Tommy Boy, 1991).

De La Soul, *Three Feet High and Rising* (Tommy Boy, 1989).

Digital Underground, *Sons of the P* (Tommy Boy, 1991).

Erik B. & Rakim, *Follow the Leader* (Uni, 1988).

Eric B. & Rakim, *Paid in Full* (Island, 1986).

Gangstarr, *Step in the Arena* (Crysalis, 1990).

Ice Cube, *Amerikkka's Most Wanted* (Profile, 1990).

Isley Brothers, "It's Your Thang," *Timeless* (T-Neck, 1969).

Kid Frost, *Hispanic Causin' Panic* (Virgin, 1990).

Kid-N-Play, *2 Hype* (Select, 1988).

Kool Moe Dee, *How Ya Like Me Now* (Jive, 1987).

L.L. Cool J., *Bad* (Def Jam, 1987).

L.L. Cool J., *Mama Said Knock You Out* (Def Jam/Columbia, 1990).

Marley Marl, *In Control: Volume 1* (Cold Chillin/Warner Bros., 1992).

MC Lyte, *Act Like You Know* (First Priority Music, 1991).

MC Lyte, *Lyte as a Rock* (First Priority Music, 1988).

MC Shan, *Down by Law* (Cold Chillin Records, 1987).

Ms. Melodie, *Diva* (Jive, 1989).

Naughty by Nature, *Naughty by Nature* (Tommy Boy, 1991).

NWA, *Niggaz4life* (Priority, 1991)

NWA, *Straight Outta Compton* (Priority, 1989).

Paris, *The Devil Made Me Do It* (Tommy Boy, 1990).

P.M. Dawn, *Of the Heart, the Soul and of the Cross* (Island, 1991).

Poor Righteous Teachers, *Holy Intellect* (Profile, 1990).

Public Enemy, *Fear of a Black Planet* (Def Jam, 1990).

Public Enemy, *It Takes a Nation of Millions to Hold Us Back* (Def Jam, 1988).

Public Enemy, *Yo! Bum Rush the Show* (Def Jam, 1987).

Queen Latifah, *All Hail the Queen* (Tommy Boy, 1989).

Queen Latifah, *Nature of a Sista* (Tommy Boy, 1991).

Roxanne Shante, "Roxanne's Revenge," *The Complete Story of Roxanne . . . The Album*, (Compleat, 1984).

Salt 'N' Pepa, *A Salt with a Deadly Pepa* (Next Plateau, 1988).

Salt 'N' Pepa, *Black's Magic* (Next Plateau, 1990).

Salt 'N' Pepa, *Cool, Hot and Vicious* (Next Plateau, 1986).

Scott-Heron, Gil, *The Revolution Will Not Be Televised* (Fly and Dutchman, 1969).

Stetsasonic, *In Full Gear* (Tommy Boy, 1988).

Terminator X, *Terminator X and the Valley of the Jeep Beats* (Columbia, 1991).

Tim Dog, *Penicillin on Wax* (Ruffhouse, 1991).

A Tribe Called Quest, *The Low End Theory* (Jive, 1990).

A Tribe Called Quest, *People's Instinctive Travels and the Paths of Rhythm* (Jive, 1990).

Yo-Yo, *Black Pearl* (Profile, 1992).

Yo-Yo, *Make Way for the Mother Lode* (Profile, 1991).

Bibliography

✦

Books

Abrahms, Roger D. *Deep Down in the Jungle: Negro Narrative Folklore from the Streets of Philadelphia*. Chicago: Aldine, 1970.

Adler, Bill. *Rap: Portraits and Lyrics of a Generation of Black Rockers*. New York: St Martin's Press, 1991.

———. *Tougher than Leather: Run DMC*. New York: Penguin, 1987.

Angus, Ian, and Sut Jhally, eds. *Cultural Politics in Contemporary America*. New York: Routledge, 1988.

Attali, Jacques. *Noise: The Political Economy of Music*. Minneapolis: University of Minnesota Press, 1985.

Bagdigian, Ben. *The Media Monopoly*. Boston: Beacon Press, 1987.

Baker, Houston. *Blues, Ideology, and Afro-American Literature: A Vernacular Theory*. Chicago: University of Chicago Press, 1984.

———. *Long Black Song: Essays in Black American Literature and Culture*. London: University Press of Virginia, 1972.

Bakhtin, Mikhail. *Speech Genres and Other Late Essays*. Austin: University of Texas Press, 1986.

Barlow, William. *Looking Up at Down: The Emergence of Blues Culture*. Philadelphia: Temple University Press, 1989.

Bell, Daniel. *The Coming of Post-Industrial Society*. New York: Basic Books, 1973.

Berman, Marshall. *All That Is Solid Melts into Air*. New York: Simon & Schuster, 1982.

Carby, Hazel V. *Reconstructing Womanhood*. New York: Oxford University Press, 1987.

Cashmore, Ellis, and Eugene McLaughlin, eds. *Out of Order? Policing Black People*. London: Routledge, 1991.

Castleman, Craig. *Getting Up: Subway Graffiti in New York*. Cambridge: MIT Press, 1982.

Center for Contemporary Cultural Studies. *The Empire Strikes Back: Race and Racism in Britain*. London: CCCS Hutchinson University Library, 1982.

Chapkis, Wendy. *Beauty Secrets: Women and the Politics of Appearance*. Boston: South End Press, 1986.

Chapple, Steve, and Reebee Garofalo. *Rock 'n' Roll Is Here to Pay*. Chicago: Nelson, 1979.

Chernoff, John Miller. *African Rhythm and African Sensibility: Aesthetics and*

Social Action in African Musical Idioms. Chicago: University of Chicago Press, 1979.

Chevigny, Paul. *Gigs: Jazz and the Cabaret Laws in New York City.* London: Routledge, 1991.

Clarke, Kenneth B. *Dark Ghetto.* New York: Harper & Row, 1965.

Cooper, Martha, and Henry Chalfant. *Subway Art.* New York: Holt, Rinehart & Winston, 1984.

Costello, Mark. *Signifying Rappers.* Boston: Ecco Press, 1989.

Crowley, Daniel. *African Folklore in the New World.* Austin: University of Texas Press, 1977.

Dannen, Frederic. *Hit Men: Powerbrokers and Fast Money inside the Music Business.* New York: Random House, 1990.

Davis, David Brion. *The Problem of Slavery in Western Culture.* Ithaca, N.Y.: Cornell University Press, 1966.

Davis, Mike. *City of Quartz: Excavating the Future in Los Angeles.* London: Verso, 1991.

Davis, Stephen. *Reggae Bloodlines.* New York: De Capo Press, 1977.

Denisoff, Serge. *Inside MTV.* New Brunswick, N.J.: Transaction Books, 1987.

Denning, Michael. *Mechanic Accents.* London: Verso, 1988.

Dundes, Alan, ed. *Mother Wit from the Laughing Barrel: Readings in the Interpretation of Afro-American Folklore.* New York: Garland, 1981.

Erenberg, Lewis A. *Steppin' Out: New York Night Life and the Transformation of American Culture, 1890–1930.* Chicago: University of Chicago Press, 1981.

Eurie, Joseph D., and James G. Spady. *Nation Conscious Rap: The Hip Hop Version.* New York: PC International, 1991.

Faludi, Susan. *Backlash: The Undeclared War against American Women.* New York: Crown, 1991.

Forester, Tom. *High-Tech Society.* Cambridge: MIT Press, 1988.

Frith, Simon, ed. *Facing the Music.* New York: Pantheon, 1988.

Frith, Simon, and Andrew Goodwin, eds. *On Record: Rock, Pop and the Written Word.* New York: Pantheon, 1990.

Gates, Henry L., Jr. *The Signifying Monkey: A Theory of African American Literary Criticism.* New York: Oxford University Press, 1988.

George, Nelson. *The Death of Rhythm and Blues.* New York: Pantheon, 1988.

———, ed. *Stop the Violence: Overcoming Self-Destruction.* New York: Pantheon, 1990.

———, George, Nelson, et al., eds. *Fresh: Hip Hop Don't Stop.* New York: Random House, 1985.

Giddings, Paula. *When and Where I Enter: The Impact of Black Women on Race and Sex in America.* New York: Bantam, 1984.

Gillespie, Angus, and Michael Rockland. *Looking for America on the New Jersey Turnpike.* New Brunswick, N.J.: Rutgers University Press, 1989.

Gilroy, Paul. *There Ain't No Black in the Union Jack.* London: Hutchinson, 1987.

Glasgow, Douglass G. *The Black Underclass: Poverty, Unemployment and Entrapment of Ghetto Youth.* New York: Vintage, 1980.

Gordon, Linda, ed. *Women, the State and Welfare.* Madison: University of Wisconsin Press, 1990.

Gramsci, Antonio. *Selections from the Prison Notebooks.* New York: International Universities Publishers, 1971.

Hager, Steve. *Hip Hop: The Illustrated History of Breakdancing, Rap Music, and Graffiti.* New York: St Martin's Press, 1984.

Hall, Stuart, et al. *Policing the Crisis.* London: Macmillan, 1977.

Hall, Stuart, and Tony Jefferson, eds. *Resistance through Rituals*. London: CCCS Hutchinson University Library, 1976.

Harvey, David. *Social Justice and the City*. Oxford: Basil Blackwell, 1988.

Hazzard, Katrina. *Jookin'*. Philadelphia: Temple University Press, 1991.

Hebdige, Dick. *Cut n Mix: Culture, Identity and Caribbean Music*. London: Methuen, 1987.

———. *Subculture: The Meaning of Style*. London: Routledge, 1979.

hooks, bell. *Ain't I a Woman: Black Women and Feminism*. Boston: South End Press, 1982.

———. *Black Looks: Race and Representation*. Boston: South End Press, 1992.

———. *Feminist Theory: From Margins to Center*. Boston: South End Press, 1984.

———. *Yearning: Race, Gender and Cultural Politics*. Boston: South End Press, 1990.

Jackson, Bruce. *Get Your Ass in the Water and Swim Like Me*. Cambridge, Mass.: Harvard University Press, 1974.

Jones, Leroi. *Blues People: The Negro Experience in White America and the Music That Developed from It*. New York: Morrow Quill, 1963.

Katz, Michael. *The Irony of Early School Reform*. Cambridge, Eng.: Cambridge University Press, 1968.

Klein, Herbert S. *African Slavery in Latin America and the Carribean*. New York: Oxford University Press, 1986.

Levine, Lawrence. *Black Culture and Black Consciousness: Afro-American Folk Thought from Slavery to Freedom*. New York: Oxford University Press, 1977.

Lewis, Lisa. *Gender Politics and MTV*. Philadelphia: Temple University Press, 1990.

Lichten, Eric. *Class, Power and Austerity*. Massachusetts: Bergin and Garvey Press, 1982.

Lipsitz, George. *A Life in the Struggle: Ivory Perry and the Culture of Opposition*. Philadelphia: Temple University Press, 1988.

———. *Time Passages: Collective Memory and American Popular Culture*. Minneapolis: University of Minnesota Press, 1990.

Lock, Graham. *Forces in Nature: The Music and Thoughts of Anthony Braxton*. New York: Da Capo Press, 1988.

Martin, Linda, and Kerry Seagrave. *Anti-Rock: The Opposition to Rock n Roll*. Hamden, Ct.: Archon Books, 1988.

Matusow, Allen J. *The Unravelling of America: A History of Liberalism in the 1960s*. New York: Harper & Row, 1984.

McClary, Susan. *Feminine Endings*. Minneapolis: University of Minnesota Press, 1991.

McClary, Susan, and Richard Leppert, eds. *Music and Society: The Politics of Composition, Performance and Reception*. New York: Cambridge University Press, 1989.

McRobbie, Angela. *Gender and Generation*. London: Macmillan Press, 1976.

———, ed. *Zoot Suits and Second-Hand Dresses: An Anthology of Fashion and Music*. Boston, Unwin Hyman, 1988.

Messerschmidt, James W. *Capitalism, Patriarchy and Crime: Toward a Socialist Feminist Criminology*. Savage, M.D.: Rowman & Littlefield, 1986.

Middleton, Richard. *Studying Popular Music*. Philadelphia: Open University Press, 1990.

Modleski, Tania. *Loving with a Vengeance: Mass-Produced Fantasies for Women*. Hamden, Ct.: Archon Books, 1982.

————, ed. *Studies in Entertainment: Critical Approaches to Mass Culture*. Bloomington: University of Indiana Press, 1986.

Mollenkopf, John. *The Contested City*. Princeton: N.J.: Princeton University Press, 1983.

Mollenkopf, John, and Manuel Castells, eds. *Dual City: Restructuring New York*. New York: Russell Sage Foundation, 1991.

Murray, Albert. *Stompin the Blues*. New York: Random House, 1976.

Nelson, Havelock, and Michael A. Gonzales. *Bring the Noise: A Guide to Rap Music and Hip Hop Culture*. New York: Crown, 1991.

Ogren, Kathy J. *The Jazz Revolution: Twenties America and the Meaning of Jazz*. New York: Oxford University Press, 1989.

Ong, Walter. *Orality and Technology: The Technologizing of the Word*. London: Methuen, 1982.

Parenti, Michael. *Inventing Reality: The Politics of the Mass Media*. New York: St Martin's Press, 1986.

Radway, Janice. *Reading the Romance*. Chapel Hill, N.C.: University of North Carolina Press, 1984.

Roberts, John Storm. *Black Music of Two Worlds*. New York: William Morrow, 1974.

Roman, Leslie, et al., eds. *Becoming Feminine: The Politics of Popular Culture*. London: Falmer Press, 1988.

Rosenberg, Terry J. *Poverty in New York City: 1980–1985*. New York: Community Service Society of New York, 1987.

Ross, Andrew. *No Respect: Intellectuals and Popular Culture*. New York: Routledge, 1989.

Ross, Andrew, and Tricia Rose, eds. *Microphone Fiends: Youth Music & Youth Culture*. New York: Routledge, 1994.

Sanjek, Russell, and David Sanjek. *American Popular Music Business in the 20th Century*. New York: Oxford University Press, 1991.

Schiller, Herbert. *Culture Inc., The Corporate Takeover of Public Expression*. New York: Oxford University Press, 1989.

Scott, James C. *Domination and the Arts of Resistance: Hidden Transcripts*. New Haven: Yale University Press, 1990.

Scott, Joan W. *Gender and the Politics of History*. New York: Columbia University Press, 1988.

Sidran, Ben. *Black Talk*. New York: Holt, Rinehart & Winston, 1971.

Simone, Timothy Maliqualim. *About Face: Race in Postmodern America*. New York: Autonomedia, 1989.

Small, Christopher. *Music of the Common Tongue*. New York: Riverrun Press, 1987.

————. *Music, Society, Education: An Examination of the Function of Music in Western, Eastern and African Cultures with Its Impact on Society and Its Use on Education*. New York: Schirmer, 1977.

Smith, Barbara, ed. *Home Girls: A Black Feminist Anthology*. New York: Kitchen Table, 1983.

Smitherman, Geneva. *Talkin' and Testifyin': The Language of Black America*. Boston: Houghton Mifflin, 1977.

Southern, Eileen. *The Music of Black Americans*. New York: Norton, 1971.

Soyinka, Wole. *Myth, Literature and the African World*. New York: Cambridge University Press, 1990.

Spencer, Jon Michael, ed. *The Emergency of Black and the Emergence of Rap. Black Sacred Music* 5, no. 1 (Spring 1991), special issue.

Stuckey, Sterling. *Slave Culture: Nationalist Theory and the Foundations of Black America*. New York: Oxford University Press, 1987.
Tabb, William. *The Long Default*. New York: Monthly Review Press, 1982.
Tate, Greg. *Flyboy in the Buttermilk*. New York: Fireside, 1992.
Tirro, Frank. *Jazz: A History*. New York, Norton, 1977.
Toop, David. *The Rap Attack: African Jive to New York Hip Hop*. London: South End Press, 1984.
———. *Rap Attack 2*. Boston: Consortium Press, 1992.
Thomson, Robert Farris. *Flash of the Spirit*. New York: Random House, 1983.
Van De Merwe, Peter. *Origins of the Popular Style*. London: Oxford University Press, 1989.
Van Sertimer, Ivan G. *They Came before Columbus*. New York: Random House, 1976.
Ventura, Michael. *Shadow Dancing in the USA*. Los Angeles, Torcher, 1985.
Wall, Cheryl A., ed. *Changing Our Own Words: Essays on Criticism, Theory and Writing by Black Women*. New Brunswick, N.J.: Rutgers University Press, 1989.
Walser, Robert. *Running with the Devil: Power, Gender, and Madness in Heavy Metal Music*. Hanover: University Press of New England, 1993.
Weitzman, Philip. *"Worlds Apart": Housing, Race, Ethnicity and Income in New York City*. New York: Community Service Society of New York, 1989.
Wepman, Dennis, Ronald Newman, and Murry Binderman. *The Life: The Lore and Folk Poetry of the Black Hustler*. Philadelphia: University of Philadelphia Press, 1976.
Williams, Patricia J. *The Alchemy of Race and Rights*. Cambridge, Mass.: Harvard University Press, 1991.
Williams, Raymond. *Keywords*. New York: Oxford University Press, 1976.
———. *The Sociology of Culture*. New York: Schocken, 1981.
Willis, Paul. *Learning to Labor: How Working-Class Kids Get Working-Class Jobs*. London: Saxon House, 1977.
Willis, Susan. *A Primer for Everyday Life*. London: Routledge, 1991.
Wilson, William J. *The Truly Disadvantaged*. Chicago: University of Chicago Press, 1987.

Articles

Aaron, Charles. "Gettin' Paid: Is Sampling Higher Education or Grand Theft Auto?" *Village Voice Rock 'n' Roll Quarterly*, Fall 1989, pp. 22–23.
Adorno, Theodore W. "On the Fetish-Character in Music and the Regression of Listening." In *The Essential Frankfurt School Reader*, ed. Andrew Arato and Eike Gebhardt, 288–289. New York: Continuum, 1982.
——— (assisted by George Simpson). "On Popular Music." In *On Record: Rock, Pop and the Written Word*, ed. Simon Frith and Andrew Goodwin. New York: Pantheon, 1990.
Allen, Harry. "Invisible Band." *Village Voice*, 18 October 1988, p. 10.
Atlanta and Alexander. "Wild Style: Graffiti Painting." In *Zoot Suits and Second-Hand Dresses: An Anthology of Fashion and Music*, ed. Angela McRobbie, 156–68. Boston: Unwin Hyman, 1988.
Austin, Joe. "A Symbol That We Have Lost Control: Authority, Public Identity, and Graffiti Writing." Unpublished paper, University of Minnesota Department of American Studies.
Baker, Houston A. "Handling Crisis: Great Books, Rap Music and the End of Western Homogeneity." *Calaloo* 13, no. 2 (Spring 1990): 173–94.

———. "Hybridity, the Rap Race, and Pedagogy for the 1990s." In *Technoculture*, ed. Andrew Ross and Constance Penley, 197–209. Minneapolis: University of Minnesota Press, 1991.

Berlant, Laura. "The Female Complaint." *Social Text* (Fall 1988): 237–59.

Carby, Hazel V. "It Jus Be's Dat Way Sometime: The Sexual Politics of Women's Blues." *Radical America* 20, no. 4 (1986): 9–22.

Cobb, Charles E. "The People Have Spoken." *The Crisis*, November 1983, p. 28.

Cooper, Barry Michael. "Raw Like Sushi." *Spin*, March 1988, p. 28.

Crenshaw, Kimberle. "Beyond Racism and Misogyny: Black Feminism and the 2 Live Crew." *Boston Review* 16, no. 6 (December 1991): 6–33.

———. "Demarginalizing the Intersection of Race and Sex: A Black Feminist Critique of Antidiscrimination Doctrine, Feminist Theory and Antiracist Politics." *University of Chicago Law Forum* 139 (1989): 139–67.

Cristgau, Robert, and Greg Tate. "Chuck D All over the Map." *Village Voice Rock 'n' Roll Quarterly*, vol. 4, no. 3, Fall 1991, pp. 12–18.

Davis, Angela Y. "Black Women and Music: A Historical Legacy of Struggle." In *Wild Women in the Whirlwind: Afro-American Culture and the Contemporary Literary Renaissance*, ed. Joanne M. Braxton and Andree Nicola McLaughlin, 3–21. New Brunswick, N.J.: Rutgers University Press, 1990.

Decker, Jeffrey L. "The State of Rap: Time and Place in Hip Hop Nationalism." *Social Text* 34 (1989): 53–84.

Denning, Michael. "The End of Mass Culture." *International Labor and Working-Class History* 37 (Spring 1990): 4–18.

———. "The Special American Conditions: Marxism and American Studies." *American Quarterly* 38, no. 3 (1986): 356–80.

Dery, Marc. "Rap!" *Keyboard*, November 1988, p. 34.

Dery, Marc. "Hank Shocklee: 'Bomb Squad' Leader Declares War on Music." *Keyboard*, September 1990, pp. 82–83, 96.

Dery, Marc, and Bob Doerschuk. "Drum Some Kill: The Beat behind the Rap." *Keyboard*, November 1988, pp. 34–36.

Di Prima, Dominique, and Lisa Kennedy. "Beat the Rap." *Mother Jones*, September–October 1990, pp. 32–35.

Dye, Peggy. "High Tech Ballroom." *Village Voice*, 5 December 1989, pp. 10–12.

Ebron, Paula. "Rapping between Men: Performing Gender." *Radical America* 23, no. 4 (1991): 23–27.

Feagin, Joe R. "The Continuing Significance of Race: Antiblack Discrimination in Public Places." *American Sociological Review* 56, no. 1 (1991): 101–16.

Fine, Elizabeth C. "Stepping, Saluting, Cracking and Freaking: The Cultural Politics of Afro-American Step Shows." *The Drama Review* 35, no. 2 (Summer 1991): 39–59.

Frith, Simon. "Picking Up the Pieces." In *Facing the Music*, ed. Simon Frith, 121–22. New York: Pantheon, 1988.

Garofalo, Reebee, "Crossing Over: 1939–1989." In *Split Image: African Americans in the Mass Media*, ed. Jannette L. Dates and William Barlow, 57–121. Washington, D.C.: Howard University Press, 1990.

Gilroy, Paul. "One Nation under a Groove: The Cultural Politics of 'Race' and Racism in Britain." In *Anatomy of Racism*, ed. David Theo Goldberg, 263–62. Minneapolis: University of Minnesota Press, 1990.

———. "Police and Thieves." In *The Empire Strikes Back*, ed. Center for Contemporary Cultural Studies, 143–82. London: CCCS Hutchinson University, 1982.

Glazer, Nathan. "On Subway Graffiti in New York." *The Public Interest* (Winter 1979): 11–33.

Goodwin, Andrew. "Sample and Hold: Pop Music in the Age of Digital Production." In *On Record: Rock, Pop and the Written Word*, ed. Simon Frith and
Andrew Goodwin, 258–73. New York: Pantheon, 1990.

Guevara, Nancy. "Women Writin' Rappin' Breakin'." In *The Year Left 2: An
American Socialist Yearbook*, ed. Mike Davis et al., 160–75. London: Verso,
1987.

Halberstam, Judith. "Starting from Scratch: Female Rappers and Feminist Discourse." *Revisions* 2, no. 2 (Winter 1989): 1–4.

Hall, Stuart. "Notes on deconstructing 'the popular'." In *People's History and
Socialist Theory*, ed. Raphael Samuel, 227–40. London: Routledge, Kegan
and Paul, 1981.

Haraway, Donna. "Situated Knowledges: The Science Question in Feminism
and the Privilege of Partial Perspective." *Feminist Studies* 14, no. 3 (Fall 1989):
575–99.

Haring, Bruce. "Many Doors Still Closed to Rap Tours." *Billboard*, 16 December
1989, p. 1.

Headley, Bernard D. "'Black on Black' Crime: The Myth and the Reality." *Crime
and Social Justice* 20 (1983): 50–62.

Holden, Steven. "Pop Life" column. *New York Times*, 17 October 1990, p. C17.

Hunter, Mead. "Interculturalism and American Music." *Performing Arts Journal*
33/34 (1989): 186–202.

Jameson, Frederic. "Reification and Utopia in Mass Culture." *Social Text* 1 (Winter 1979): 137, 139.

Katz, Cindi, and Neil Smith. "L.A. Intifada: Interview with Mike Davis." *Social
Text* 33 (1993): 19–33.

Kelley, Robin D. G. "Kickin' Reality, Kickin' Ballistics: The Cultural Politics
of Gangsta Rap in Postindustrial Los Angeles." In *Droppin' Science: Critical Essays on Rap Music and Hip Hop Culture*, ed. Eric Perkins. Philadelphia:
Temple University Press, 1994.

Kerber, Linda K. "Diversity and Transformation of American Studies." *American Quarterly* 41, no. 3 (September 1986): 415–31.

Keyes, Cheryl. "Verbal Art Performance in Rap Music: The Conversation of the
80s." *Folklore Forum* 17 (Fall 1984): 143–52.

Leppert, Richard, and George Lipsitz. "'Everybody's Lonesome for Somebody': age, the body and experience in the music of Hank Williams." *Popular
Music* 9, no. 3 (1990): 259–74.

Levy, Alan, and Barbara L. Tischler. "Into the Cultural Mainstream: The Growth
of American Music Scholarship." *American Quarterly* 42, no. 1 (March 1990):
57–73.

Light, Alan. "Ice-T." *Rolling Stone*, 20 August 1992, pp. 32, 60.

Lipsitz, George. "The Struggle for Hegemony." *Journal of American History* 75,
no. 1 (1988): 146–50.

Lott, Eric. "Double-V, Double-Time: Bebop's Politics of Style." *Calaloo* 11,
no. 3 (1988): 597–605.

Marsh, Dave, and Phyllis Pollack. "Wanted for Attitude." *Village Voice*, 10 October 1989, pp. 33–37.

Malanowski, Jamie. "Top Hip Hop." *Rolling Stone*, 13 July 1989, pp. 77–78.

Maultsby, Portia K. "Africanisms in African-American Music." In *Africanisms in
American Culture*, ed. Joseph E. Holloway, 185–210. Bloomington: Indiana
University Press, 1990.

McAdams, Janine, and Deborah Russell. "Rap Breaking Through to Adult Market." *Hollywood Reporter*, 19 September 1991, pp. 4, 20.

McClary, Susan. "Living to Tell: Madonna's Resurrection of the Fleshly." *Genders* 7 (Spring 1990): 2–21.

McRobbie, Angela. "Settling Accounts with Subcultures: A Feminist Critique." In *On Record: Rock, Pop and the Written Word*, ed. Simon Frith and Andrew Goodwin, 66–80. New York: Pantheon, 1990.

Mercer, Kobena. "Black Hair/Style Politics." In *Out There: Marginalization and Contemporary Cultures*, ed. Russell Ferguson et al., 247–64. Cambridge: MIT Press, 1990.

———. "Monster Metaphors: Notes on Michael Jackson's 'Thriller'." In *Zoot Suits and Second-Hand Dresses: An Anthology of Fashion and Music*, ed. Angela McRobbie, 50–73. Boston: Unwin Hyman, 1988.

Mitchell-Kernan, Claudia. "Signifying." In *Mother Wit from the Laughing Barrel: Readings in the Interpretation of Afro-American Folklore*, ed. Alan Dundes, 310–28. New York: Garland, 1981.

Pearlman, Jill. "Rap's Gender Gap." *Option* (Fall 1988): 23–36.

Pierce, H. Bruce. "Blacks and Law Enforcement: Towards Police Brutality Reduction." *Black Scholar* 17 (1986): 49–54.

Pratt, Ray. "Popular Music, Free Space, and the Quest for Community." *Popular Music and Society* 13, no. 4 (1989): 59–76.

Reed, Adolph J., Jr. "The Liberal Technocrat." *Nation*, 6 February 1988, pp. 167–70.

———. "The Rise of Louis Farrakhan." *Nation*, 21 January 1991, pp. 1, 51–56; 28 January 1991, pp. 86–92 (two-part article).

———. "The 'Underclass' as Myth and Symbol: The Poverty of Discourse about Poverty." *Radical America* 24, no. 1 (Jan–Mar 1990, pub. 1992): 20–40.

Reed, Adolph J., Jr., and Julian Bond, eds. "Equality: Why We Can't Wait." *Nation*, 9 December 1991, pp. 733–37.

Reeves, Marcus. "Ear to the Street." *The Source*, March 1993, p. 18.

Schwichtenberg, Catherine. "Feminist Cultural Studies." *Critical Studies in Mass Communication* 6, no. 2 (1989): 202–208.

Senghor, Leopold Sendar. "Standards critiques de l'art Africain." *African Arts/Arts d'Afrique* 1, no. 1 (Autumn 1967): 6.

Shecter, John. "Chocolate Ties." *The Source*, July 1993, p. 18.

Shusterman, Richard. "The Fine Art of Rap." *New Literary History* 22, no. 3 (Summer 1991): 613–32.

Smith, Duncan. "The Truth of Graffiti." *Art & Text* 17: 84–90.

Snead, James A. "On Repetition in Black Culture," *Black American Literature Forum* 15, no. 4 (1981): 146–54.

Spillers, Hortense. "Interstices: A Small Drama of Words." In *Pleasure and Danger: Exploring Female Sexuality*, ed. Carol Vance, 73–100. Boston: Routledge, Kegan Paul, 1984.

Stephanson, Anders. "Interview with Cornel West." In *Universal Abandon: The Politics of Postmodernism*, ed. Andrew Ross, 269–86. Minneapolis: University of Minnesota Press, 1988.

Tannenbaum, Rob. "Sucker MC." *Village Voice*, 4 December 1990, p. 69.

Thomas, Richard, and Homer Hawkins. "White Policing of Black Populations: A History of Race and Social Control in America." In *Out of Order? Policing Black People*, ed. Ellis Cashmore and Eugene McLaughlin, 65–86. London: Routledge, 1991.

Thompson, Robert Ferris. "Kongo Influences on African American Artistic Culture." In *Africanisms in American Culture*, ed. Joseph E. Holloway, 148–84. Bloomington: University of Indiana Press, 1990.

Tucker, Bruce. "Tell Tchaikovsky the News: Postmodernism, Popular Culture and the Emergence of Rock n Roll." *Black Music Research Journal* 9, no. 2 (1989): 271–94.

Van Ripper, Frank. "Ford to New York: Drop Dead." *New York Daily News*, 30 October 1975, p. 1.

Walkowitz, Daniel J. "New York: A Tale of Two Cities." In *Snowbelt Cities: Metropolitan Politics in the Northeast and Midwest since WW II*, ed. Richard M. Bernard. Bloomington Indiana University Press, 1990.

Watrous, Peter. "It's Official: Rap Music Is in the Mainstream." *New York Times*, 16 May 1988, C11.

Watts, Jerry G. "It Just Ain't Righteous: On Witnessing Black Crooks and White Cops." *Dissent* 90 (1983): 347–53.

West, Cornel. "The New Cultural Politics of Difference." In *Out There: Marginalization and Contemporary Cultures*, ed. Russell Ferguson et al., 19–38. Cambridge: MIT Press, 1990.

Williams, Raymond. "The Analysis of Culture." In *The Long Revolution*. London: Chatto and Windus, 1961.

Willis, Andre Craddock. "Rap Music and the Black Musical Tradition: A Critical Assessment." *Radical America* 23, no. 4 (1991): 29–38.

Wilson, Ollie. "Black Music as Art." *Black Music Research Journal* 3 (1983): 1–22.

Wise, Gene. "Paradigm Drama." In "American Studies: A Cultural Institutional History of the Movement." *American Quarterly* 31, bibliography issue (1979): 293–337.

Index

✦

Adorno, T. W., 71, 72, 209(n71)
"Adventures of Grandmaster Flash on the Wheels of Steel, The," 53–54
Afrika Bambaataa, 51, 53, 56
Afrodiasporic traditions: influence on hip hop of, 23, 25, 27, 36, 49, 61, 189(n4); influence on rap of, 75, 85, 197(n10); rhythm and repetition in, 66–70. *See also* Caribbean music
Ahlerich, Milt, 128
Allen, Harry, 73, 85–86
All That Is Solid Melts into Air (Berman), 31
"All Wrong" (Ice Cream Tee), 162
American Family Association, 129
Antoinette, 163
Apocalypse 91 (Public Enemy), 123
"Arizona" (Public Enemy), 123
Art world, 46–47, 194(n52)
Ashhurst-Watson, Carmen, 16, 169
Astor, Patti, 46
Attali, Jacques, 70, 71, 72
Audubon Ballroom, 116, 119, 121–23
Austin, Joe, 46

"Baby Got Back" (Sir-Mix-a-Lot), 169
Backspin, 53
Bagdikian, Ben, 29
Baker, Houston A., 23, 151
Barnes, Dee, 178–79
Basquiat, Jean-Michel, 35, 194(n52)
Bass, frequencies, 75–80
Beastie Boys, 4
Be Bop, 6
Bell Biv Divoe (BBD), 172–73
Berlant, Laura, 162–63

Berman, Marshall, 31
Bernard, James, 8
BET (Black Entertainment Television), 8, 119, 206(n35)
Big Daddy Kane, 3, 189(n6), 192(n40)
Billboard, 130
Black culture: and black experience, 21–27; crossover and, 4–6, 83–84; as danger to social order, 133, 207(n49); female contributions to, 151–53; repetition in, 198(nn 18, 24); and sexuality, 168; style and individuality in, 206(n36). *See also* Hip hop; Rap
Black feminism. *See* Feminism, black women and
Black Panthers, 55
Black Sheep, 4
Blesh, Rudi, 67
Blow, Kurtis, 56, 75, 196(n87)
Blues music: and black experience, 23; sexism in, 24, 104; use of technology, 199(n30)
"Bomb, The" (Ice Cube), 172
Bomb Squad, 199(n36)
Boogie Down Productions, 107, 108–109
Boss, 59, 174
Boston Herald, 134
Brand Nubian, 4
Bray, Kevin, 10, 187(n9)
Break beat, 73–74, 194(n54); records, 199(n28). *See also* Rupture
Breakdancing: and black experience, 22, 27; description, 34, 47–51; and incorporation, 194(n64); self-naming and, 36; style/moves, 38–39, 194(n56). *See also* Hip hop

"Breaks, The" (Kurtis Blow), 56, 196(nn 80, 87)
B-Real, 67
"Bridge, The" (MC Shan), 200(n44)
Brown, Chuck, 87
Brown, James, 70, 90, 92
"Buffalo Stance" (Neneh Cherry), 162
Bush, George, 183
Busta Rhymes, 67
Butts, Reverend Calvin, 122, 183–84
Bytches with Problems (BWP), 123, 155, 203(n13)

C&C Music Factory, 51
Cabaret laws, 133
"Can't Truss It" (Public Enemy), 1
Capitalism. *See* Commercialization
Capoiera, 49
Carby, Hazel, 23, 153–54
Caribbean music, 75, 189(n4), 199(n31)
Carter, Jimmy, 33
Carter, Ron, 78
Castleman, Craig, 43, 44
Castro, Daisy (Baby Love), 48
Censorship, 3, 14–15, 17, 120, 184
Chalfant, Henry, 42, 46
Chic, 202(n69)
Chocolate, 12
Chuck D (Carl Ryder), 99, 116–19, 122, 134, 179, 183, 187(n6), 189(n6), 199(n36)
Chung House of Metal, 76
Chunky and Pappy, 48
Classical music (Western), 65, 69
Class oppression, 61, 114, 119–20. *See also* Inequality; Racism
Clinton, Bill, 183
Clinton, George, 92
Clugston, Gary, 76
Columbia University, 121
"Come into My House" (Queen Latifah), 163
"Comin' Back Strapped" (BWP), 123
Commercialization, 24, 40–41, 56–57, 58. *See also* Marketing/sales
Compton's Most Wanted, 59
Confrontation, 35–36, 48, 194(n59), 195(n73). *See also* Violence
Considine, J. D., 81
Conyers, John, 141
Cooper, Martha, 42
"Cop Killer" (Ice-T), 130, 183

Cowboy, 54
Crazy Legs, 35, 36, 48, 49, 50
Crenshaw, Kimberle, 181
Crews/posses: breakdancing, 48; graffiti, 43–44; importance of, 10–11, 34; rap, 55–56
Criminality: defining, 208(n58); social control ideology and black, 125–26, 130–33, 135–45; war on drugs and black, 106, 121
Critics, 80–84
Crossover, 4–6, 83–84, 187(n6). *See also* Incorporation
Culture: definition, 198(n16); European, 68–69. *See also* Black culture
Culture Freedom, 67
Cut. *See* Break beat
Cypress Hill, 59

Daddy-O, 79, 89
D'Agostino, John, 137–39, 209(n71)
Dance music, 83–84, 199(n36)
Das Efx, 3, 67
"Date Rape" (A Tribe Called Quest), 150
Davis, Angela, 153
Davis, Mike, 19–20
Def Jam, 6, 16
Deindustrialization, 22, 25. *See also* Socioeconomic forces
De La Soul, 4, 58, 150
Dery, Mark, 75, 76
"Description of a Fool" (A Tribe Called Quest), 150
"Devil Made Me Do It, The" (Paris), 102–103
Disco, 47, 211(n13)
Discourse/dialogue: and issues of social control, 99–106, 125–26, 129–45 (*see also* Power relationships); and popular music, 148; women rappers and sexual, 147–51, 161–63, 170–75, 181–82, 210(nn 8, 11). *See also* Rap
Discrimination, public space, 126–29, 207(nn 43, 44). *See also* Racism
Disposable Heroes of Hiphoprisy, 175
Distortion, 74–75
DJs: names of, 36; role in rap development, 51–54, 55–56, 211(n13); use of technology, 34. *See also specific individuals*
D-Nice, 123
Dr. Dre, 59, 178–79

Quinones, Lee, 45

Racism, xiii–xiv, 61, 208(nn 54, 67);
    and feminism, 177–82; gendered,
    203(n13); institutional, 99–106,
    124–45, 204(n14) (*see also* Police/
    security); as rap topic, 106, 111–14.
    See also Discrimination, public space;
    Inequality
Rammelzee, 45, 194(n52)
Rap: Afrodiasporic influences, 75, 85,
    197(n10) (*see also* Afrodiasporic tra-
    ditions); black experience and under-
    standing, xii–xiv, 1–2, 14–20, 23–27,
    62–72, 95–96, 184–85, 196(n87);
    composition and production, 39,
    73–90, 93–95, 197(nn 6, 10, 13),
    200(n40); crossover appeal, 4–6,
    187(n6); gangsta, 4, 59, 174, 190(n16),
    195(n74); history and description,
    2–4, 6–8, 34, 51–59, 211(n13); legal
    issues, 90–93; as social criticism, 99–
    124; as threat to social order, 1–2,
    124–45; and videos, 8–14 (*see also*
    Videos, music). *See also* Hip hop;
    Women rappers
"Rap, Symbolism and Fear, On" (*New York
    Times*), 81
"Rapper's Delight," xi, 3, 56, 195(n78),
    196(n80)
"Raw" (Big Daddy Kane), 192(n40)
"Real Face of Rap: The 'black music' that
    isn't either, The" (*New Republic*), 81
"Recipe of a Hoe" (Boss), 174
Record companies. *See* Music industry
Red Alert, 35, 57, 206(n33)
Redding, Otis, 161
Redman, 59
Reeves, Marcus, 50
Reggae music, 199(n31), 204(n18)
Regional differentiation, 60
Renaissance, 66
Repetition: role in rap of, 66–74, 75; role
    in Western and black cultures, 198(nn
    18, 24)
Resistance: to moral restrictions on
    women, 166–67; rap as expression of,
    99–124; and women rappers, 146–47,
    161–66, 170–71, 173–75
Revenge fantasies, 113–14, 128, 174. *See
    also* Police/security
Rhymes. *See* Lyrics
Rhythm: role in rap of, 64–74

Rhythm and blues (R&B). *See* Blues
    music
Robinson, Sylvia, 3, 56, 195(n78)
"Rock Dis Funky Joint" (Poor Righteous
    Teachers), 67
Rock 'n' roll: attacks on, 129–30; influence
    on rap, 51–52; as reflection of society,
    23
Rock Steady Crew, 35, 48
Roland TR-808, 75–76
"Roxanne Roxanne" (UTFO), 57, 163
"Roxanne's Revenge" (Roxanne Shante),
    57, 162–63, 196(n81), 211(n19)
"Rump Shaker" (Wrecks-N-Effect), 169
Run DMC, 3, 51–52, 58, 195(n66)
Rupture, 38–39, 67–74
Ryder, Carl. *See* Chuck D

Sadler, Eric (Vietnam), 74–75, 77, 80, 89,
    93, 199(n36)
Salt, 35, 56, 149, 175, 182; on feminism,
    176, 177
Salt 'N' Pepa, 86–87, 163, 212(n31);
    commercial success of, 4, 57, 154;
    and male-female relationships, 151,
    155, 156–58, 211(n25); on sexuality,
    166–67, 170, 212(n29)
Sample Some of Disc, Sample some of D.A.T.
    (George Clinton), 92
Sampling: importance to rap of, 73; select-
    ing passages, 78–80, 200(n41); use in
    composition, 88–90, 200(n44). *See
    also* Legal issues; Technology
Samuels, David, 80–81
"Say That Then" (Oaktown 3-5-7), 162
Scott, James, 100, 110, 114, 148
Scratching, 53
Seen, 44, 45
"Self-Destruction" (STV), 140, 141–42
Sequence, 56, 57
Sexism: as obstacle to women in hip hop,
    44, 57–58, 170; and rap, xiii–xiv, 1,
    15, 103–104, 171–73; society and pre-
    valence of, 15–16, 24, 61, 206(n37);
    women rappers and, 147–48, 149–51,
    178, 210(n8)
Sexuality, 166–75
Shabazz, Betty, 122
Shabba Ranks, 67
"Shake Your Thang" (Salt 'N' Pepa),
    166–67, 212(n29)
Shante, Roxanne, 3, 57, 162–63, 196(n81),
    211(n19)

UNIVERSITY PRESS OF NEW ENGLAND publishes books under its own imprint and is the publisher for Brandeis University Press, Brown University Press, University of Connecticut, Dartmouth College, Middlebury College Press, University of New Hampshire, University of Rhode Island, Tufts University, University of Vermont, and Wesleyan University Press, and Salzburg Seminar.

ABOUT THE AUTHOR

TRICIA ROSE is Assistant Professor of History and Africana Studies at New York University and author of numerous articles on black culture, rap music, and contemporary popular culture.

Library of Congress Cataloging-in-Publication Data

Rose, Tricia.
    Black noise : rap music and black culture in contemporary America / by Tricia Rose.
        p.   cm.—(Music culture)
    Includes bibliographical references and index.
    ISBN 0–8195–5271–2.—ISBN 0–8195–6275–0 (pbk.)
        1. Rap (Music)—History and criticism.   2. Afro-Americans—Music—History and criticism.   3. Popular culture—United States.
    I. Title.   II. Series.
    ML3531.R67   1994
    782.42164—dc20   93-41386
    ⊗